Greenopia

the urban dweller's guide to
green living
Los Angeles

eat · shop · live green

PUBLISHED BY The Green Media Group, LLC
Founder Gay Browne
Publisher Terrye Bretzke
Writer/Editor Nancy Arbuckle
Research Ferris Kawar, Ron Durgin, Doug Mazeffa
Design Lightbourne, Inc.

The Green Media Group, LLC
P.O. Box 1706 Santa Monica CA 90406-1706 USA
310-917-1100 Fax 310-917-1109
www.greenopia.com

Second edition
ISBN 978-0-9785064-21

Additional titles available from the publisher:
Greenopia San Francisco Bay Area
Greenopia New York City

Greenopia guides are available at volume discounts and custom cover printing. Please contact The Green Media Group, LLC for further information at (310) 917-1100, fax (310) 917-1109, or e-mail us at booksales@greenopia.com.

Greenopia is a group of dedicated professionals from diverse backgrounds that have come together with a common goal. We are all looking to do our part to create a better world for ourselves and to leave a lighter footprint on the one we leave behind for our families and future generations. We hope that dedication is reflected in the pages that follow and that this guide becomes a resource you use every day.

The work of our research and publishing teams was extensive, and we gratefully acknowledge their unceasing commitment: from the development of our criteria, to the exhaustive on-the-ground review of thousands of businesses, to evaluating and vetting the hundreds of businesses that qualified, and for bringing it all together in a handy guide. Our web team has also done an incredible job creating an exciting companion to our printed guides. They have worked hard to make the Greenopia listings accessible online and are developing ways to build community, capture user feedback, and offer our readers more information on ways to green their own lives.

Greenopia thanks its incredible staff and everyone who made this guide what it is: Alayha Aquarian, Ryan Andersen, Elizabeth Barry, Joy Cernac, Susan Cohen, Christina Coron, Jennifer Coscia, Hannah Davey, Stephanie Hanford, Lisa Harrison, Craig Henderson, Seth Maislin, Stef McDonald, Jennifer Roberts, and Laura Sellers.

And from the Greenopia Team, many thanks to all of our families and loved ones for their support and understanding throughout the long hours we were absent from their lives during the creation of this guide.

Eating Out   1

Eating In   37

Being Beautiful   67

Getting Goods   87

Caring for Critters   107

We would like to recognize and thank our Los Angeles Advisory Council and the experts who contributed their knowledge to each section of the guide. We are indebted to this stellar group of individuals who gave us their time and shared their expertise to help us ensure the accuracy and quality of our listings and to give us input on the guide content and criteria overall. Their collaboration and guidance were invaluable. We are enormously grateful for their input, advice, experience, and enthusiasm.

Suzanne Biegel, Chief Catalyst and Consultant, Greenopia

Chef Eddie J., Enlightened Food Group of Santa Monica

Mary Cordaro, Environmental Consultant and Certified Bau-Biologist, Founder/President, H3Environmental

Monica Gilcrest, National Resource Center Coordinator, Global Green

Steve Glenn, Founder and CEO of LivingHomes, LLC

Jane Kennedy, Owner, Palmetto

Marilee Kuhlman, Owner/Designer, Comfort Zones Gardens Designs

Michelle L'Don, West Coast Sales Director, Organic Vintners

Yoni Levenbach, CEO, Orchids Without Borders

Andy Lipkis, Founder and President, TreePeople

Linda Loudermilk, CEO and DCF, Loudermilk, Inc.

Christine SE Magar, Green Building Architect and Sustainability Advisor, President, Greenform

Chris Paine, Writer/Director, "Who Killed the Electric Car?"

Akasha Richmond, Chef/Owner, Akasha Restaurant/Bar/Bakery

David Rosenstein, President, Intex Solutions

Amelia Saltsman, Author and Publisher, Blenheim Press

Joe Sehee, Executive Director, Green Burial Council

Nancy Sutley, Deputy Mayor for Energy and Environment, City of Los Angeles

Deirdre Wallace, Founder and President, The Ambrose Hotel and The Ambrose Collection

Lance Williams, Ph.D., Executive Director, Los Angeles Chapter, U.S. Green Building Council

Todd Warner, Owner, Tailwaggers/Tailwashers

Gregg Wendt, Enright Premier Wealth Advisors, Inc.

Marvilyn Wright, Director of Green Real Estate, KJM Real Estate

We would also like to express our appreciation to the Monterey Bay Aquarium Foundation for the use of their Seafood Watch Guide, the Environmental Working Group for allowing us to reprint their Pesticides in Produce information, and to Amelia Saltsman for creating our Eating in Season chart in addition to her other work on the guide.

Welcome to the second edition of *Greenopia Los Angeles*, with 700 new listings to keep you in step with the city's ever-growing green community. We're thrilled to present more than 1,400 of the greenest local businesses in categories that  mirror your life: food, clothing, building, cleaning, and more!

Greenopia is designed to help you lead a healthier lifestyle and leave a lighter footprint on the earth. I created it for very personal reasons: A lifelong asthmatic myself, I have a child who was diagnosed with autism-related learning disabilities, linked to high mercury levels. Determined to reduce the toxins in our lives, my husband and I built the first green home in Pacific Palisades. But finding resources wasn't easy. So I created a go-to guide.

Whether you're looking for a nontoxic dry cleaner or organic coffee shop, eco-friendly sheets, or all natural baby gifts, you'll find them in our user-friendly book. What you won't find is advertising; no business paid to be included. All listings are research-based and approved by a panel of experts.

Carrying more than 50 different questionnaires—one for each category in the guide—our researchers combed Los Angeles on foot to uncover the green secrets of each neighborhood and to interview business owners. Each company must meet several standards to be awarded our *Green Leaf Certification*, which shows you its level of eco-commitment at a glance.

Visit our website, www.greenopia.com, for further details on our rating process and to give feedback on our listings so we can keep tracking L.A.'s green scene. Together—one choice at a time—we can create a healthier planet.

Spread the word!

Gay Browne

Gay Browne, Founder

About Greenopia

This second edition of *Greenopia Los Angeles* updates all the information we gathered for our first 2006 guide and includes more than 700 new green businesses—over 1,400 in all. Our goal is to present you with a comprehensive guide to the most eco-friendly businesses, services, and organizations around L.A. We personally surveyed every corner of the Los Angeles area to uncover, identify, and evaluate green businesses. We marched through the doors of hundreds of restaurants, stores, salons, hotels, and transport services to ensure their adherence to our criteria.

This guide is not a paid directory. Companies cannot pay to be included. The businesses listed must meet our guidelines and qualifications. All categories are screened differently as each requires questions that are tailored to that particular type of service or business. In each section we provide an introduction that outlines why sustainability is particularly important in that category. We also share what criteria we use in our evaluation and a description of how the ratings are applied for each category. We look at, for example, the percentage of organic products sold by a grocer, the number of sustainable home-building projects of a general contractor, or if a pet groomer uses all natural shampoos and nontoxic flea treatments in its services. We also look at what the business is doing in its day-to-day operations to demonstrate its commitment to environmentally-friendly practices. We reviewed, among other things, whether they have a recycling or energy-efficiency program in place, if their delivery or service vehicles run on alternative fuel, or for a restaurant, if they participate in a composting or biodiesel-recycling program.

Every listed business and organization must meet our minimum qualifying standard to be a Greenopia-designated business and receive a "Greenopia Certified Business" award. In many categories we use our own ✐ *Green-Leaf Award* system to identify relative performance among listed businesses on key measures of their eco-friendly services and products. Businesses can earn from one to four leaves. Those that earn four leaves meet our highest standards.

We invite your comments about the businesses and services featured in the guide. It is our desire to make this guide and our website interactive so that you can play an active role in identifying and supporting the green merchants in your area, and encourage businesses to become a part of the Greenopia community. If you discover a business that we have not included, or if you're a business owner yourself and we missed you, please let us know. You will find us at **greenopia.com.**

As more businesses adopt green practices, we as consumers have increased opportunities to make ecologically smart choices. Together we will have a positive and powerful environmental impact.

How to Use This Guide

We hope you will find Greenopia comprehensive and easy to use. We have divided the guide into ten chapters that we feel best represent areas of daily living. Within each chapter, we've broken out the various retailers, services, and organizations by category—52 in all. Browse the Table of Contents for all our categories, or turn to the index to find specific businesses alphabetically, or by region and category.

Each chapter is introduced by a local expert, many of whom served on our local Advisory Council (see page VI). They offer great advice and even share their own path to eco-awareness. At the end of select chapters, and scattered throughout the guide, we've included charts, definitions, guidelines, and practical tips for healthier, more sustainable living—all designed to show you that a greener lifestyle is accessible and possible to achieve.

The local green businesses, services, and resources presented here are the core of Greenopia. Below is a sample listing with a brief explanation of how a typical one works:

❶ Erewhon Natural Foods Market ❷ 🌿🌿🌿🌿
❸ 7660 Beverly Blvd. LA 90036 · **323-937-0777**
Mon-Sat 8am-10pm Sun 9am-9pm   www.erewhonmarket.com
❹ Large selection of organically grown produce, groceries, and macrobiotic staples. Wide variety of natural remedies including vitamins, herbs, and homeopathics. Visit website for their own Health-e-Coupons.

❶ Businesses are listed in alphabetical order within the category.

❷ The number of leaves awarded the business is based on the criteria stated at the beginning of the category. Some categories are not leaf awarded, so a leaf rating will not always appear in the listing.

❸ Everything you need to locate or contact the business: street address, city, zip code, phone or other information, hours, and web address, if any.

❹ Greenopia's description of the eco-friendly products or services offered by the business, along with noteworthy additional green elements about the business or service.

Also look for other relevant listing information in the criteria statement. For example, in *Restaurants and Cafés*, the listing shows one or more "**$**" to denote the average price of an entrée, as well as a "**C**" if catering is offered.

What we don't include in our listings is what you, as a customer, might experience: How satisfied you were with the service; if the quality was what you expected; whether you would recommend the business or service to others.

We encourage you to comment on the businesses, services, and resources you find in Greenopia. Visit greenopia.com to write a review and share your experiences with others.

It Has to Taste Good

BY AKASHA RICHMOND

Chefs want to work with the best ingredients they can find. That's the bottom line. And the best ingredients are often the "greenest." They were grown locally, by a farmer the chef very likely has a personal relationship with.

I like to think back to when the movie business in Hollywood was just beginning and real stars like Clark Gable lived on farms. Farms! In fact, Mr. Gable himself sold his farm-fresh eggs to the studio where he worked. Talk about locally sourced! Those days may be long gone but professional chefs (and home cooks, too) can try to recreate them by buying produce at farmers' markets, by patronizing restaurants where they know there is a commitment to quality and sustainability, and by working to protect local agricultural lands.

Not only does the food you eat need to taste good, it has to be good for you. You have to know what makes you feel good when you eat it. Are you a vegetable and salad person? A protein person? A soy milk drinker? These are things we need to learn about ourselves and, having done so, can find the best organic and local sources for those foods that nourish our bodies best.

My mom was a really good cook so I got introduced to healthy eating early on. We had whole wheat bread, yogurt, and protein shakes before anyone else was even thinking along those lines. My mom bought vegetables at an open-air market and purchased poultry at a ranch stand. I grew up eating really good food.

When the natural foods movement began to take off, the food was so unappealing, it was giving wholesome meals a bad name. That's why I started cooking as a profession. Remember, just because food is healthy, it doesn't have to taste bad. Although that perception still persists in some people's minds, others are starting to make really good choices about what they eat, where they buy it, and where it comes from.

About that last point, it is really important to know the farms and companies that supply the restaurants you frequent. Look for their names on the menu. Ask the chef. Don't settle for a simple "we use organic foods whenever possible." This could mean that the grapes are flown in from Chile, the beef from Uruguay. Know the chefs whose restaurants you visit. Many do benefits for the environment. Support them in their commitment. They in turn will support the best suppliers and the greenest ingredients, and you'll be treated to a tastier meal than you could have imagined.

AKASHA RICHMOND

Akasha Richmond is a caterer known for her passion for organic and natural cooking. Her "green" culinary expertise has been featured at the E! Entertainment Golden Globes Party, EMA Awards, backstage at the Grammy's, Farm Aid, and at the Sundance Film Festival. Akasha is now the proprietor of her first restaurant, AKASHA, in Culver City.

Restaurants and Cafés

One of the most intimate moments we share with our planet is when we're holding a fork. The food we eat comes from the earth and turns into the stuff we're made of. Every day, more restaurants and cafés are recognizing that a healthy planet yields healthy food, which ends up making healthy people. That sounds tasty to us. But not every establishment offering green eats makes a big deal out of it, so we looked below the surface to find healthy and natural fare from across the cuisine spectrum suitable for any type of budget.

Although we looked at all sorts of ways a restaurant or café might demonstrate its commitment to sustainability (recycling programs, energy and water conservation, composting, etc.), our primary focus was on the food, as we expect yours is.

Our leaf awards are based on the following:

- the percentage of produce purchased that is either certified organic and/or locally grown without pesticides and chemical fertilizers.

- the percentage of fresh poultry and eggs that is certified organic, free-range/cage-free or locally raised, free-range/cage-free without the use of hormones and/or antibiotics.

- the percentage of dairy products and grains that are certified organic.

- the source of the seafood—whether it was wild-caught or farm raised, and, if farm raised, the composition of its diet.

- the percentage of fresh meat (or meat substitutes such as soy) that is certified organic and/or grass fed and produced without the use of hormones and antibiotics.

- the percentage of certified organic coffee, tea, juice, alcohol, and other nondairy beverages.

Of food and/or beverages served during any given one-week period:

      🌿   at least 25% meet the above criteria.

      🌿🌿   at least 50% meet the above criteria.

      🌿🌿🌿   at least 75% meet the above criteria.

      🌿🌿🌿🌿   90% or more meet the above criteria.

Average price of an entrée:

      $ $10 or less

      $$ $11-$20

      $$$ $21-$30

      $$$$ $31 and up

      C   Provides catering services

AMERICAN

BLD ✐✐✐ **$$ C**
7450 Beverly Blvd. LA 90036 • **323-930-9744**
Mon-Fri 7am-12am Sat-Sun 8am-12am www.bldrestaurant.com
Serves American comfort food using local farmers' market produce, organic
free-range poultry and eggs, wild-caught fish, and hormone-free meats;
composting program.

Bloom Cafe ✐✐ **$$**
5544 W. Pico Blvd. LA 90019 • **323-934-6900**
Daily 9am-10pm www.bloomcafe.com
Café focusing on organic seasonal produce from local farms. Uses
biocompostable takeout containers.

Boa Steakhouse ✐✐ **$$$$ C**
101 Santa Monica Blvd. Santa Monica 90401 • **310-899-4466**
8462 W. Sunset Blvd. West Hollywood 90069 • **323-650-8383**
Hours vary by location www.boasteak.com
Some organic produce and meats; some wild-caught fish.

Coral Tree Café ✐✐✐ **$$ C**
6600 N. Topanga Canyon Blvd. Canoga Park 91303 • **818-587-3330**
17499 Ventura Blvd. Encino 91316 • **818-789-8733**
11645 San Vicente Blvd. LA 90049 • **310-979-8733**
10250 Santa Monica Blvd. LA 90064 • **310-553-8733**
Hours vary by location www.coraltreecafe.net
Organic eggs, produce, and other organic ingredients. Organic coffee and
teas. Vegetarian and vegan options.

Grace Restaurant ✐✐ **$$$$ C**
7360 Beverly Blvd. LA 90036 • **323-934-4400**
Tue-Thu 6pm-10:30pm Fri-Sat 6pm-11pm Sun 6pm-10pm
www.gracerestaurant.com
Organic, farmers' market produce; hormone-free meats; wild-caught fish.

Heirloom Bakery and Café ✐ **$**
807 Meridian Ave. Ste. C South Pasadena 91030 • **626-441-0042**
Tue-Fri 6am-6pm Sat-Sun 8am-3pm
Local farmers' market produce; organic tea; organic, fair trade coffee;
organic, house-baked bread.

Hungry Cat, The ✐✐ **$$$**
1535 N. Vine St. Hollywood 90028 • **323-462-2155**
Mon-Sat 12pm-2am Sun 10am-12am www.thehungrycat.com
Some organic meat and produce; wild-caught fish; grass-fed, hormone-free
beef. Raw bar.

Interim Café (formerly Newsroom Café) ✐✐✐✐ **$**
530 Wilshire Blvd. Santa Monica 90401 • **310-319-9100**
Mon-Fri 8am-9pm Sat 9am-7pm Sun 9am-3pm
Organic produce, poultry, meats, grains; wild-caught fist. Some organic,
nondairy beverages.

Joey's Café ✐ **$ C**
8301 Santa Monica Blvd. West Hollywood 90069 • **323-822-0671**
Daily 8am-10pm
Some organic produce, poultry, grains; some wild-caught fish.

Let's Be Frank Dogs ✏✏✏✏ $ C
Helms Ave. bet. Washington and Venice Blvds. LA 90034 • **415-515-8084**
Tue-Fri 11:30am-3:30pm Sat-Sun 11:30am-4:30pm www.letsbefrankdogs.com
Hot dog cart. Local, grass-fed beef dogs; heritage pork brats; organic
condiments, juices, sodas.

M Café de Chaya ✏✏✏✏ $$ C
7119 Melrose Ave. LA 90046 • **323-525-0588**
Mon-Sat 9am-10pm Sun 9am-9pm www.mcafedechaya.com
Contemporary macrobiotic cuisine; mostly vegetarian and vegan fare.
Locally grown organic produce and brown rice; organic, seasonal desserts,
coffee, and green tea.

Mäni's Bakery Café ✏ $
519 S. Fairfax Ave. LA 90036 • **323-938-8800**
2507 Main St. Santa Monica 90405 • **310-396-7700**
Daily 7:30am-8pm www.manisbakery.com
Bakery and café. Some organic ingredients; fruit juice-sweetened desserts.

Mayberry ✏ $
1028 Swarthmore Ave. Pacific Palisades 90272 • **310-454-6467**
Daily 7:30am-9pm
Some organic poultry, grains, produce. Outdoor dining; kid- and dog-
friendly.

Natural Soul Food Non-Profit Café ✏✏✏ (Donations only)
1444 W. Martin Luther King Jr. Blvd. LA 90062 • **323-298-0005**
Daily 9:30am-9:30pm www.naturalsoulfood.org
Some organic produce, grains, and nondairy beverages; organic poultry,
wild-caught fish. Nonprofit café; prices are set by customer.

Patrick's Roadhouse ✏ $$
106 Entrada Dr. Santa Monica 90402 • **310-459-4544**
Mon-Fri 7am-3pm Sat-Sun 8am-4pm www.patricksroadhouse.info
Organic meats; some organic produce, poultry, grains. Wild-caught and
organic, farm-raised fish.

Simon LA ✏ $$$
8555 Beverly Blvd. LA 90048 • **310-358-3979**
Daily 6:30am-10:30pm www.sofitel.com
Some organic and natural ingredients; some organic chicken; some wild-
caught fish.

Skratch ✏✏✏ $ C
3867 Hughes Way Culver City 90232 • **310-558-3400**
Mon-Fri 11am-8pm (seasonal) www.skratchbasics.com
Organic produce, poultry, meats, dairy; wild-caught fish. Biodegradable
takeout containers.

Standard 24/7 Restaurant, The ✏ $$ C
8300 Sunset Blvd. West Hollywood 90069 • **323-650-9090**
550 S. Flower St. LA 90071 • **213-892-8080**
Daily 24 hrs Lounge open til 2am www.standardhotels.com
Coffeeshop atmosphere. Some organic produce, poultry, meats, and grains;
some wild-caught fish.

Swingers ✏✏ $
8020 Beverly Blvd. LA 90048 • **323-653-5858**
802 Broadway Santa Monica 90401 • **310-393-9793**
Hours vary by location www.committedinc.com
Retro diner. Some organic ingredients; many vegetarian and vegan options.

Wilshire ▱▱▱▱ $$$
2454 Wilshire Blvd. Santa Monica 90403 • **310-586-1707**
Mon-Fri 12pm-2:30pm, 6pm-10pm Sat 6pm-10pm www.wilshirerestaurant.com
Seasonal, American cuisine; many organic ingredients. Supports local
farmers. Late night and *prix fixe* menus.

AMERICAN (CONTEMPORARY)

A Votre Sante ▱▱▱ $$ C
13016 San Vicente Blvd. LA 90049 • **310-451-1813**
Mon 10am-10pm Tue-Fri 8am-10pm Sat 9am-10pm Sun 9am-9pm
www.avotresantela.com
Health-oriented cuisine; vegetarian options. Hormone-free chicken; organic
greens and produce; organic pancakes and oats; organic coffee and tea.

Abode Restaurant & Lounge ▱▱▱ $$$$
1541 Ocean Ave. Santa Monica 90401 • **310-394-3463**
Mon-Thu 5:30pm-10pm Fri-Sat 6pm-12pm Sun 6pm-10pm
Happy Hour Sun-Fri 5pm-7pm www.aboderestaurant.com
Seasonal, artisanal cuisine using organic, sustainable ingredients. Dining
tables and other interior elements made from sustainable woods.

Akasha ▱▱▱▱ $$$ C
9543 Culver Blvd. Culver City 90232 • **310-845-1700**
Bakery: Mon-Sat 7am-6pm Restaurant/bar: Mon-Thu 11:30am-11pm
Fri-Sat 11:30am-12:30am www.akasharestaurant.com
New American cuisine. Sustainable ingredients and seafood, free-range and
organic poultry and meats. Organic produce and dairy. Locally roasted, fair trade
coffee. Extensive organic and sustainable wine, beer, and spirits selection.

Backyard, The ▱▱▱ $$
930 Hilgard Ave. LA 90024 • **310-443-8211**
Seasonal hours
Serves Contemporary American/Californian cuisine using free-range poultry
and eggs; grass-fed, hormone-free meats. Organic dairy, produce, grains,
coffee, tea, juice.

Bistro 767 ▱▱▱ $$$ C
767 Deep Valley Dr. Rolling Hills Estates 90274 • **310-265-0914**
Tue-Sat 5:30pm-10pm www.bistro767.com
Organic produce, poultry, meats, grains; many locally purchased ingredients.

Blue Velvet ▱▱ $$$
750 S. Garland Ave. LA 90017 • **213-239-0061**
Mon-Thu 11:30am-2:30pm, 5:30pm-10:30pm Fri 11:30-2:30pm, 5:30pm-11pm
Sat 5:30pm-11pm www.bluevelvetrestaurant.com
Organic produce (some from on-site rooftop garden); some organic, free-range
poultry and eggs; wild-caught fish; some grass-fed, hormone-free meats.

Blvd, The ▱▱ $$$$
9500 Wilshire Blvd. Beverly Hills 90210 • **310-275-5200**
Daily 6:30am-10:30pm www.fourseasons.com
Organic, local produce; organic, free-range poultry, eggs; wild-caught and
sustainably farmed fish; hormone-free meats.

Craft ▱▱▱▱ $$$$ C
10100 Constellation Blvd. LA 90067 • **310-279-4180**
Mon-Fri 11:30am-2:30pm Mon-Thu 5pm-10pm Fri-Sat 5pm-11pm
www.craftrestaurant.com
Organic produce, poultry, meats, dairy, grains. Wild-caught and organic,
farm-raised fish.

Cut ✑ $$
9500 Wilshire Blvd. Beverly Hills 90210 • **310-276-8500**
Mon-Sat 5:30pm-10:30pm Sidebar 5:30pm-1:30am www.wolfgangpuck.com
Steakhouse featuring some organic grass-fed beef and other hormone-free
meats; some locally grown organic produce.

Danny's Venice Deli ✑ $$
23 Windward Ave. Venice 90291 • **310-566-5610**
Mon-Fri 10:30am-10pm Sat-Sun 10am-10pm www.dannysvenicedeli.com
Kosher deli and restaurant. Some organic ingredients.

Edendale Grill, The ✑✑ $$$
2838 Rowena Ave. LA 90034 • **323-666-2000**
Mon-Thu 5:30pm-10pm Fri-Sat 5:30pm-11:30pm Sun 10am-3pm, 5:30pm-10pm
www.edendalegrill.com
Some organic produce; some hormone-free meats, poultry; wild-caught fish.

Firefly Bistro ✑ $$$
1009 El Centro St. South Pasadena 91030 • **626-441-2443**
Tue-Fri 11:30am-2:30pm, 5:30pm-10pm Sat-Sun 10am-2:30pm, 5:30pm-10pm
www.eatatfirefly.com
Modern American cuisine using some organic ingredients.

Food ✑✑✑ $ C
10571 W. Pico Blvd. LA 90064 • **310-441-7770**
Mon-Fri 8am-8pm Sat 8am-6pm Sun 8am-3pm www.food-la.com
Local, organic produce; free-range poultry, eggs; wild-caught and hormone-
free, farm-raised fish; grass-fed, hormone-free meats. Some organic dairy,
grains, beverages.

Foundry, The ✑✑ $$$
7465 Melrose Ave. LA 90046 • **323-651-0915**
Tue-Sun 6am-11pm www.thefoundryonmelrose.com
Some organic, locally grown produce; free-range poultry; wild-caught fish.
Certified organic nondairy beverages.

Full O' Life Health Food Restaurant ✑✑ $
2515 W. Magnolia Rd. Burbank 91506 • **818-845-7411**
Mon-Fri 11am-3:30pm Sun 11am-3pm
Organic ingredients; naturally-raised poultry. Sugar-free, white flour-free
desserts.

Granville Café ✑ $$
121 N. San Fernando Blvd. Burbank 91502 • **818-848-4726**
Mon-Thur 11am-10pm Fri 11am-11pm Sat 8am-11pm Sun 8am-10pm
www.granvillecafe.com
Some organic produce; free-range, hormone-free poultry and farm-raised
fish. Organic coffee.

Josie ✑✑✑✑ $$$$
2424 Pico Blvd. Santa Monica 90405 • **310-581-9888**
Mon-Sat 6pm-close Sun 5:30pm-close www.josierestaurant.com
Healthy approach to classic cuisine and comfort foods. Farmers' market
produce; grass-fed, hormone-free meats; free-range, hormone-free poultry.
Organic coffee and teas.

Mike and Anne's ✑ $$$ C
1040 Mission St. South Pasadena 91030 • **626-799-7199**
Tue-Fri 11am-2:30pm, 5:30pm-9:30pm Sat-Sun 8:30am-2:30pm, 5:30pm-9:30pm
Farmers' market produce; locally produced cheese, coffee, beer; wild-
caught fish.

Napa Valley Grille ⌀⌀ $$$ C
1100 Glendon Ave. LA 90024 • **310-824-3322**
Mon-Fri 11:30-11pm Sat 11am-11pm Sun 11am-9pm www.napavalleygrille.com
Some organic produce, farm-raised fish; some wild-caught fish.

Sunset Restaurant, The ⌀ $$$
6800 Westward Beach Rd. Malibu 90265 • **310-589-1007**
Tue-Fri 5pm-10pm Sat-Sun 11am-10pm www.thesunsetrestaurant.com
Pacific Rim-inspired cuisine. Organic poultry, meats; some wild-caught fish.

Terra Restaurant ⌀⌀ $$$
21337 Pacific Coast Hwy. Malibu 90265 • **310-456-1221**
Tue-Sun 6pm-10pm Sun 11am-3pm Bar 5pm-10pm
Some organic produce, grains, dairy; free-range poultry, eggs; wild-caught
fish; grass-fed, hormone-free meats. Citrus, tomatoes grown on-site.

Utopia ⌀⌀⌀ $ C
2311 Santa Monica Blvd. Santa Monica 90404 • **310-315-4375**
Mon-Fri 8am-4pm Sat 9am-3pm
Organic produce, poultry, meats, grains, dairy; wild-caught fish; organic
coffee, tea.

Watercress A Café ⌀⌀⌀ $
13565 Ventura Blvd. Sherman Oaks 91423 • **818-385-1448**
Mon-Sat 10am-6pm www.watercresscafe.com
Seasonal, home-style cooking. Mostly organic ingredients; minimal use of
salt, oil, refined sugar.

Yonni's ⌀ $ C
1714 N. Wilcox Ave. Hollywood 90028 • **323-962-1020**
Daily 9am-9pm www.yonnis.com
Some organic ingredients; free-range chicken; organic coffee, tea. Outdoor
dining; takeout.

ASIAN

Blue Hen ⌀⌀⌀⌀ $ C
1743 Colorado Blvd. LA 90041 • **323-982-9900**
Mon-Fri 11:30am-3pm, 5:30pm-9:30pm Fri 11:30am-3pm, 5:30pm-10pm
Sat 5pm-10pm Sun 5pm-9pm www.eatatbluehen.com
Serves Vietnamese food using free-range poultry and eggs; grass-fed,
hormone-free meats. Organic dairy, produce; some organic grains. Supports
local farms, sustainable farming practices.

China Beach Bistro ⌀⌀ $
2024 Pacific Ave. Venice 90291 • **310-823-4646**
Mon-Tue, Thu-Sun 11am-10pm www.chinabeachbistro.com
Cuisine from central Vietnam. Some organic ingredients. Vegetarian
options.

Fresh in the Box ⌀⌀ $
13354 Washington Blvd. LA 90066 • **310-301-9100**
Mon-Sat 11am-9:30pm
Japanese cuisine using many organic ingredients.

Happi Songs Asian Tavern ⌀ $$
460 S. La Brea Ave. LA 90036 • **323-936-7622**
Mon-Thu 11:30am-3pm, 6pm-11pm Fri 6pm-12am Sat 3pm-12am Sun 3pm-11pm
www.happisongs.com
Pan-Asian cuisine. Some organic ingredients; some wild-caught fish.

Inaka Natural Foods Restaurant   ␥␥   **$$**
131 S. La Brea Ave. LA 90036 • **323-936-9353**
Tue-Fri 12pm-2:30pm, 6pm-9:45pm Sat 5:30pm-9:45pm Sun 5:30pm-9pm
Japanese macrobiotic cuisine. Some organic produce, grains, wild-caught
fish. Vegetarian options.

Kiyokawa   ␥␥␥   **$$$$**   **C**
265 S. Robertson Blvd. Beverly Hills 90211 • **310-358-1900**
Mon-Fri 12pm-3pm, 6pm-10pm Sat 6pm-10pm www.kiyokawa-restaurant.com
Natural Japanese cuisine. Mostly organic produce, free-range, hormone-
free poultry; some wild-caught fish.

Restaurant 2117   ␥␥␥   **$$**
2117 Sawtelle Blvd. LA 90025 • **310-477-1617**
Tue-Sat 12pm-2:30pm, 6pm-10pm Sun 5:30pm-9pm www.restaurant2117.com
Japanese cuisine. Locally grown organic produce; grass-fed, hormone-free
meats; free-range chicken; wild-caught fish.

Shima   ␥␥␥   **$$$$**
1432 Abbot Kinney Blvd. Venice 90291 • **310-314-0882**
Tue-Sat 6pm-10:30pm
Japanese cuisine. Wild-caught fish; organic produce, eggs, grains,
nondairy beverages.

Sushi Roku   ␥␥   **$$$**   **C**
8445 W. 3rd St. LA 90048 • **323-655-6767**
33 Miller Alley Pasadena 91103 • **626-683-3000**
1401 Ocean Ave. Santa Monica 90401 • **310-458-4771**
Hours vary by location www.sushiroku.com
Japanese cuisine. Wild-caught fish; some organic produce; hormone-free
meats; free-range chicken.

ASIAN FUSION

Casa De Tree   ␥␥␥␥   **$**
2543 Pacific Coast Hwy. Ste. E Torrance 90505 • **310-784-0455**
Tue-Sat 8:30am-8pm www.casadetree.com
Bakery and vegan deli featuring a blend of Japanese and French recipes.
Uses seasonal organic produce, grains, beverages. No artificial additives.

Chaya Venice   ␥   **$$-$$$**
110 Navy St. Venice 90291 • **310-396-1179**
Mon-Fri 11:30am-2:30pm Daily 6pm-close www.thechaya.com
Some organic ingredients. Full sushi bar; some wild-caught and organic,
farm-raised fish.

Green Zone Restaurant   ␥␥   **$$**
534 E. Valley Blvd. Ste. 5 San Gabriel 91776 • **626-288-9300**
Tue-Sat 11:30am-3pm, 5:30pm-10pm Sun 11:30am-3pm, 5:30pm-9pm
www.greenzonerestaurant.com
Organic produce, poultry, dairy; wild-caught fish. Some organic nondairy
beverages.

Ma' Kai Restaurant & Lounge   ␥␥   **$$$**
101 Broadway Ave. Santa Monica 90401 • **310-434-1511**
Daily 11:30am-12am www.makailounge.com
Organic, free-range, cage-free poultry; some organic meats, grains,
produce; some wild-caught fish.

Red I Seven ⌀⌀ $$
700 N. San Vicente Blvd. West Hollywood 90069 • **310-289-1587**
Mon-Fri 11:30am-3pm www.wolfgangpuck.com
Some organic produce, grains, coffee, tea. Free-range, cage-free poultry;
wild-caught fish.

3 on Fourth ⌀⌀ $$$ C
1432A Fourth St. Santa Monica 90401 • **310-395-6765**
Mon-Thu 11:30am-2:30pm, 5:30pm-10pm Fri-Sat 11:30am-2:30pm, 6pm-11pm
www.3onfourth.com
Japanese, French, American cuisine using organic, sustainable ingredients.

X'otik Kitchen ⌀⌀⌀ $$ C
6121 Washington Blvd. Culver City 90232 • **310-280-3961**
Mon-Sat 11am-8pm www.xotikkitchen.com
Mostly organic produce; free-range chicken; grass-fed beef; wild-caught fish.

CALIFORNIAN

Ammo ⌀⌀⌀⌀ $$ C
1155 N. Highland Ave. LA 90038 • **323-871-2666**
Mon-Thu 11:30am-3pm, 5:30pm-10pm Fri 11:30am-3pm, 5:30pm-11pm
Sat 10am-3pm, 5:30pm-11pm Sun 10am-3pm, 5:30pm-10pm
www.ammocafe.com
Mostly locally grown or sustainably harvested, organic produce; wild-
caught fish; hormone-free meats and poultry; organic coffee and teas.
Participates in composting program.

Axe ⌀⌀⌀⌀ $$$
1009 Abbot Kinney Blvd. Venice 90291 • **310-664-9787**
Tue-Thu 11:30am-3pm, 6pm-10pm Fri 11:30am-3pm, 6pm-10:30pm Sat 9am-3pm,
6pm-10:30pm Sun 9am-3pm, 5:30pm-9:30pm www.axerestaurant.com
Seasonal, market-driven menu; mostly local, organic ingredients. Interior
designed with sustainable woods, handmade jute lamps. Composts and
participates in biodiesel recycling program.

Bistro 45 ⌀⌀⌀ $$$ C
45 S. Mentor Ave. Pasadena 91106 • **626-795-2478**
Tue-Thu 11:30am-2pm, 6pm-9pm Fri 11:30am-2pm, 6pm-9:30pm
Sat 6pm-9:30pm Sun 5pm-9pm www.bistro45.com
Locally purchased produce; grass-fed, hormone-free beef; free-range
chicken; organic fish. Vegetarian options.

Café Pinot ⌀ $$$
700 W. Fifth St. LA 90071 • **213-239-6500**
Mon-Fri 11:30am-2:30pm, 5pm-10pm Sat 5pm-10:30pm Sun 5pm-9:30pm
www.patinagroup.com
Wild-caught and sustainable, farm-raised fish; some organic produce,
meats, poultry, eggs, grains.

Café Vida ⌀⌀⌀ $$ C
15317 Antioch St. Pacific Palisades 90292 • **310-573-1335**
Daily 8am-9pm
Mostly organic ingredients; wild-caught fish. Vegetarian options.

Calitalia (formerly Native Cafe) ⌀⌀ $$$ C
23536 Calabasas Rd. Calabasas 91302 • **818-223-9600**
Tue-Thu 11:30am-2:30pm, 5pm-10pm Fri 11:30am-2:30pm, 5pm-11pm
Sat-Sun 11pm
Californian and Italian cuisine. Some organic produce, poultry, meats; wild-
caught fish. Musical entertainment in the Native Lounge. Take a massage
break in the Relaxation Lounge.

Campanile ✐✐✐ $$$$ C
624 S. La Brea Ave. LA 90036 • **323-938-1447**
Mon-Wed 11:30am-2:30pm, 6pm-10pm Thu-Fri 11:30am-2:30pm, 5:30pm-11pm
Sat 9:30am-1:30pm, 5:30pm-11pm Sun 9:30am-1:30pm
www.campanilerestaurant.com
Organic, locally grown produce; organic poultry, eggs, grains; wild-caught fish.

Canelé ✐ $$ C
3219 Glendale Blvd. LA 90039 • **323-666-7133**
Tue-Sat 5:30pm-10:30pm Sun 5pm-10pm www.canele-la.com
California and Mediterranean cuisine. Farmers' market-based ingredients;
organic produce, poultry, meats. Some wild-caught fish.

Cheebo ✐✐✐ $$$
7533 W. Sunset Blvd. LA 90046 • **323-850-7070**
Mon-Thu 8am-11pm Fri-Sat 8am-12am Sun 8am-11pm www.cheebo.com
Locally grown produce; grass-fed, hormone-free beef; free-range chicken,
organic eggs. Vegan and vegetarian options.

Comfort Café at Fred Segal ✐✐✐ $ C
420 Broadway Ave. Santa Monica 90401 • **310-395-6252**
Mon-Sat 10am-7pm Sun 12pm-6pm www.cafeatfredsegal.com
Some organic poultry, meats, dairy, grains. Serves organic coffee, tea.

Flowering Tree, The ✐✐ $
8253 Santa Monica Blvd. West Hollywood 90046 • **323-654-4332**
Mon-Thu 9am-9pm Fri-Sat 9am-3pm
Organic, local produce; free-range poultry; grass-fed, hormone-free beef.
Vegan and vegetarian options. Interior designed using bamboo flooring,
low-VOC paint.

Ford's Filling Station ✐✐✐ $$ C
9531 Culver Blvd. Culver City 90252 • **310-202-1470**
Mon-Sat 11am-11pm www.fordsfillingstation.net
California seasonal cuisine using many organic ingredients.

Getty Center Restaurant, The ✐✐ $$-$$$ C
1200 Getty Center Dr. LA 90049 • **310-440-6810**
Tue-Thu 11:30am-2:30pm Fri-Sat 11:30am-2:30pm, 5pm-9pm Sun 11am-3pm
www.bamco.com
Californian/Mediterranean cuisine using local, sustainable ingredients.

Grill, The ✐✐ $$$ C
101 Wilshire Blvd. Santa Monica 90401 • **310-576-7777**
Daily 7am-2pm, 5:30pm-10pm www.fairmont.com/santamonica
Located in the Fairmont Miramar Hotel. Uses some organic ingredients.

Harvest, The ✐✐ $$$
13018 San Vicente Blvd. LA 90049 • **310-458-6050**
Tue-Sat 5:30pm-10pm www.theharvestrestaurant.com
Californian/Mediterranean cuisine using ingredients from Santa Monica
farmers' market. Some organic produce; organic meats, wild-caught fish.

Hugo's Restaurant ✐✐ $$
12851 Riverside Dr. Studio City 91607 • **818-761-8985**
8401 Santa Monica Blvd. West Hollywood 90069 • **323-654-3993**
Mon-Fri 7:30am-10pm Sat-Sun 8am-10pm www.hugosrestaurant.com
Many organic ingredients; some wild-caught fish. Vegetarian options.

Inn of the Seventh Ray 🍃🍃🍃🍃 $$$ C
128 Old Topanga Canyon Rd. Topanga 90290 • **310-455-1311**
Mon-Fri 11:30am-3pm, 5:30pm-10pm Sat 10:30am-3pm, 5:30pm-10pm
Sun 9:30am-3pm, 5:30pm-10pm www.innoftheseventhray.com
Local, organic produce. Hormone-free, organic meat; cage-free poultry;
wild-caught fish. Organic bakery, raw menu. Vegan and vegetarian options.

Jack Sprat's Grille 🍃 $$ C
10668 W. Pico Blvd. LA 90064 • **310-837-6662**
Mon-Thu 11:30am-9pm Fri 11:30am-10pm Sat 9:30am-10pm Sun 9:30am-8pm
www.jackspratsgrille.com
Some organic produce, poultry, meats, grains; wild-caught and organic,
farm-raised fish.

Joe's Restaurant 🍃🍃🍃 $$$ C
1023 Abbot Kinney Blvd. Venice 90291 • **310-399-5811**
Tue-Thu 12pm-2:30pm, 6pm-10pm Fri 12pm-2:30pm, 6pm-11pm
Sat 11am-2:30pm, 6pm-11pm Sun 11am-2:30pm www.joesrestaurant.com
Organic poultry, dairy; some organic produce, meats; wild-caught fish.

Literati 2 🍃🍃 $$$
12081 Wilshire Blvd. LA 90025 • **310-479-3400**
Seasonal hours www.literati2.com
Local, seasonal produce; grass-fed meats, free-range poultry, wild-caught
fish. Some organic ingredients. Hosts private parties.

Lucques 🍃🍃🍃 $$$ C
8474 Melrose Ave. LA 90069 • **323-655-6277**
Mon 6pm-10pm Tue-Sat 12-2:30pm, 6pm-11pm Sun 5pm-10pm
www.lucques.com
Mostly organic ingredients. Extensive wine selection. Outdoor seating.

Michael's Restaurant 🍃🍃🍃 $$$$ C
1147 Third St. Santa Monica 90403 • **310-451-0843**
Mon-Thu 12pm-2:30pm, 6pm-10pm Fri 12pm-2:30pm, 6pm-10:30pm
Sat 6pm-10:30pm www.michaelssantamonica.com
Mostly organic produce, meats; some organic poultry, wild-caught fish.

Naturally 🍃 $
15200 Sunset Blvd. Ste. 105 Pacific Palisades 90272 • **310-459-1010**
Mon-Fri 8:30am-5:30pm Sat 9:30am-4:30pm
Some organic produce, poultry, dairy; wild-caught fish. Vegetarian options.

Nine Thirty 🍃🍃🍃 $$$
930 Hilgard Ave. LA 90024 • **310-443-8211**
Daily 6:30am-11am 5pm-11pm www.ninethirtyw.com
Organic produce, dairy, grains, coffee, tea, juice. Free-range poultry, eggs;
grass-fed, hormone-free meats.

Paddington's Tea Room 🍃🍃🍃 $$$ C
355 S. Robertson Blvd. Beverly Hills 90211 • **310-652-0624**
Daily 11am-6pm www.paddingtonstearoom.com
Most ingredients from local farmers' markets. Organic produce, meat,
poultry. Some organic grains, tea, dairy.

Patina 🍃🍃 $$$$ C
141 S. Grand Ave. LA 90012 • **213-972-3331**
Mon-Fri 11am-2pm, 5pm-11pm Sat-Sun 5pm-11pm (Performance Eve.) or
Sat-Sun 5pm-9:30pm (Non-Performance Eve.) www.patinagroup.com
Upscale Californian, French-inspired cuisine. Many organic, local
ingredients; extensive cheese selection. Cooking classes available.

Rustic Canyon 🌿🌿🌿 $$$
1119 Wilshire Blvd. Santa Monica 90401 • **310-393-7050**
Mon-Thu 11:30am-2:30pm, 5:30pm-10:30pm Fri 11:30am-2:30pm, 5:30pm-
11:30pm Sun 5:30pm-10:30pm www.rusticcanyonwinebar.com
Neighborhood restaurant and wine bar. Farmers' market-inspired dishes;
mostly local, organic ingredients. Supports sustainable, local farming practices.

Sante La Brea 🌿🌿 $
345 N. La Brea Ave. LA 90036 • **323-857-0412**
Mon-Sat 8am-10pm Sun 8am-9pm www.santecuisine.com
Organic and locally grown produce; grass-fed, hormone-free beef; free-
range chicken. Vegetarian and vegan options.

Spago 🌿🌿🌿 $$$$
176 N. Canon Dr. Beverly Hills 90210 • **310-385-0880**
Mon-Fri 11:30am-2pm Sat 12pm-2pm Mon-Sun 5pm-close
www.wolfgangpuck.com
Organic, locally grown produce; organic poultry, eggs, grains; wild-caught
and organic, farm-raised fish.

Table 8 🌿🌿 $$$
7661 Melrose Ave. LA 90046 • **323-782-8258**
Mon-Sat 6pm-10pm www.table8restaurants.com
Locally purchased, farmers' market produce; hormone-free, grass-fed
meats; free-range poultry. Vegetarian options.

Tender Greens 🌿🌿🌿 $ C
9532 Culver Blvd. Culver City 90232 • **310-842-8300**
Daily 11:30am-9:30pm www.tendergreensfood.com
Locally grown, organic produce from small farms. Organic poultry, meats,
grains; artisanal wines.

Urth Caffé 🌿🌿🌿🌿 $ C
267 S. Beverly Dr. Beverly Hills 90210 • **310-205-9311**
2327 Main St. Santa Monica 90405 • **310-314-7040**
8565 Melrose Ave. West Hollywood 90069 • **310-659-0628**
Hours vary by location www.urthcaffe.com
Locally purchased produce; hormone-free dairy; free-range eggs; organic
coffee, tea. Vegan and vegetarian options.

Whist 🌿🌿 $$$
1819 Ocean Ave. Santa Monica 90401 • **310-260-7500**
Daily 7am-10pm www.viceroysantamonica.com
Located in the Viceroy Hotel. Farmers' market-inspired cuisine. Organic
poultry, meats, dairy, grains; some organic produce.

FRENCH

Canyon Bistro in Topanga, The 🌿🌿 $$
120 N. Topanga Canyon Ste. 119 Topanga 90290 • **310-455-7800**
Tue-Fri 11am-10pm Sat-Sun 10am-10pm www.canyonbistro.com
Eclectic combination of French, Asian, and American cuisine. Some organic
ingredients. Serves weekend brunch.

Chameau 🌿🌿🌿 $$$ C
339 N. Fairfax Ave. LA 90036 • **323-951-0039**
Tue-Sat 6pm-10pm www.chameaurestaurant.com
Organic, locally grown produce; grass-fed, hormone-free beef; free-range
chicken. Vegetarian options.

Figaro Bistro ✐✐✐ $$
1802 N. Vermont Ave. LA 90027 • **323-662-1587**
Mon-Sun 8:30am-10:30pm
Southern French-inspired cuisine. Organic ingredients; some wild-caught fish.

Hampton's ✐✐ $$$
2 Dole Dr. Westlake Village 91362 • **818-575-3000**
Mon-Sat 5:30pm-10pm Sun 10:30am-2pm
www.fourseasons.com/westlakevillage
French/Californian cuisine. Some organic poultry, meat, produce; some wild-caught fish.

Mélisse ✐✐✐ $$$$ C
1104 Wilshire Blvd. Santa Monica 90401 • **310-395-0881**
Tue-Thu 6pm-9:30pm Fri 6pm-10pm Sat 5:45pm-10pm www.melisse.com
Traditional French cuisine with contemporary American influence. Uses local organic produce, wild-caught fish, organic meats, and free-range poultry; some organic beverages and wines.

Mes Amis Restaurant ✐✐✐ $$ C
1739 N. Vermont Ave. LA 90027 • **323-665-7810**
Mon, Thu-Fri 11am-11pm Sat-Sun 9am-11pm
Provençale cuisine using predominantly organic ingredients.

Pinot Bistro ✐ $$$
12969 Ventura Blvd. Studio City 91604 • **818-990-0500**
Mon 12pm-2pm Tue-Thu 12pm-2pm, 5:30pm-9:30pm Fri 2pm-2pm, 5:30pm-10pm Sat-Sun 5:30pm-9pm www.patinagroup.com
Some organic poultry; some wild-caught and organic, farm-raised fish.

750ml ✐✐✐ $$$ C
966 Mission St. South Pasadena 90130 • **626-799-0711**
Mon-Sun 5pm-11pm www.750ml.com
Locally grown produce, free-range and organic meats, wild-caught fish.

Sona Restaurant ✐✐✐ $$$$ C
401 N. La Cienaga Blvd. LA 90048 • **310-659-7708**
Tue-Fri 6pm-10pm Sat 5:30pm-11pm www.sonarestaurant.com
Locally-grown, organic produce; hormone-free meats; wild-caught fish. Extensive list of organic wines.

ITALIAN

Blue Table ✐✐✐ $$
4774 Park Granada Calabasas 91302 • **818-222-5195**
Mon-Fri 10am-8pm Sat 10am-5pm www.blue-table.com
European deli. Many organic ingredients. Some wild-caught and organic, farm-raised fish.

Ca' del Sole ✐✐✐ $$$ n
4100 Cahuenga Blvd. Toluca Lake 91602 • **818-985-4669**
Mon-Thu 11am-3pm, 5:30pm-9:30pm Fri 11am-3pm, 5:30pm-10pm
Sat 5:30pm-10pm Sun 11am-9pm www.cadelsole.com
Locally produced, organic ingredients. Free-range, hormone-free poultry; grass-fed meats. Biodegradable takeout containers. Houses the Chef Is Chef Culinary School.

Café Carolina ✐✐ $$
17934 Ventura Blvd. Encino 91316 • **818-881-8600**

Café Carolina (cont.)
Mon-Thu 5:30pm-9:30pm Fri-Sat 5:30pm-10pm Sun 5:30pm-9:30pm
www.organiccafecarolina.com
Neighborhood trattoria. Locally grown ingredients; some organic and vegetarian options.

Capo $\mathcal{O}$ $$$$ C
1810 Ocean Ave. Santa Monica 90401 • 310-394-5550
Tue-Fri 6pm-10pm Sat 6pm-11pm
Some organic produce; hormone-free meats and poultry; wild-caught fish.

Fresco Ristorante $\mathcal{OO}$ $$$ C
514 S. Brand Blvd. Glendale 91204 • 818-247-5541
Tue-Fri 11:30am-2pm, 5:30pm-10pm Sat-Sun 5:30-10pm
www.fresco-ristorante.com
Organic, local produce; wild-caught fish; free-range, hormone-free chicken.
Organic coffee, tea.

Il Grano $\mathcal{OO}$ $$$
11359 Santa Monica Blvd. LA 90025 • 310-477-7886
Mon-Fri 11:30am-2pm Mon-Sat 5:30pm-10pm www.ilgrano.com
Seasonal, farmers' market produce; wild-caught fish. Some organic ingredients.

Kreation Kafe Organic $\mathcal{OOO}$ $$ C
1023 Montana Ave. Santa Monica 90403 • 310-458-4880
Daily 8am-10pm
Locally grown organic produce; hormone-free meats, poultry, fish.

Modo Mio Cucina Rustica $\mathcal{O}$ $$ C
15200 Sunset Blvd. Ste. 106 Pacific Palisades 90272 • 310-459-0979
Mon-Thu 11:30am-3pm, 5pm-10pm Fri 11:30am-3pm, 5pm-10:30pm
Sat 5pm-10:30pm Sun 5pm-10pm www.modomiocucinarustica.com
Northern Italian cuisine. Some organic produce, poultry, meats; wild-caught fish.

Osteria Mozza $\mathcal{OO}$ $$$
6602 Melrose Ave. LA 90038 • 323-297-0100
Mon-Sat 5:30pm-11pm www.mozza-la.com
Some organic produce, meats, poultry; some wild-caught fish.

Pace Restaurant $\mathcal{OOO}$ $$$ C
2100 Laurel Canyon Blvd. LA 90046 • 323-654-8583
Mon-Fri 5:30pm-11pm Sun 10am-3pm www.peaceinthecanyon.com
Organic produce, dairy, grains, meats, poultry; wild-caught and organic, farm-raised fish.

Pizzeria Mozza $\mathcal{OO}$ $$
641 N. Highland Ave. LA 90036 • 323-297-0101
Daily 12pm-12am www.mozza-la.com
Some organic produce, poultry, meats; some wild-caught fish.

LATIN AMERICAN

Ciudad $\mathcal{OOO}$ $$$ C
445 S. Figueroa St. LA 90071 • 213-486-5171
Mon-Tue 11:30am-9pm Wed-Thu 11:30am-11pm Fri 11:30am-12am Sat 5pm-12am Sun 5pm-9pm Weekday Happy Hour www.ciudad-la.com
Locally purchased produce; wild-caught fish, grass-fed, hormone-free beef; cage-free poultry. Vegetarian options. Participates in biodiesel program.

Mama's Hot Tamales Café 🌿🌿 $ C
2124 W. Seventh St. LA 90057 • 213-487-7474
Mon-Sun 11am-3:30pm www.mamas-hot-tamales.com
Organic produce from farmers' market; some organic grains, dairy, beverages. Vegetarian options.

MEDITERRANEAN

A.O.C. 🌿🌿🌿 $$$$ C
8022 W. 3rd St. LA 90048 • **323-653-6359**
Mon-Fri 6pm-11pm Sat 5:30pm-11pm Sun 5pm-10pm www.aocwinebar.com
Upscale wine bar with more than 50 offerings by the glass. Mediterranean-style tapas and small plates made with local, organic produce; farm-raised organic fish; and other organic ingredients.

Courtyard Restaurant, The 🌿 $$ C
8543 Santa Monica Blvd. West Hollywood 90069 • **310-358-0301**
Mon-Thu 4:30pm-12am Fri 4:30pm-1am Sat 9pm-1am Sun 4:30pm-10pm
www.dinecourtyard.com
Some local, organic produce; hormone-free chicken, beef; wild-caught fish.

Elf Café 🌿🌿🌿🌿 $$
2135 W. Sunset Blvd. LA 90026 • **213-484-6829**
Wed-Sun 6pm-11pm
Organic, sustainable, locally grown ingredients. Vegan and vegetarian options.

Little Door, The 🌿🌿🌿 $$$$ C
8164 W. 3rd St. LA 90048 • **323-951-1210**
Mon-Thu 6pm-10:30pm Fri-Sat 6pm-11:30pm Sun 6pm-10:30pm
www.thelittledoor.com
Seasonal ingredients from farmers' markets and local sources. Organic produce, poultry, grains, dairy; wild-caught and organic, farm-raised fish.

Simon's Café 🌿 $$ C
4515 Sepulveda Blvd. Sherman Oaks 91403 • **818-783-6698**
Mon-Fri 11:30am-2:30pm, 5:30pm-10pm Sat 5:30pm-10pm www.simonscafe.com
Original Mediterranean cuisine. Some organic ingredients; wild-caught fish. Participates in biodiesel program. Offers cooking classes.

MEXICAN

Border Grill 🌿🌿 $$ C
1445 Fourth St. Santa Monica 90401 • **310-451-1655**
Mon-Thu 11:30am-10pm Fri-Sat 11:30am-11pm Sun 11:30am-10pm
www.bordergrill.com
Wild-caught fish; grass-fed, hormone-free beef; cage-free poultry. Vegetarian options.

Hugo's Tacos 🌿🌿 $
4749 Coldwater Cyn. Studio City 91607 • **818-762-7771**
Mon-Thu 10am-10pm Fri-Sat 10am-11pm Sun 10am-10pm www.hugostacos.com
Organic rice, beans, and tortillas; wild-caught and organic, farm-raised fish; some organic produce.

La Serenata de Garabaldi 🌿🌿 $$$ C
10924 W. Pico Blvd. LA 90064 • **310-441-9667**
1842 E. First St. LA 90033 • **323-265-2887**
1416 Fourth St. Santa Monica 90401 • **310-656-7017**
Hours vary by location www.laserenataonline.com
Some organic, locally grown produce; some organic poultry, meats, grains; some wild-caught fish.

MIDDLE EASTERN

Addi's Tandoor 🌿🌿 $$
800 Torrance Blvd. Redondo Beach 90505 • **310-540-1616**
Mon-Thu 11am-2:30pm, 5:30pm-10pm Fri 11am-2:30pm, 5:30pm-10:30pm Sat
12pm-3pm, 5:30pm-10:30pm www.addistandoor.com
Serves Indian/Pakistani cuisine using some organic produce, rice, tea.
Some hormone-free meats, free-range poultry, wild-caught fish.

Green Earth Café 🌿🌿🌿 $ C
22990 Ventura Blvd. Woodland Hills 91364 • **818-222-2033**
Mon-Sat 11am-9:30pm
Homemade Persian cuisine; organic produce, poultry, meats.

PIZZA

Bravo Pizzeria 🌿 $
2400 Main St. Santa Monica 90405 • **310-392-7466**
Mon-Thu 10:30am-1:30am Fri-Sat 10:30am-3:30am Sun 10:30am-1:30am
www.bravosantamonica.com
Pizza and Italian cuisine. Some organic ingredients.

Pitfire Pizza Co., The 🌿🌿 $ C
2018 Westwood Blvd. LA 90025 • **310-481-9860**
108 W. Second St. LA 90012 • **213-808-1200**
5211 Lankershim Blvd. North Hollywood 91601 • **818-980-2949**
Hours vary by location www.pitfirepizza.com
Ingredients from farmers' markets; organic heirloom tomatoes and other
organic produce, poultry, dairy, and grains.

SEAFOOD

Gulfstream 🌿 $$$
10250 Santa Monica Blvd. LA 90067 • **310-553-3636**
Mon-Sat 11:30am-10pm Sun 11:30am-9pm www.hillstone.com
Hormone-free poultry, farm-raised fish, some wild-caught fish.

Providence 🌿🌿 $$$$
5955 Melrose Ave. LA 90038 • **323-460-4170**
Mon-Fri 6pm-10pm Fri 12pm-2:30pm Sat 5:30pm-10pm Sun 5:30pm-9pm
www.providencela.com
Specializes in wild-caught seafood and shellfish. Some organic ingredients.

Water Grill, The 🌿🌿 $$$$
544 S. Grand Ave. LA 90071 • **213-891-0900**
Mon-Tue 11:30am-5:30pm Wed-Fri 11:30am-9:30pm Sat 5pm-9:30pm Sun
4:30pm-8:30pm www.watergrill.com
Seasonal seafood; wild-caught fish. Organic produce, poultry, and meats.

VEGETARIAN/VEGAN/RAW

Café Vegan 🌿 $
7669 Beverly Blvd. LA 90036 • **323-937-3100**
Daily 11am-11pm
Vegan cuisine. Organic produce and tea; all natural beverages.

California Vegan 🌿🌿🌿 $ C
12113 Santa Monica Blvd. Unit 207 LA 90025 • **310-207-4798**
7300 Sunset Blvd. Unit A LA 90046 • **323-874-9079**
Daily 11am-10:30pm www.californiavegan.com

California Vegan (cont.)

Vegetarian and vegan Thai food. Mostly organic ingredients. Organic soy and almond milk. Participates in biodiesel program.

Casa de Souza Coffee House 🍃🍃🍃 $

634 N. Main St. LA 90012 • **213-687-0363**
Mon-Fri 10am-7pm Sat 10am-9pm Sun 11am-6pm
All vegetarian, mostly vegan food. Local, organic produce; organic grains. Organic coffee roasted on premises.

Cook's Double Dutch 🍃🍃 $$ C

9806 Washington Blvd. Culver City 90232 • **310-280-0991**
Mon-Fri 12pm-2:30pm www.cooksdoubledutch.com
Vegetarian and vegan cuisine featuring local, organic produce; some organic wines.

Cru 🍃🍃🍃🍃 $$

1521 Griffith Park Blvd. LA 90026 • **323-667-1551**
Mon, Wed-Sun 12pm-10pm www.crusilverlake.com
All-organic, gourmet, raw, vegan cuisine.

Euphoria Loves Rawvolution 🍃🍃🍃🍃 $ C

2301 Main St. Santa Monica 90405 • **310-392-9501**
Daily 9am-9:30pm www.euphorialovesrawvolution.com
Raw, vegan cuisine. Organic, locally grown ingredients. Raw food deli, packaged raw food snacks. Participates in composting program. Visit their Beauty and Wisdom lifestyle boutique.

Fatty's & Co 🍃🍃🍃 $$

1627 Colorado Blvd. LA 90041 • **323-254-8804**
Wed-Sat 5pm-10pm Sun 5pm-9pm www.fattyscafe.com
Vegetarian and vegan cuisine. Organic, local ingredients. Rennet-free cheese; organic, fair trade coffee and tea; some organic wines.

Figtree's Café 🍃🍃🍃 $$ C

429 Ocean Front Walk Venice 90291 • **310-392-4937**
Daily 8am-7pm www.figtreescafe.com
Beachfront café serving vegetarian and vegan cuisine; many organic ingredients.

Flore Vegan Cuisine 🍃🍃🍃🍃 $

3818 W. Sunset Blvd. Silverlake 90026 • **323-953-0611**
Tue-Fri 10am-9pm Sat-Sun 10am-1pm, 3pm-9pm
Vegan cuisine using mostly organic ingredients. Outdoor seating; kid friendly.

Follow Your Heart Market & Café 🍃🍃🍃🍃 $

21825 Sherman Way Canoga Park 91303 • **818-348-3240**
Daily 8am-9pm www.followyourheart.com
One of the oldest vegetarian eateries in Southern California. Home-style, vegetarian comfort food. Many local, organic ingredients. Also visit their on-site natural foods grocery store.

Golden Bridge 🍃🍃🍃🍃 $

6322 De Longpre Ave. LA 90028 • **323-936-4172**
Mon-Thu 10am-9pm Fri-Sat 10am-4pm www.goldenbridgeyoga.com
Vegan café. Organic produce, coffee, tea, nondairy beverages.

Green Temple, The 🍃🍃🍃 $$

1700 S. Catalina Redondo Beach 90277 • **310-944-4525**

Tue-Thu 11am-9pm Fri-Sat 11am-10pm Sun 9am-4pm, 5pm-9pm
www.greentemple.net
Vegan and vegetarian options. Organic grains; organic coffee and tea.

Happy Veggie Restaurant ⌀ $ C
709 N. Pacific Coast Hwy. Redondo Beach 90277 • **310-379-5035**
Mon-Sat 11am-9pm www.happyveggie.com
Vegan and vegetarian restaurant offering Asian fusion cuisine using some
organic ingredients; no MSG.

Leaf Cuisine ⌀⌀⌀⌀ $ C
11938 W. Washington Blvd. LA 90066 • **310-390-6005**
14318 Ventura Blvd. Sherman Oaks 91423 • **818-907-8779**
Hours vary by location www.leafcuisine.com
Live, raw, vegan foods; juice bar. Mostly organic ingredients. Raw food prep
cooking classes.

M Café de Chaya ⌀⌀⌀⌀ $$ C
7119 Melrose Ave. LA 90046 • **323-525-0588**
Mon-Sat 9am-10pm Sun 9am-9pm www.mcafedechaya.com
Contemporary macrobiotic cuisine; mostly vegetarian and vegan fare.
Locally grown organic produce and brown rice; organic, seasonal desserts,
coffee, and green tea.

Madeleine Bistro ⌀⌀⌀⌀ $$ C
18621 Ventura Blvd. Tarzana 91356 • **818-758-6971**
Seasonal hours www.madeleinebistro.com
French-inspired, pan-ethnic vegan cuisine. Organic produce, grains.
Organic beer and beverages.

Native Foods ⌀⌀⌀⌀ $$ C
1110 Gayley Ave. LA 90024 • **310-209-1055**
Daily 11am-10pm www.nativefoods.com
Vegetarian and vegan Californian cuisine. Organic grains, coffee, and tea;
mostly organic produce. Kid-friendly. Cooking classes.

Pure Luck Restaurant ⌀⌀ $
707 Heliotrope Dr. LA 90027 • **323-660-5993**
Mon-Sat 11am-12am
Vegan cuisine. Organic produce, fair trade coffee.

RAW by Juliano and Ariel ⌀⌀⌀⌀ $ C
609 Broadway Santa Monica 90401 • **310-587-1552**
Mon-Thu 10am-10pm Fri-Sat 10am-11pm Sun 10am-10pm www.planetraw.com
Raw, vegan cuisine. All-organic ingredients.

Real Food Daily ⌀⌀⌀⌀ $$
414 N. La Cienega Blvd. LA 90048 • **310-289-9910**
514 Santa Monica Blvd. Santa Monica 90401 • **310-451-7544**
Hours vary by location www.realfood.com
Organic vegan cuisine. Seasonal, locally grown produce.

Soul Vegetarian Restaurant ⌀⌀ $$ C
4067 W. Pico Blvd. LA 90019 • **323-734-4037**
Mon-Fri 11am-9pm Sat-Sun 9am-9pm www.soulvegetarian.com
All-vegan restaurant. Organic, locally purchased produce; raw and cooked foods.

Spot, The ⌀⌀⌀⌀ $ C
110 Second St. Hermosa Beach 90254 • **310-376-2355**
Daily 11am-10pm www.worldfamousspot.com

Spot, The (cont.)
Natural food restaurant. Organic whole grains, poultry, produce; nongrain and nondairy options.

Taste of the Goddess Café ✎✎✎✎ **$$**
7373 Beverly Blvd. LA 90036 • **323-933-1400**
Mon 11am-7pm Tue-Sat 11am-9pm Sun 12pm-6pm www.tasteofthegoddess.com
Live, vegan cuisine. Organic produce, grains, nondairy beverages; juice bar.

Terra Bella Café ✎✎✎✎ **$**
1408 Pacific Coast Hwy. Redondo Beach 90277 • **310-316-8708**
Mon-Sat 10:30am-9pm Sun 11am-4pm www.terrabellacafe.com
Gourmet living cuisine from local, organic, seasonal produce. Organic nondairy beverages. Many herbs grown on-site.

Tierra Café ✎✎✎ **$**
818 Wilshire Blvd. LA 90017 • **213-629-1402**
Mon-Fri 7am-3:30pm
Organic, vegetarian fast-food restaurant. Vegan options.

Vegan Express ✎ **$**
3217 W. Cahuenga Blvd. LA 90068 • **323-851-8837**
Mon-Thu 11am-9pm Fri-Sat 11am-10pm Sun 11am-9pm
Produce from farmers' market; some organic ingredients.

Vegan Factory ✎✎ **$**
19014 Ventura Blvd. Tarzana 91356 • **818-342-3286**
Mon-Fri 11am-10pm Sat-Sun 12pm-10pm www.veganfactory.com
Thai vegan food. Some organic produce, grains, beverages.

Vegan Glory ✎✎✎ **$**
8393 Beverly Blvd. LA 90048 • **323-653-4900**
Daily 11am-10pm www.veganglory.com
Vegan and vegetarian Thai fusion cuisine. Locally grown produce; organic rice.

Vegan Joint, The ✎✎ **$ C**
10438 National Blvd. LA 90034 • **310-559-1357**
Mon-Thu 11am-9pm Fri-Sat 11am-10pm Sun 11am-9pm www.theveganjoint.com
All-vegan, Thai-based cuisine. Locally purchased, mostly organic produce. No refined sugar or MSG.

Vegetable Delight Restaurant ✎ **$ C**
17823 Chatsworth St. Granada Hills 91344 • **818-360-3997**
Tue-Sun 11:30am-9:30pm
Chinese vegetarian cuisine. Some organic ingredients.

Wine Bars and Breweries

Your favorite restaurant serves organic food. The specialty market around the corner has organic and hormone-free artisan cheeses. That loaf of bread you just bought is made from sustainably harvested wheat. Just thinking about it makes you want to celebrate with a nice glass of wine . . . or maybe a bottle of brew!

Well, shouldn't that refreshment be sustainably produced? We think so. In fact, conventional wine grape growing is responsible for a whole bunch of environmental ills—depletion of soil fertility (a critical factor in wine quality), ground water pollution, and destruction of beneficial insects and birds. What's more, vineyard workers are exposed to toxic chemicals as are nearby communities.

The same is true for the barley and hops that are used to make beer. Hops are particularly prone to fungus damage so those produced conventionally rely heavily on the use of fungicides. Similarly, herbicides, insecticides, and fossil fuel fertilizers are used on conventionally grown beer-making grains.

Throw in the fossil fuel used to transport the heavy glass bottles, the refrigeration required, and you've got a recipe for resource depletion. That means it's time to check out your local microbrewery. Beer can be produced in small vats and thus lends itself to urban production. So by supporting your local brewpub, you'll be building the local economy and saving a boatload of fossil fuel.

When it comes to wine, always ask for ones made from grapes that have been sustainably grown. Their quality just seems better; maybe because organic vintners tend to spend more time in their fields since raising grapes in an ecologically friendly way seems to be a more "hands-on" process. Dig a little deeper into the wine list. Make sure those somme-liers know their sustainable stuff.

Because this is an emerging field requiring strict adherence to USDA guidelines (see page 60), and since both supply and customer demand fluctuate, we have reduced our minimum threshold for inclusion in the guide. To be listed, at least 15% of the wines and beers served by an establishment must be organic and/or biodynamic (see page 58). We also looked at whether the business demonstrates a commitment to quality organic wines and beers by actively promoting them to its patrons.

Bottle Rock
3847 Main St. Culver City 90232 • **310-386-9463**
Mon-Thu 12pm-11pm Fri-Sat 12pm-2am Sun 12pm-11pm
www.bottlerock.com
Wine bar with decent selection of organic wine and beer; some organic ingredients in tapas menu.

Good Microbrew and Grill ✑

3725 W. Sunset Blvd. LA 90026 • **323-660-3645**
Mon-Thu 11am-10pm Fri-Sat 9am-11pm Sun 11am-10pm
www.goodmicrobrew.com
Microbrewery with good selection of organic beers.

Library Ale House ✑

2911 Main St. Santa Monica 90405 • **310-314-4855**
Daily 11:30am-12am www.libraryalehouse.com
Restaurant and bar with a small selection of organic beers and wines.

Otheroom, The ✑

1201 Abbot Kinney Blvd. Venice 90291 • **310-396-6230**
Daily 5pm-2am www.theotheroom.com
Wine and beer bar specializing in handcrafted beer and boutique wine with
some organic options. Features emerging local artist exhibits.

WineStyles Pacific Palisades ✑

1970 Monument Ste. 116 Pacific Palisades 90272 • **310-454-6960**
Mon-Sat 11am-8pm Sun by appt. www.winestyles.net/pacificpalisades
Wine boutique and club that offers organic wines for sale. Conducts
tastings and events featuring organic wines.

☕ Coffee and Tea Houses

Coffee and tea are the most commonly consumed beverages in the world
after water. And coffee houses and tea shops have played a major role in
human civilization ever since people got the hankering for something hot
to drink (and maybe a little something to eat on the side).

Coffee and tea also have huge ecological and social impacts. Much of
today's coffee crop is grown in technified "sun farms" rather than in the
shady rainforest understory. Coffee "sun farms" rely heavily on chemical
fertilizers and pesticides and harbor 90% fewer bird species than shade
plantations. In fact, shade grown coffee farms play a key role in the
conservation of migratory birds.

Keep in mind that not all shade grown coffee is organic and not all
organic coffee is shade grown. We hope you will do your best to find
an ecologically-friendly product that you like. Growing coffee and tea
in a sustainable fashion preserves healthy ecosystems and protects
wildlife. And while you're reading those labels, check for fair trade
certification. This indicates that growers are getting a living wage for
their harvest.

In short, there's a long story behind that little latté and a quite a tale
behind that pot of tea. It's one we're sure you'll be happy to get to know.
*(Oh, and don't forget to bring your own mug or cup if that coffee or tea
is to go!)*

We have determined leaf awards based primarily on the percentage of
coffees and teas that are served and available to purchase that are certified organic. However, because many of these establishments also use

Coffee and Tea Houses (cont.)

a wide range of milk products and offer prepared food items, we have factored in whether or not there are certified organic options in these areas as well. We also evaluated the percentage of juices, soft drinks, and smoothie ingredients that are certified organic.

> ⌀ at least 25% of all of the products served and available for sale meet the above criteria.
>
> ⌀⌀ at least 50% of all of the products served and available for sale meet the above criteria.
>
> ⌀⌀⌀ at least 75% of all of the products served and available for sale meet the above criteria.
>
> ⌀⌀⌀⌀ 90% or more of all of the products served and available for sale meet the above criteria.

Fair Trade

Fair trade certification helps farmers in the developing world get a fair price for their crops. It also helps to ensure good working conditions and preserves agricultural traditions. Fair trade certification also has significant environmental benefits in that it supports the preservation of watersheds, virgin forests, wildlife, and the conservation of water. It also maintains a prohibition against the use of genetically modified organisms. (See page 105 for more information about fair trade.)

Abbot's Habit ⌀
7554 W. Sunset Blvd. Hollywood 90046 • **323-512-5278**
1401 Abbot Kinney Blvd. Venice 90291 • **310-399-1171**
Hours vary by location
Café offers organic coffee and tea; organic soy milk; organic, raw leaf wraps.

Acadie Handcrafted French Crepes ⌀⌀
213 Arizona Ave. Santa Monica 90405 • **310-395-1120**
Mon-Wed 8am-8pm Thu-Sun 8am-9pm www.crepescompany.com
Crêperie serving organic coffee and tea.

Aroma Coffee and Tea Company ⌀⌀
4360 Tujunga Ave. Studio City 91604 • **818-508-7377**
Mon-Sat 6am-11pm Sun 7am-11pm www.aromacoffeeandtea.com
Organic, fair trade coffee and loose tea; backyard seating.

Buster's Ice Cream & Coffee Stop ⌀⌀
1006 Mission St. South Pasadena 91030 • **626-441-0744**
Mon-Wed 7am-7pm Thu 7am-8pm Fri-Sun 7am-10pm
Serves organic coffee, some organic tea; offers some fair trade choices.

Buzz Coffee ⌀⌀
7623 Beverly Blvd. LA 90036 • **323-634-7393**
Mon-Fri 7am-9pm Sat-Sun 8am-9pm
Café offers selection of organic coffee and tea.

Café Mimosa ✐✐
395 S. Topanga Canyon Blvd. Topanga 90290 • **310-455-4341**
Mon-Sat 6:30am-2pm Sun 7:30am-2pm
Selection of organic coffee, tea, pastries, soup, and snacks.

Café*Sol*r ✐✐✐✐
Beverly/Vermont Red Line Metro Station LA 90004 • **310-601-7520**
Mon-Fri 6:30am-12pm www.cafesolr.com
Coffee cart serving organic, fair trade, and locally roasted coffee and tea;
organic soy milk. Biodegradable cups and sleeves.

Caffe Etc. ✐✐
6371 Selma Ave. Hollywood 90028 • **323-464-8824**
Daily 7am-11pm www.caffeetc.com
Café serving locally roasted coffee; organic vegan and vegetarian prepared
foods.

City Bakery, The ✐✐✐
225 26th St. Brentwood 90049 • **310-656-3040**
Mon-Sat 7am-7pm Sun 7am-6pm www.thecitybakery.com
Organic coffee, baked goods, sandwiches, and salads.

Coffee Cellar ✐✐✐
2122 W. Seventh St. LA 90057 • **213-487-7474**
Daily 11am-3:30pm www.coffeecellar.com
100% organic, fair trade coffee. Also carries shade-grown and bird-friendly
varieties.

Coffee Fix ✐✐✐
12508 Moorpark St. Studio City 91604 • **818-762-0181**
Mon-Fri 7am-7pm Sat 8am-7pm Sun 9am-7pm
Neighborhood spot serving 100% organic coffee, some organic tea; pastries.

Conservatory for Coffee, Tea, and Cocoa, The ✐
10117 Washington Blvd. Culver City 90232 • **310-558-0436**
Mon-Fri 7am-6pm Sat 8am-2:45pm www.conservatorycoffeeandtea.com
On-site roasting of organic, fair trade coffee; selection of organic teas;
organic soy milk. Tables made from recycled plastic.

Cow's End, The ✐
34 Washington Blvd. Marina Del Rey 90292 • **310-574-1080**
Daily 6am-12am www.cowsend.com
Café offers some organic coffee and tea options; some organic muffins and
pastries.

Dr. Tea's Tea Garden and Herbal Emporium ✐✐✐✐
8612 Melrose Ave. West Hollywood 90069 • **310-657-9300**
Mon-Sat 8am-12pm Sun 8am-12pm www.teagarden.com
Specializes in organic tea and tea products; organic foods and juices.

18th Street Coffee House ✐✐
1725 Broadway Santa Monica 90404 • **310-264-0662**
Mon-Thu 7am-7pm Fri 7am-6:30pm Sat 8:30am-6pm
Neighborhood spot serving organic coffee and tea; outdoor patio.

Euphoria Loves Rawvolution ✐✐✐✐
2301 Main St. Santa Monica 90405 • **310-392-9501**
Mon-Sun 9am-9:30pm www.euphorialovesrawvolution.com
Organic teas, juices, and elixirs. Received Santa Monica Sustainable
Quality Award. Green Business Certified.

Grateful Bread 🌿
1518 Montana Ave. Santa Monica 90403 • **310-394-7178**
Mon-Sat 7am-7pm Sun 8am-4pm www.gratefulbread.org
Bakery offering organic coffee and nondairy beverages.

Groundwork Coffee Co. 🌿🌿🌿
1501 N. Cahuenga Blvd. Hollywood 90028 • **323-871-0107**
811 Traction Ave. LA 90013 • **213-626-8850**
108 W. Second St. LA 90012 • **213-620-9668**
2908 Main St. Santa Monica 90405 • **310-392-9243**
671 Rose Ave. Venice 90291 • **310-396-9469**
3 Westminster Ave. Venice 90291 • **310-452-2706**
Hours vary by location www.lacoffee.com
One of the first certified organic roasters in Southern California. Wide
variety of 100% certified organic, fair trade, shade grown, single source
coffees; organic teas.

Healing Tree Apothecary & Tea Bar, The 🌿🌿🌿
2711 E. Thousand Oaks Blvd. Thousand Oaks 91362 • **805-497-4438**
Mon-Sat 10:30am-6:30pm Sun 11am-5pm www.healingtreeproducts.com
Tea bar offering a wide selection of organic teas. Also sells natural health
care products in its apothecary.

Interim Café (formerly Newsroom Café) 🌿🌿🌿🌿
530 Wilshire Blvd. Santa Monica 90401 • **310-319-9100**
Mon-Fri 8am-9pm Sat 9am-7pm Sun 9am-3pm
Organic coffee, tea, juice, dairy products, and food items.

Jack n' Jill's 🌿🌿
342 N. Beverly Dr. Beverly Hills 90210 • **310-247-4500**
510 Santa Monica Blvd. Santa Monica 90401 • **310-656-1501**
Hours vary by location www.eatatjacknjills.com
Certified organic coffee, tea, and some juices; some organic food items.

Johnnie's Coffee Café 🌿
13455 Maxella Ave. Marina Del Rey 90292 • **310-301-9489**
Mon-Sat 7am-5pm Sun 8am-5pm
Organic coffee and tea. Outdoor seating.

Kaffee Wien 🌿🌿
8629 1/2 Melrose Ave. West Hollywood 90069 • **310-855-1136**
Mon-Fri 7:30am-6pm Sat-Sun 9am-4pm
Organic coffee, tea, chocolate, and soy milk.

Kaldi Coffee and Tea 🌿
3147 Glendale Blvd. LA 90039 • **323-660-6005**
Mon-Thu 6:30am-9pm Fri 6:30am-10pm Sat 7am-10pm Sun 7am-8pm
Organic tea; some organic, fair trade coffee. On-site coffee roasting.

Karma Coffee House 🌿🌿🌿
1544 North Cahuenga Blvd. Hollywood 90028 • **323-460-4188**
Daily 8am-12am www.karmacoffeehouse.com
Handcrafted, slow-roasted, organic, fair trade coffee; organic vegan dishes.
Nightly entertainment.

King's Café 🌿🌿
5506 Sawtelle Blvd. Culver City 90230 • **310-398-9019**
Mon-Tue 7am-12am Wed 7am-10pm Thu-Fri 7am-12am Sat 8am-10pm
Organic coffee and some organic tea. Monthly live entertainment.

Le Pain Quotidien ✏✏✏✏
9630 Santa Monica Blvd. Beverly Hills 90210 • **310-859-1100**
11702 Barrington Ct. LA 90049 • **310-476-0969**
320 S. Robertson Blvd. LA 90048 • **310-858-7270**
8607 Melrose Ave. LA 90069 • **310-854-3700**
451 Manhattan Beach Blvd. Manhattan Beach 90266 • **310-546-6411**
88 W. Colorado Blvd. Pasadena 91105 • **626-396-0956**
316 Santa Monica Blvd. Santa Monica 90401 • **310-393-6800**
13045 Ventura Blvd. Studio City 91604 • **818-986-1929**
1055 Broxton Ave. Westwood 90024 • **310-824-7900**
Hours vary by location www.lepainquotidien.com
Bakery serving organic coffee; organic pies, pastries, omelets, soups, and salads.

Literati Café ✏✏✏
12081 Wilshire Blvd. LA 90025 • **310-231-7484**
Mon-Fri 7am-11pm Sat-Sun 8am-11pm www.literaticafe.com
Selection of organic coffee and tea; organic produce and grains.

Mäni's Bakery Café ✏✏✏
519 S. Fairfax Ave. LA 90036 • **323-938-8800**
2507 Main St. Santa Monica 90405 • **310-396-7700**
Daily 7:30am-8pm www.manisbakery.com
Bakery and café with organic food and baked goods. Desserts sweetened with fruit juice.

Marie et Cie ✏
11704 Riverside Dr. Valley Village 91607 • **818-508-5049**
Mon-Fri 6am-10pm Sat-Sun 8am-8pm
Organic coffee and tea. Outdoor seating; free Wi-Fi. Also sells gifts, accessories, home furnishings.

Novel Café ✏✏✏
212 Pier Ave. Santa Monica 90405 • **310-396-8566**
Mon-Fri 7am-1am Sat-Sun 8am-12am www.novelcafe.com
Organic coffee, tea, dairy products; organic juices; some organic food items.

Planet Earth Eco Café ✏✏✏✏
509 Pier Ave. Hermosa Beach 90254 • **310-318-1888**
Tue-Fri 7am-5pm Sat-Sun 9am-3pm www.planetearthsweetshop.com
Organic, fair trade coffee and tea from small grower cooperatives; other organic beverages and vegan food options; Ayurvedic herbal tonics and E3Live tonics.

Psychobabble Coffee House ✏
1866 N. Vermont Ave. LA 90027 • **323-664-7500**
Daily 7am-2am www.psychobabblecafe.com
Selection of organic tea. Live entertainment (comedy and cabaret nights); free DSL.

Rainbow Acres ✏✏✏✏
13208 W. Washington Blvd. LA 90066 • **310-306-8330**
Mon-Fri 7am-9pm Sat-Sun 8am-8pm
Organic coffee and espresso bar inside market.

Rooibos Tea House ✏✏✏✏
533 N. Fairfax Ave. LA 90036 • **323-658-7832**
401½ S. Fairfax Ave. LA 90036 • **323-658-7832**
Mon-Fri 10am-5pm Sun 12pm-7pm www.africanredtea.com
Organic tea. Selection of soap, skin care items, and health products made with teas.

Shakti's Elements 🍃🍃🍃🍃
717 Broadway Santa Monica 90401 • **310-576-2008**
Mon-Fri 7:30am-7:30pm Sat 8am-7:30pm Sun 8am-6pm
www.shaktiselements.com
Organic coffee and tea bar inside yoga studio and retail space.

Silverlake Coffee Co. 🍃🍃
2388 Glendale Blvd. Ste 13 LA 90039 • **323-913-0388**
Mon-Fri 6:30am-9pm Sat-Sun 7:30am-9pm
Organic coffee and tea; fresh brews one organic coffee each day.

Spot, The 🍃🍃
4455 Overland Ave. Culver City 90230 • **310-559-8868**
Mon-Thu 6:30am-10pm Fri 6:30am-12am Sat 9am-12am Sun 9am-10pm
www.thespotcafelounge.com
Selection of organic tea, coffee, dairy beverages, and food items. Live entertainment.

Stroh's Gourmet 🍃🍃
1239 Abbot Kinney Blvd. Venice 90291 • **310-450-5119**
Mon-Fri 7am-5pm Sat-Sun 7am-7pm
Organic coffee and beverages.

UnUrban 🍃🍃
3301 Pico Blvd. Santa Monica 90405 • **310-315-0056**
Mon-Sat 7am-12am Sun 8am-8pm
Organic coffee, tea, sandwiches, and soups.

Urth Caffé 🍃🍃🍃🍃
267 S. Beverly Dr. Beverly Hills 90210 • **310-205-9311**
2327 Main St. Santa Monica 90405 • **310-314-7040**
8565 Melrose Ave. West Hollywood 90069 • **310-659-0628**
Hours vary by location www.urthcaffe.com
Carries own brand of exclusively organic coffee and hand-selected fine teas. Hormone-free dairy.

Utopia 🍃🍃🍃🍃
2311 Santa Monica Blvd. Santa Monica 90404 • **310-315-4375**
Mon-Fri 8am-4pm Sat 9am-3pm
Organic coffee, tea. Some organic breakfast and lunch offerings.

Velocity Café 🍃🍃
2127 Lincoln Blvd. Santa Monica 90405 • **310-314-3368**
Mon-Sat 5:30am-6pm www.velocity-cafe.com
Organic coffee and tea. Free Internet for customers.

Venice Grind 🍃🍃🍃🍃
12224 Venice Blvd. LA 90066 • **310-397-2227**
Mon-Fri 6am-10pm Sat-Sun 7am-10pm www.venicegrind.com
Organic coffee and tea. Baked goods from local bakeries. Art exhibits.

Waterlily Café 🍃
120 S. Topanga Blvd. Topanga 90290 • **310-455-0401**
Mon-Fri 7am-5pm Sat-Sun 8am-5pm
Organic coffee, tea, juice; some organic ingredients in sandwiches and salads.

Yogo Presso 🍃🍃
5245 W. Rosencrans Ave. Hawthorne 90250 • **310-297-6870**
Mon-Fri 7:30am-8:30pm Sat 11am-8pm
Organic coffee and frozen yogurt.

Zeli Coffee Bar
639 Foothill Blvd. La Canada 91011 • **818-790-2315**
695 E. Colorado Blvd. Pasadena 91101 • **626-356-9901**
Hours vary by location
Neighborhood café serving selection of organic coffee and tea.

Zen Zoo Tea
1517 N. Vine St. Hollywood 90028 • **323-962-9969**
Mon-Thu 9am-9pm Fri-Sat 10am-11pm Sun 9am-9pm www.zenzootea.com
Carries a wide selection of organic teas. Live entertainment; art exhibits.

Juice Bars

The advent of juice bars and smoothie shops has been a real boon to those of us who like our fruit in a cup and our vitamins on the go. Keeping our immune systems healthy has gotten easier and, if we choose organic options, we can keep our planetary systems healthy as well. And when you sidle up to that juice bar, don't forget to have a reusable cup in hand to avoid using disposable polystyrene or plastic!

We have determined leaf awards based primarily on the percentage of juices and soft drinks offered that are certified organic. We have also factored in the percentage of smoothie ingredients and dairy products used that are certified organic, as well as the percentage of prepared food items that are certified organic.

Of all the products served or available for sale, and the ingredients used:

at least 25% meet the above criteria.

at least 50% meet the above criteria.

at least 75% meet the above criteria.

at least 90% meet the above criteria.

Beverly Hills Juice
8382 Beverly Blvd. LA 90048 • **323-655-8300**
Mon-Fri 7am-6pm Sat 10am-6pm www.beverlyhillsjuice.com
Juices and beverages made with organic produce from farmers' markets.

Interim Café (formerly Newsroom Café)
530 Wilshire Blvd. Santa Monica 90401 • **310-319-9100**
Mon-Fri 8am-9pm Sat 9am-7pm Sun 9am-3pm
Organic juice and coffee; food menu offers mostly organic items.

Leaf Cuisine
11938 W. Washington Blvd. LA 90066 • **310-390-6005**
14318 Ventura Blvd. Sherman Oaks 91423 • **818-907-8779**
Hours vary by location www.leafcuisine.com
Organic juices, smoothies; raw, organic, vegan food items. Teaches raw food prep classes.

Mr. & Mrs. Organic ✿✿✿✿
22140 Ventura Blvd. Woodland Hills 91364 • **818-704-8448**
Mon-Fri 10am-7pm Sat 10am-6pm
Organic juices and other beverages; raw salads and sandwiches.

One Life Natural Foods ✿✿✿✿
3001 Main St. Santa Monica 90405 • **310-392-4501**
Daily 8am-9pm
Juice bar and deli offering organic juices, produce, and vitamins.

Rainbow Acres ✿✿✿✿
13208 W. Washington Blvd. LA 90066 • **310-306-8330**
4756 Admiralty Way Marina Del Rey 90292 • **310-823-5373**
Mon-Fri 7am-9pm Sat-Sun 8am-8pm
Organic juice bar located inside the market.

Taste of the Goddess Café ✿✿✿✿
7373 Beverly Blvd. LA 90036 • **323-933-1400**
Mon 11am-7pm Tue-Sat 11am-9pm Sun 12am-6pm
www.tasteofthegoddess.com
Organic juice bar. Also serves raw, vegan cuisine made with organic ingredients.

Vitamin Bar, The ✿✿✿✿
23823 West Malibu Rd. Malibu 90265 • **310-317-4833**
Mon-Sat 9am-6pm Sun 11am-4pm
Juice bar offering offering a variety of beverages made with organic produce. Also sells organic vitamins, beauty and body care products.

 Bakeries

Enter a bakery that serves up organic treats and you've entered a world where good taste and good health join in perfect combination. And they do so in a sustainable way.

A loaf of whole grain bread, a pie plump with organic apples, some wholesome breakfast muffins—look for food that is both delicious and environmentally friendly. It's out there waiting for you.

The bakeries included here were given leaf awards based on the percentage of grains and total dairy products used that is certified organic. We also factored in the percentage of produce used that is certified organic and/or locally grown without pesticides and chemical fertilizers. We also looked at the percentage of total beverages purchased that is certified organic.

✿	at least 25% of the goods offered meet the above criteria.
✿✿	at least 50% of the goods offered meet the above criteria.
✿✿✿	at least 75% of the goods offered meet the above criteria.
✿✿✿✿	90% or more of the goods offered meet the above criteria.

Bakeries (cont.)

Akasha �️✍✍✍
9543 Culver Blvd. Culver City 90232 • **310-845-1700**
Mon-Sat 7am-6pm www.akasharestaurant.com
Offers New American dishes and baked goods made with sustainable
ingredients. Organic drinks. Menu also available for catering or to-go.

Casa De Tree ✍✍✍✍
2543 Pacific Coast Hwy. Ste. E Torrance 90505 • **310-784-0455**
Tue-Sat 8:30am-8pm www.casadetree.com
Organic bakery and vegan deli café serving pastries, coffee, and tea;
French- and Japanese-inspired menu items.

City Bakery, The ✍✍✍
225 26th St. Brentwood 90049 • **310-656-3040**
Mon-Sat 7am-7pm Sun 7am-6pm www.thecitybakery.com
Organic baked goods made fresh daily on premises; sandwiches and
salads; organic coffee and tea.

Le Pain Quotidien ✍✍✍✍
9630 Santa Monica Blvd. Beverly Hills 90210 • **310-859-1100**
11702 Barrington Ct. LA 90049 • **310-476-0969**
320 S. Robertson Blvd. LA 90048 • **310-858-7270**
8607 Melrose Ave. LA 90069 • **310-854-3700**
451 Manhattan Beach Blvd. Manhattan Beach 90266 • **310-546-6411**
88 W. Colorado Blvd. Pasadena 91105 • **626-396-0956**
316 Santa Monica Blvd. Santa Monica 90401 • **310-393-6800**
13045 Ventura Blvd. Studio City 91604 • **818-986-1929**
1055 Broxton Ave. Westwood 90024 • **310-824-7900**
Hours vary by location www.lepainquotidien.com
Bakery serving organic pies, pastries, omelets, soups, salads, and coffee.

Leda's Bake Shop ✍✍
13722 Ventura Blvd. Sherman Oaks 91423 • **818-386-9644**
Mon-Sat 10:30am-6pm www.ledasbakeshop.com
Uses many organic ingredients in cupcakes, cookies, and other baked
goods.

Little Next Door ✍✍✍
8142 W. 3rd St. LA 90048 • **323-951-1010**
Daily 9am-9:30pm www.thelittledoor.com
French café and artisan marketplace offering organic baked goods,
handmade local jams.

Mäni's Bakery Café ✍✍
519 S. Fairfax Ave. LA 90036 • **323-938-8800**
2507 Main St. Santa Monica 90405 • **310-396-7700**
Hours vary by location www.manisbakery.com
Bakery is also full-service restaurant with organic options and fruit juice-
sweetened desserts.

Chocolatiers and Dessert Shops

A masterfully made dessert rich in organic ingredients, a chocolate torte made from cacao grown without harm to the planet—ice cream made from milk free of hormones and other additives, these are not only delicious and pleasurable treats for you, they also treat the planet well. Maybe your diet is at odds with your dessert, but there's no need to go off your green values when it's time to indulge.

The chocolatiers and dessert purveyors included here were given leaf awards based on the percentage of certified organic ingredients used in their menu items. To determine this, we looked into the percentage of chocolate and dairy products they use that is certified organic. We also took a look at all the prepared chocolate and non-chocolate food items and determined what percentage is certified organic. In addition, we factored in whether or not the chocolate used qualified for fair trade certification.

> ✐ at least 25% of the ingredients in the desserts/ chocolate goods and/or at least 25% of the prepared food items are certified organic.
>
> ✐✐ at least 50% of the ingredients in the desserts/ chocolate goods and/or at least 50% of the prepared food items are certified organic.
>
> ✐✐✐ at least 75% of the ingredients in the desserts/ chocolate goods and/or at least 75% of the prepared food items are certified organic.
>
> ✐✐✐✐ 90% or more of the ingredients in the desserts/ chocolate goods is certified organic and/or at least 90% of the prepared food items are certified organic.

Compartes Chocolatier ✐✐
912 S. Barrington Ave. LA 90049 • **310-826-3380**
Mon-Sat 10am-6pm www.compartes.com
Handcrafted, artisinal chocolates prepared with organic, market-fresh, seasonal ingredients. All packaging is recyclable; package reuse is encouraged.

Intemperantia Chocolates ✐✐✐
15324 Antioch St. Pacific Palisades 90272 • **310-459-4703**
Mon-Fri 10-6 Sat 12-6 www.intemperantia.com
Selection of organic and fair trade chocolate; no artificial ingredients, flavorings, or colors. Take their chocolate quiz online!

Mäni's Bakery Café ✐✐
2507 Main St. Santa Monica 90405 • **310-396-7700**
519 S. Fairfax Ave. LA 90036 • **323-938-8800**
Hours vary by location www.manisbakery.com
Bakery and café offering organic treats and desserts sweetened with fruit juice.

Sno:la ∅∅∅
244 N. Beverly Dr. Beverly Hills 90210 • **310-274-2435**
Mon-Thu 11-10 Fri-Sat 11-11 Sun 11-10 www.snolayogurt.com
Frozen yogurt made with organic milk and natural ingredients; no refined white sugar. Uses biocompostable takeout containers. Counters and benches made from repurposed and recycled materials.

21 Choices Frozen Yogurt ∅
85 W. Colorado Blvd. Pasadena 91105 • **626-304-9521**
817 W. Foothill Blvd. Claremont 91711 • **909-621-7175**
Hours vary by location www.21choices.com
All natural frozen yogurt made with some organic fruit and ingredients; no syrups or artificial flavorings.

Urth Caffé ∅∅
267 S. Beverly Dr. Beverly Hills 90210 • **310-205-9311**
8565 Melrose Ave. West Hollywood 90069 • **310-659-0628**
2327 Main St. Santa Monica 90405 • **310-314-7040**
Hours vary by location www.urthcaffe.com
Fresh-baked desserts using locally purchased produce, free-range eggs, hormone-free dairy, and other organic ingredients. Organic coffee, coffee drinks, and teas. Vegan options.

∅ GREEN TIP

Takeout Containers: Worst to First

1. Styrofoam—Will outlive all of us, becoming a permanent part of our environment. Its production poses health risks. Many cities are passing laws banning it.

2. Plastic Containers—Made from ever-more-limited petroleum. Recycling helps a little but only a fraction actually gets recycled. Also, there's pollution in the production and health risks as well.

3. Cardboard Boxes—Food-soiled paper and cardboard cannot be recycled and a lot of paper products contain harmful chlorine or bleach. However, some cities have composting programs for soiled cardboard, and clean cardboard can be recycled.

4. Bio-Products—Manufactured from starchy agricultural products and/or plant fibers. Most need special conditions to biodegrade properly and all require energy and scarce resources to produce. Bio-products mixed with recyclable plastics create insoluble sorting problems, often leaving whole batches of recyclable plastic useless. Good news—better options are coming!

5. Aluminum Foil—Can be washed and reused. Can be recycled if clean. Oxidizes in landfill without emissions.

6. Recycled Paper Products—Saves energy and trees; reduces pollution. Seek 100% recycled material.

7. **Bring Your Own (BYO)**—Be creative: jars, mugs, your own Tupperware®, empty yogurt containers. Whatever you bring, it must be clean.

In the words of the U.S. Department of Agriculture, "Organic food is produced by farmers who emphasize the use of renewable resources and the conservation of soil and water to enhance environmental quality for future generations." Thus "organic" refers to a specific set of standards used throughout the entire process of food production. Food that is certified organic comes from farms (in the United States or in other countries) that have been inspected and approved under the USDA's guidelines by a government-approved certifier. Organic certification prohibits the use of most conventional pesticides, synthetic fertilizers, sewage sludge, bioengineering, and irradiation (also called "ionizing radiation" or "cold pasteurization"). Organic meat, eggs, poultry, and dairy come from animals not treated with antibiotics or growth hormones. Certified organic food is, by definition, free from genetically modified organisms (GMOs). Also, any handling or processing of organic food must be done by certified companies.

ORGANIC CONTENT/SINGLE-INGREDIENT FOODS
Check package labeling carefully and look for signs at the supermarket to guide you to organic foods. The USDA's strict labeling rules help you know the exact organic content of the food you buy. The USDA Organic seal also tells you that a product is at least 95% organic. Look for the word *organic* and a small sticker version of the USDA Organic seal on vegetables or pieces of fruit. The word *organic* and the seal may also appear on packages of meat, cartons of milk or eggs, cheese, and other single-ingredient foods.

ORGANIC LABELING/MULTI-INGREDIENT FOODS
Federal organic legislation allows four labeling categories for the wide variety of products that use organic ingredients. Products made entirely with certified organic ingredients and methods can be labeled "100% organic." Products with 95% to 100% organic ingredients can use the word *organic* on packaging, advertising, etc. Both may also display the USDA organic seal. A third category, containing a minimum of 70% organic ingredients, can be labeled "made with organic ingredients." In addition, products can also display the logo of the individual certification body that approved them. Products made with less than 70% organic ingredients cannot advertise this information to consumers and can only mention this fact in the product's ingredient statement, not on the front of the package. Similar percentages and labels apply in the European Union.

SMALL AND TRANSITIONAL FARMERS
Although organic certification is an excellent way to ensure the quality and eco-friendliness of the food you buy, not all farmers and food producers are officially certified. The organic certification process is rigorous and often expensive. Small farms in particular may not be certified, or may be "transitional," meaning they are on their way to certification. If you go to farmers' markets, the best way to understand what you're buying and how it is grown is to talk to the farmer or vendor. Local farmers may be happy to show you around their farms so you can see for yourself as well.

HOW TO USE THIS GUIDE

The seafood in this guide may occur in more than one column based on how it is caught, where it is from, etc. Please read all columns and be sure to check labels or ask questions when shopping or eating out: Where is the sea-food from? Is it farmed or wild-caught? How was it caught?

MAKE CHOICES FOR HEALTHY OCEANS

Your consumer choices make a difference:

Best Choices are abundant, well managed, and caught or farmed in environmentally friendly ways.

Good Alternatives are an option, but there are concerns with how they're caught or farmed—or with the health of their habitat due to other human impacts.

Avoid for now as these are caught or farmed in ways that harm other marine life or the environment.

BEST CHOICES

Abalone (farmed)
Barramundi (US farmed)
Catfish (US farmed)
Clams, Mussels, Oysters (farmed)
Cod: Pacific (Alaska longline)†
Crab: Dungeness
Halibut: Pacific†
Lobster: Spiny (US)
Pollock (Alaska wild)†
Rockfish: Black (CA, OR)
Sablefish/Black Cod (Alaska†, BC)
Salmon (Alaska wild)†
Sardines
Scallops: Bay (farmed)
Shrimp: Pink (OR)
Spot Prawn (BC)
Striped Bass (farmed)
Sturgeon, Caviar (farmed)
Tilapia (US farmed)
Trout: Rainbow (farmed)
Tuna: Albacore (US†, BC troll/pole)
Tuna: Skipjack (troll/pole)
White Seabass

KEY

BC=British Columbia   CA=California   OR=Oregon
WA=Washington   Mid-Atlantic=North Carolina to New York
Northeast=Connecticut to Maine

* Limit consumption due to concerns about mercury or other contaminants. Visit www.oceansalive.org/eat.cfm.

† Some or all of this fishery is certified as sustainable to the Marine Stewardship Council standard. Visit www.msc.org.

GOOD ALTERNATIVES

Basa/Tra (farmed)
Clams, Oysters* (wild)
Cod: Pacific (trawled)
Crab: King (Alaska), Snow, imitation
Dogfish (BC)*
Flounders, Soles (Pacific)
Lingcod*
Lobster: American/Maine
Mahi mahi/Dolphinfish (US)
Rockfish (hook & line caught from Alaska, BC)
Sablefish/Black Cod (CA, OR, WA)
Salmon (CA, OR, WA wild)
Sanddabs: Pacific
Scallops: Sea (Canada and Northeast)
Shrimp (US farmed or wild)
Spot Prawn (US)
Squid
Sturgeon (wild from OR, WA)
Swordfish (US longline)*
Tuna: Bigeye, Yellowfin (troll/pole)
Tuna: canned light*
Tuna: canned white/Albacore*

AVOID

Chilean Seabass/Toothfish*
Cod: Atlantic
Crab: King (imported)
Dogfish (US)*
Grenadier/Pacific Roughy
Lobster: Spiny (Caribbean imported)
Mahi mahi/Dolphinfish (imported)
Monkfish
Orange Roughy*
Rockfish (trawled)
Salmon (farmed, including Atlantic)*
Scallops: Sea (Mid-Atlantic)
Shark*
Shrimp (imported farmed or wild)
Sturgeon*, Caviar (imported wild)
Swordfish (imported)*
Tuna: Albacore, Bigeye, Yellow fin (longline)*
Tuna: Bluefin*

Seafood WATCH The Seafood Watch Guide has been reprinted with the permission of the Monterey Bay Aquarium Foundation. Visit www.seafoodwatch.org for more seafood recommendations and the latest updated information.

Flavor: The Path to Greenlightenment

BY AMELIA SALTSMAN

Since you are reading this book, you already are concerned about how to feed your family safely and well. Fortunately, when we dine in, there is a simple, pleasurable path to follow in these complicated times: seek flavor and diversity in the ingredients you use to prepare your meals.

Think about it. If a strawberry is meltingly juicy, sweet, and red all the way through, or an armload of Swiss chard is vibrantly deep green from the rich soil in which it was grown, chances are good the crop was sustainably farmed. When a passionate farmer raises varieties bred for flavor first, nurtures them to perfect ripeness, and then rushes them to market within twenty-four hours of harvest, these are our tangible clues to his or her sense of responsibility in the field. The same is true for fish, meats, eggs, and cheeses: how were they caught, raised, or produced and how do they taste? Today, when words like *organic* are loaded with multiple meanings, we must look to the food and the farmer to help us find the answers.

Fruits and vegetables taste best grown in season. Seasonality often indicates local production, and, of course, local signifies season. Shop where seasonal ingredients are sold and you'll know what's "in" or "out" in your area.

And, if variety is the spice of life, it is also our greatest weapon against industrial agriculture and its emphasis on single crops. Purple asparagus, white zucchini, red-fleshed potatoes, and striped beets keep dinner interesting and ensure crop diversity. Many of the "new" delicacies we see at farmers' markets are actually old varieties rescued from oblivion by our enjoyment of them.

So whether you shop at a farmers' market, co-op, a "green" market, or use a CSA (Community-Supported Agriculture), look for flavor and diversity. When purchasing ready-made foods or hiring caterers, look for evidence of the seasonal and local choices the cook makes. At least this one thing is simple: When the raw ingredients taste great, everything we hope to find in our food—sustainability, sound nutrition, seasonality, local production, ease of preparation—tends to fall into place. What a pleasant way to do good—for our bodies and the environment.

AMELIA SALTSMAN

Los Angeles-born Amelia Saltsman is a television host, cooking teacher, and writer. She is the author of *The Santa Monica Farmers' Market Cookbook: Seasonal Foods, Simple Recipes, and Stories from the Market and Farm* (www.ameliasaltsman.com).

Most of us spend a significant portion of our food budget every week at our local grocery store. We recommend spending that all-important grocery money on products that are healthier for you and the planet.

A good way to start is by buying organic and/or locally grown products. Organic products are better for your health, and organic agriculture is better for the environment. And food that's locally grown tends to be picked at its freshest and tastiest. Its purchase directly supports nearby farms and helps sustain local communities, while at the same time reducing the amount of fuel consumed and pollution created by transporting the products to market.

Conscious shopping also demands that we purchase nonfood items (personal care products, cleaning supplies, paper products) that are also environmentally friendly. Look for shampoos and toothpastes that are organic or all natural. Household cleaners can be full of toxins and many paper products are whitened with chlorine. Look for alternatives. Read the labels carefully on everything you buy. That's what we do!

We have evaluated our grocery stores in fifteen product areas: produce, meat and meat alternatives, poultry, eggs, fish, dairy products, canned and dry goods, nondairy beverages, prepared foods, frozen foods, personal care items, personal care tools, cleaning products, cleaning tools, and paper goods.

- For produce, we checked the percentage purchased that is certified organic and/or locally grown without pesticides and chemical fertilizers.

- For fresh meat (beef, lamb, pork, and game) and meat alternatives (tofu, soy), we determined the percentage that is certified organic and/or grass fed and produced without the use of hormones and antibiotics.

- For fresh poultry and eggs, we evaluated the percentage purchased that is certified organic, free-range/cage-free and/or locally raised, free-range/cage-free without the use of hormones and antibiotics.

- With fish, we checked into whether it was wild caught or sustainably farm raised and processed without chemical treatment. (We have included a Seafood Guide on page 34 to help you make healthy and sustainable seafood choices.)

- For dairy products, we checked the percentage of certified organic options or ones that were locally produced without hormones and antibiotics.

- We looked into the percentage of certified organic canned and dry goods, nondairy beverages, and frozen foods.

- For prepared foods, we determined the percentage made with certified organic ingredients and/or locally grown ingredients without pesticides and chemical fertilizers.

- For personal care products (toothpaste, shampoos, deodorants, etc.), we looked into the percentage that is organic or all natural.

- For personal care tools (hairbrushes, toothbrushes, nail files, etc.) and household cleaning tools (mops, sponges, etc.), we determined the percentage made with environmentally-friendly materials.

- We checked the percentage of available household cleansers, soaps, and detergents that are nontoxic.

- For household paper products (paper towels, toilet paper, etc.), we looked at the percentage made from recycled content and whitened without chlorine.

> ✐ at least 25% of products meet the above criteria.
>
> ✐✐ at least 50% of products meet the above criteria.
>
> ✐✐✐ at least 75% of products meet the above criteria.
>
> ✐✐✐✐ at least 90% of products meet the above criteria.

Genetic Engineering (GE)

Genetic Engineering is a radical new way to grow food. Unlike traditional breeding, genetic engineering manipulates the genes and DNA of plants and animals to create new life forms, or Genetically Modified Organisms (GMOs), that would never occur in nature. This creates new and unpredictable health and environmental risks. To create GE crops, genes from bacteria, viruses, plants, and animals are inserted into plants like soybeans, corn, canola, and cotton. Try to avoid all products containing GMOs. However, since GE products are not generally labeled, the best way to avoid eating them is to purchase organically grown food.

Co-opportunity ✐✐✐✐
1525 Broadway Santa Monica 90404 • **310-451-8902**
Daily 7am-10pm www.coopportunity.com
Cooperative natural grocer carrying organic bulk foods, produce, meats, fish, eco-friendly cleaning products, natural pet products, organic beer and wine. Membership not required.

Country Natural Food Store ✐✐✐✐
415 S. Topanga Canyon Topanga 90290 • **310-455-3434**
Mon-Fri 8am-6pm Sat 8am-6pm
Neighborhood grocery store offering all natural and organic goods.

Erewhon Natural Foods Market ✑✑✑✑
7660 Beverly Blvd. LA 90036 • **323-937-0777**
Mon-Sat 8am-10pm Sun 9am-9pm   www.erewhonmarket.com
Large selection of organically grown produce, groceries, and macrobiotic staples. Wide variety of natural remedies including vitamins, herbs, and homeopathics. Visit website for their own Health-e-Coupons.

Follow Your Heart Market & Café ✑✑✑✑
21825 Sherman Way Canoga Park 91303 • **818-348-3240**
Daily 8am-9pm www.followyourheart.com
Full-service natural grocer catering to vegans and vegetarians. Manufactures its own Follow Your Heart® products. Carries locally sourced organic produce; gifts, books, health and beauty products, and more. Product experts on hand. Café in back of store.

Full O' Life ✑✑✑
2515 W. Magnolia Blvd. Burbank 91505 • **818-845-8343**
Mon-Thu 8am-8pm Fri 8am-4pm Sun 9:30am-6pm www.fullolife.com
Natural food market with organic and locally grown produce; eco-friendly cleaning, paper, beauty, and health products.

Grassroots Natural Market and Kitchen ✑✑✑
1119 Fair Oaks Ave. South Pasadena 91030 • **626-799-0156**
Mon-Fri 8am-7pm Sat 9am-7pm Sun 9am-5pm
Carries organic prepared food, produce, meats, cleaning supplies. Organic juice bar.

Health Food City ✑✑✑
3651 E. Foothill Blvd. Pasadena 91107 • **626-351-8616**
140 W. Valley Blvd. Ste. 102 San Gabriel 91776 • **626-288-3498**
Hours vary by location www.healthfoodcity.com
Offers organic canned and dry goods, frozen food items; organic and all natural personal care products and health books; nontoxic cleaning supplies.

Healthy Discounts ✑✑✑
14427 Ventura Blvd. Sherman Oaks 91423 • **818-995-7684**
Mon-Sat 9am-8pm Sun 10am-6pm
Natural grocer specializing in supplements and vitamins; offers some organic prepared foods.

Mr. Wisdom Hari Krishna Restaurant and Specialty Health Food Store ✑✑✑✑
3526 W. Slauson Ave. LA 90043 • **323-295-1517**
Mon-Fri 9:30am-7pm Sat 10am-6pm
Neighborhood market adjacent to restaurant. Offers a variety of organic and all natural grocery items. On-premises organic wheat and barley grass farm.

Nature Mart ✑✑✑
2080 Hillhurst Ave. LA 90027 • **323-660-0052**
Daily 7am-10pm
Full-line grocery store with organic produce and health foods; large bulk selection; eco-friendly household and beauty products.

One Life Natural Foods ✑✑✑
3001 Main St. Santa Monica 90405 • **310-392-4501**
Daily 9am-9pm
Features juice bar, deli, organic produce, vitamins, natural cosmetics, and herb room.

Pacific Coast Greens 🌱🌱🌱🌱
22601 Pacific Coast Hwy. Malibu 90265 • **310-456-0353**
Daily 8am-8pm
Full-service organic and all natural grocery store. In-store deli and catering
available.

Rainbow Acres 🌱🌱🌱🌱
13208 W. Washington Blvd. LA 90066 • **310-306-8330**
4756 Admiralty Way Marina Del Rey 90292 • **310-823-5373**
Hours vary by location
Family-owned, full-service natural foods grocery store. In-store deli.
Washington Blvd. store offers larger selection.

Simply Wholesome 🌱🌱
4508 W. Slauson Ave. LA 90043 • **323-294-2144**
Mon-Sat 8:30am-10pm Sun 10am-9pm
Health food store catering to vegetarians and vegans. Offers some organic
or all natural grocery, personal care, and household items.

Sprouts Farmers Market 🌱🌱🌱
4230 Pacific Coast Hwy. Torrance 90505 • **424-903-7062**
Daily 8am-10pm www.sprouts.com
Full-service grocery store specializing in farm-fresh organic and local
produce. Large selection of organic and all natural goods and grocery
items. Provides cloth and recycled plastic grocery bags. In-store deli.

Trader Joe's 🌱🌱
230 E. Alameda Ave. Burbank 91502 • **818-848-4299**
10330 Mason Ave. Chatsworth 91311 • **818-341-3010**
9290 Culver Blvd. Culver City 90232 • **310-202-1108**
1566 Colorado Blvd. Eagle Rock 90041 • **323-257-6422**
17640 Burbank Blvd. Encino 91316 • **818-990-7751**
130 N. Glendale Blvd. Glendale 91205 • **818-637-2990**
11114 Balboa Blvd. Granada Hills 91344 • **818-368-6461**
475 Foothill Blvd. La Canada 91011 • **818-790-6373**
3433 Foothill Blvd. La Crescenta 91214 • **818-249-3693**
10850 National Blvd. LA 90064 • **310-470-1917**
263 S. La Brea Ave. LA 90036 • **323-965-1989**
2738 Hyperion Ave. LA 90027 • **323-665-6774**
3456 S. Sepulveda Ave. LA 90034 • **310-836-2458**
1800 Rosencrans Blvd. Manhattan Beach 90266 • **310-202-1108**
1821 Manhattan Beach Blvd. Manhattan Beach 90266 • **310-372-1274**
604 W. Huntington Dr. Monrovia 91016 • **626-358-8884**
345 S. Lake Ave. Pasadena 91101 • **626-395-9553**
467 Rosemead Blvd. Pasadena 91107 • **626-351-3399**
610 S. Arroyo Pkwy. Pasadena 91105 • **626-568-9254**
28901 S. Western Ave. Rancho Palos Verdes 90275 • **310-832-1241**
1761 S. Elena Ave. Redondo Beach 90277 • **310-316-1745**
7260 N. Rosemead Blvd. San Gabriel 91775 • **626-285-5862**
3212 Pico Blvd. Santa Monica 90405 • **310-581-0253**
14119 Riverside Dr. Sherman Oaks 91423 • **818-789-2771**
613 Mission St. South Pasadena 91030 • **626-441-6263**
11976 Ventura Blvd. Studio City 91604 • **818-509-0168**
451 Avenida de los Arboles Thousand Oaks 91360 • **626-599-3700**
10130 Riverside Dr. Toluca Lake 91602 • **818-762-2787**
19720 Hawthorne Blvd. Torrance 90503 • **310-793-8585**
2545 Pacific Coast Hwy. Torrance 90503 • **310-326-9520**
6751 Fallbrook Ctr. West Hills 91307 • **818-883-4134**
7304 Santa Monica Blvd. West Hollywood 90046 • **323-851-9772**
8611 Santa Monica Blvd. West Hollywood 90069 • **310-338-9238**
8645 S. Sepulveda Blvd. Westchester 90045 • **310-338-9238**
21055 Ventura Blvd. Woodland Hills 91364 • (Opening early 2008)

Trader Joe's (cont.)

Hours vary by location www.traderjoes.com
Full-service neighborhood market offering many organic and all natural choices and its own Trader Joe's brand products sourced with no GMO ingredients; nontoxic household and personal care products.

Vicente Foods ✍

12027 San Vicente Blvd. LA 90049 • **310-472-5215**
Mon-Sat 8am-10pm Sun 9am-9pm www.vicentefoods.com
Full-line, independently owned, neighborhood grocery store offering some organic and all natural products.

VP Discount Health & Food Mart ✍✍✍

1127 W. Huntington Dr. Arcadia 91007 • **626-821-1028**
607 N. Glendale Ave. Glendale 91206 • **818-240-1948**
8001 Beverly Blvd. LA 90048 • **323-658-6506**
Hours vary by location
Organic produce, grocery items; vitamins; vegan and vegetarian options.

Whole Foods Market ✍✍✍✍

239 N. Crescent Dr. Beverly Hills 90210 • **310-274-3360**
760 S. Sepulveda Blvd. El Segundo 90245 • **310-333-1900**
331 N. Glendale Ave. Glendale 91206 • **818-548-3695**
11666 National Blvd. LA 90064 • **310-996-8840**
11737 San Vicente Blvd. LA 90049 • **310-826-4433**
6350 W. 3rd St. LA 90036 • **323-964-6800**
19340 Rinaldi St. Northridge 91326 • **818-363-3933**
465 S. Arroyo Pkwy. Pasadena 91105 • **626-204-2266**
3751 E. Foothill Blvd. Pasadena 91107 • **626-351-5994**
405 N. Pacific Coast Hwy. Redondo Beach 90277 • **310-376-6931**
2201 Wilshire Blvd. Santa Monica 90403 • **310-315-0662**
12905 Riverside Dr. Sherman Oaks 91423 • **818-762-5548**
4520 Sepulveda Blvd. Sherman Oaks 91403 • **818-382-3700**
740 N. Moorpark Thousand Oaks 91360 • **805-777-4730**
2655 Pacific Coast Hwy. Torrance 90505 • **310-257-8700**
7871 W. Santa Monica Blvd. West Hollywood 90046 • **323-848-4200**
1050 S. Gayley Ave. Westwood 90024 • **310-824-0858**
21347 Ventura Blvd. Woodland Hills 91364 • **818-610-0000**
Hours vary by location www.wholefoodsmarket.com
Full-service grocery store offering many organic and some fair trade products; bulk selection; natural body care products; alternative pharmacy; organic beer and wine. Provides catering. In-store bakery, deli, and fresh meat/fish counters.

Wild Oats Marketplace ✍✍✍✍

1425 Montana Ave. Santa Monica 90403 • **310-576-4707**
500 Wilshire Blvd. Santa Monica 90401 • **310-395-4510**
Daily 7am-10pm www.wholefoodsmarket.com
Neighborhood-style natural grocer offering many organic and some fair trade products; natural body care products; alternative pharmacy; organic beer and wine; bakery and deli. Recently merged with Whole Foods and will be renamed as Whole Foods Market.

Farmers' Markets and Community-Supported Agriculture

Both Farmers' Markets and Community-Supported Agriculture are bringing the farm to the family. We are getting closer to the source of our food and it feels good. Kids are starting to see where their carrots come from and we are all falling in love again with fresh, tree-ripened peaches.

There's nothing like a good farmers' market or a weekly box from a nearby CSA. Farmers' markets and local agriculture are about the food and about the community. The produce is fresh and changes naturally with the seasons.

You may notice that some of the food at a farmers' market is not certified organic. Often small farmers cannot afford to go through the certification process. It is still important to support these farmers and buy locally grown food. Some vendors will clearly mark their area with signs that say "organic" or "pesticide free." If you're not sure, ask—the farmers are happy to talk to you about their produce and farming practices.

All farmers' markets listed here meet our criteria, as they are on the front lines of the locally grown movement and offer a variety of organic products. That direct growing and purchasing relationship between producer and consumer is what we are all about. But, given the variation among vendors within a market, we have viewed all markets equally and not given leaf awards to any individual market.

Similarly for CSAs, all meet our criteria for inclusion and support the values we care most about. By joining a CSA, you are shopping locally in a very fundamental way, eating in season, providing for land stewardship and building a strong local economy.

Certified Farmers' Market (CFM)

These are locations that have been approved by the local county agricultural commissioner for farmers to sell agricultural products directly to consumers.

Community-Supported Agriculture (CSA)

When you buy a share in a local farm operation, you are part of what is called Community-Supported Agriculture. This means you have joined a regional community of growers and consumers and are sharing in both the risks and the benefits of food production. Typically, members or "shareholders" of the farm pay in advance to cover the costs of the farm. In return, they receive shares of the farm's produce throughout the growing season. By direct sales to community members, growers receive better prices for their crops and a steadier income.

FARMERS' MARKETS

Alhambra CFM
100 S. Monterey St. Alhambra 91801 • **626-570-5081**
Sun 8:30am-1pm Year-round www.cafarmersmarkets.com

Arts District - Little Tokyo CFM
200 N. Spring St. LA 90012 • **323-600-8660**
Thu 10am-2pm Year-round www.downtownfarmersmarket.org

Atwater Village CFM
3250 Glendale Blvd. LA 90039 • **323-463-3171**
Sun 10am-2pm Year-round www.farmernet.com

Beverly Hills CFM
Civic Center Dr. at N. Foothill Rd. LA 90210 • **310-550-4796**
Sun 9am-1pm Year-round www.cafarmersmarkets.com

Brentwood CFM
741 Gretna Green Way LA 90046 • **818-591-8161**
Sun 9am-2:30pm Year-round www.rawinspiration.org

Burbank CFM
E. Olive Ave. at S. Glenoaks Blvd. Burbank 91502 • **626-308-0457**
Sat 8am-12:30pm Year-round www.cafarmersmarkets.com

Calabasas Old Town CFM
Mulholland Dr. at Calabasas Rd. Calabasas 91364 • **818-591-8161**
Sat 8am-1pm Year-round www.rawinspiration.org

Century City CFM
1800 Ave. of the Stars LA 90067 • **818-591-8161**
Thu 11am-3pm Year-round www.rawinspiration.org

Culver City CFM
Main St. at Culver Blvd. Culver City 90232 • **310-253-5775**
Tue 2pm-7pm Year-round www.cafarmersmarkets.com

Downtown L.A. (Bank of America Plaza) CFM
333 S. Hope St. LA 90071 • **818-591-8161**
Fri 11am-3pm Year-round www.rawinspiration.org

Downtown L.A. CFM
650 W. Fifth St. LA 90071 • **818-591-8161**
Wed 11:30am-3pm Year-round www.rawinspiration.org

Echo Park Farmers' Market
Logan St., South of Sunset Blvd. LA 90026 • **323-463-3171**
Fri 3pm-7pm Year-round www.farmernet.com

El Segundo CFM
Main St. at Pine Ave. El Segundo 90245 • **310-615-2649**
Thu 3pm-7pm Year-round www.cafarmersmarkets.com

Encino ONEgeneration CFM
Victory Blvd. at White Oak Van Nuys 91406 • **818-708-6611**
Sun 8am-1pm Year-round www.onegeneration.org/farmer_market.asp

Gardena CFM
Van Ness Ave. at El Segundo Blvd. LA 90019 • **323-777-1755**
Sat 6:30am-12:30pm Year-round www.cafarmersmarkets.org

Glendale CFM
100 N. Brand Blvd. Glendale 91203 • **818-548-2005**
Thu 9:30am-1:30pm Year-round www.cafarmersmarkets.com

Hermosa Beach CFM
Valley Dr. at Eighth St. Hermosa Beach 90266 • **310-376-0951**
Fri 12pm-4pm Year-round www.farmernet.com

Hollywood CFM
1600 Ivar Ave. Hollywood 90028 • **323-463-3171**
Sun 8am-1pm Year-round www.farmernet.com

Hollywood Sears CFM
5601 Santa Monica Blvd. Hollywood 90038 • **323-463-3171**
Wed 12pm-5:30pm Year-round www.farmernet.com

L.A. Adams/Vermont CFM
1432 W. Adams Blvd. LA 90097 • **323-777-1755**
Wed 2pm-6pm Year-round www.farmernet.com

L.A. Central Avenue CFM
4410 McKinley Ave. LA 90011 • **323-463-3171**
Sat 8am-2pm Year-round www.farmernet.com

L.A. Chinatown CFM
727 N. Hill St. LA 90012 • **213-680-0243**
Thu 2pm-6pm Year-round www.farmernet.com

L.A. Eagle Rock CFM
2100 Merton Ave. LA 90041 • **323-225-5466**
Fri 4pm-9pm (summer), Fri 5pm-8pm (winter) www.farmernet.com

L.A. Haramabee CFM
5730 Crenshaw Blvd. LA 90043 • **323-292-5550**
Sat 10am-4pm Year-round www.cafarmersmarkets.com

L.A. (Old L.A.) CFM
5703 Marmion Way LA 90042 • **323-255-5030**
Tue 3pm-8pm Year-round www.farmernet.com

L.A. 7th and Figueroa
Seventh St. at Figueroa St. LA 90017 • **213-953-7176**
Thu 10am-4pm Year-round www.farmernet.com

La Cañada Flintridge CFM
1346 Foothill Blvd. LA 91011 • **818-591-8161**
Sat 9am-1pm Year-round www.rawinspiration.org

La Cienega CFM
1801 La Cienega Blvd. LA 90034 • **562-495-1764**
Thu 3pm-7:30pm (summer), Thu 3pm-7pm (winter) www.farmernet.com

Larchmont Village CFM
209 N. Larchmont Blvd. LA 90004 • **818-591-8161**
Sun 10am-2pm Year-round www.rawinspiration.org

Leimert Park Village CFM
Degnan Blvd. at 43rd St. Vision theatre parking lot LA 90008 • **323-463-3171**
Sat 9am-2pm Year-round www.farmernet.com

Malibu CFM
23555 Civic Center Way Malibu 90265 • **310-457-4537**
Sun 10am-3pm Jun-Nov www.malibufarmersmarket.com/cms

Manhattan Beach CFM
13th St. at Morningside Dr. Manhattan Beach 90266 • **310-379-9901**
Tue 12pm-6pm (summer), Tue 12pm-4pm (winter)
www.mbfarmersmarket.com

Mar Vista Farmers' Market
Grandview Ave. at Venice Blvd. Venice 90291 • **310-861-4444**
Sun 9am-2pm Year-round www.marvistafarmersmarket.org

Melrose Place CFM
8400 Melrose Pl. West Hollywood 90069 • **818-591-8161**
Sun 10am-2pm Year-round www.rawinspiration.org

Northridge CFM
9301 Tampa Ave. Northridge 91324 • **805-643-6458**
Wed 5pm-9pm March-Oct www.farmernet.com

Pacific Palisades CFM
1037 Swarthmore Ave. Pacific Palisades 90272 • **818-591-8161**
Sun 8am-1pm Year-round www.rawinspiration.org

Palos Verdes CFM
Hawthorne at Silverspur Rd. Rolling Hills Estate 90274 • **310-324-3994**
Sun 9am-1pm Year-round www.farmernet.com

Pasadena Victory Park CFM
N. Sierra Madre Blvd. at Paloma St. Pasadena 91107 • **626-449-0179**
Sat 8:30am-12:30pm Year-round www.farmernet.com

Pasadena Villa Park CFM
363 E. Villa St. Pasadena 91101 • **626-449-0179**
Tue 8:30am-12:30pm Year-round www.farmernet.com

Redondo Beach CFM
Veteran's Park at Harbor Dr. Redondo Beach 90277 • **310-372-1171**
Thu 8am-1pm Year-round www.farmernet.com

Santa Monica Pico CFM
2200 Virginia Ave. Santa Monica 90404 • **310-458-8712**
Sat 8am-1pm Year-round www.cafarmersmarkets.com

Santa Monica Saturday Organic CFM
Arizona Ave. at Third St. Santa Monica 90401 • **310-458-8712**
Sat 8:30am-1pm Year-round www.cafarmersmarkets.com

Santa Monica Sunday CFM
Main St. at Ocean Prk. Santa Monica 90405 • **310-458-8712**
Sun 9:30am-1pm Year-round www.cafarmersmarkets.com

Santa Monica Wednesday CFM
Arizona Ave. at Second St. Santa Monica 90401 • **310-458-8712**
Wed 8:30am-1:30pm Year-round www.cafarmersmarkets.com

Silverlake CFM
3700 Sunset Blvd. LA 90026 • **323-661-7771**
Sat 8am-1pm Year-round www.sunsetjunction.org

South Pasadena CFM
Mission St. at Meridian Ave. South Pasadena 91030 • **818-786-6612**
Thu 4pm-8pm (summer), Thu 4pm-7pm (winter) www.farmernet.com

Studio City CFM
Ventura Pl. at Ventura Blvd. Studio City 91604 • **818-655-7744**
Sun 8am-1pm Year-round www.farmernet.com

Toluca Lake CFM
4500 N. San Cola Ave. Toluca Lake 91602 • **818-845-0754**
Sun 9:30am-2:30pm Year-round www.cnfmca.com

Torrance CFM
2200 Crenshaw Blvd. Torrance 90016 • **310-328-2809**
Tue 8am-1pm Year-round www.farmernet.com

Venice CFM
Venice Blvd. at Venice Way Venice 90291 • **310-399-6690**
Fri 7am-11am Year-round www.farmernet.com

Watts Healthy CFM
Central Ave. at 103rd St. LA 90002 • **323-463-3171**
Hours irregular, call ahead www.farmernet.com

West Hollywood CFM
N. Vista St. at Fountain Ave. West Hollywood 90046 • **323-848-6502**
Mon 9am-2pm Year-round www.cafarmersmarkets.org

West L.A. CFM
11338 Santa Monica Blvd. LA 90025 • **310-284-7855**
Sun 9am-2pm Year-round www.farmernet.com

Westchester CFM
7000 W. Manchester Ave. Westchester Park Westchester 90045
310-582-5850
Wed 8:30am-1pm Year-round www.farmernet.com

Westwood Farmers' Market
Davis Ave. at Constitution Ave. Westwood 90024 • **310-861-8188**
Thu 12pm-7pm Year-round www.westwoodfarmersmarket.com

Westwood Village CFM
1036 Broxton Ave. West L.A./Westwood Village 90024 • **310-430-2919**
Sun 10am-3pm Year-round www.farmernet.com

COMMUNITY-SUPPORTED AGRICULTURE ▬▬▬▬

EarthWorks Community Farm
1210 Lerma Rd. South El Monte 91733 • **323-224-2550 x202**
Sat 10am-12pm Year-round www.ewent.org
Community farm provides youth with job and life skills, nutrition and organic farming training, employment, and leadership development. Produce stand open Saturdays. Delivers produce to senior centers and shelters.

Tierra Miguel Foundation, CSA
14910 Pauma Valley Dr. Pauma Valley 92601 • **760-742-4213**
Call or visit website for delivery schedule www.tierramiguelfarm.org
Produces and delivers organic produce to CSA members. Foundation works toward sustainable farm practice awareness and land conservation.

Vital Zuman Organic Farm
29127 Pacific Coast Hwy. Malibu 90265 • **310-457-4356**
Tue-Sat 12pm-5pm Year-round www.vitalzuman.com
Family farm and cooperative work retreat. Grows exclusively chemical-free, organic products. Farm stand open throughout the year; produce box orders available by appointment and sold at local farmers' markets.

These grocery and produce delivery services deliver fresh, healthy food and sustainably made nonfood items to your door. Not only can they save you valuable hours every week, many also offer fast and convenient online ordering capabilities.

We reviewed these delivery services in thirteen product areas: produce, fresh meat and meat alternatives, poultry and eggs, fish, dairy products, canned and dry goods, nondairy beverages, prepared foods, personal care products and tools, household cleansers and cleaning tools, and household paper products.

- For produce, we calculated the percentage that is certified organic and/or locally grown without pesticides and chemical fertilizers.

- For fresh meat (beef, lamb, pork, and game) and meat alternatives (tofu, soy), we determined the percentage that is certified organic and/or grass fed and produced without the use of hormones and antibiotics.

- For fresh poultry and eggs, we evaluated the percentage that is certified organic, free-range/cage-free and/or locally raised, free-range/cage-free without the use of hormones and antibiotics.

- With fish, we checked into whether it was wild caught or sustainably farm raised and processed without chemical treatment. (We have included a Seafood Guide on page 34 to help you make healthy and sustainable seafood choices.)

- For dairy products, we checked the percentage of certified organic options or ones that were locally produced without hormones and antibiotics.

- We looked at the percentage of certified organic canned and dry goods, and nondairy beverages.

- For prepared foods, we determined the percentage made with certified organic ingredients and/or locally grown ingredients without pesticides and chemical fertilizers.

- For personal care products (toothpaste, shampoos, deodorants, etc.), we looked into the percentage that is organic or all natural.

- For personal care tools (hairbrushes, toothbrushes, nail files, etc.) and household cleaning tools (mops, sponges, etc.), we determined the percentage made with environmentally-friendly materials.

- We checked the percentage of household cleansers, soaps, and detergents that are nontoxic.

- For household paper products (paper towels, toilet paper, etc.), we looked at the percentage made from recycled content and whitened without chlorine.

∅ at least 25% of products meet the above criteria.

∅∅ at least 50% of products meet the above criteria.

∅∅∅ at least 75% of products meet the above criteria.

∅∅∅∅ at least 90% of products meet the above criteria.

Bohemian Baby ∅∅∅∅
Marina Del Rey • **800-708-7605**
Order online or call to set up account; delivers and ships Tue and Thu
www.bohemian-baby.com
Delivers 100% organic baby food, full baby and toddler meals; caters 1st birthday parties. Products also sold in Whole Foods and other local retailers.

Dervaes Gardens ∅∅∅∅
631 Cypress Ave. Pasadena 91103 • **626-795-8400**
Call to set up account; delivery and pickup available by appt. only
www.dervaesgardens.com
Family-owned business delivering seasonal, organic, locally grown vegetables, herbs, fruits, and edible flowers to Los Angeles area clients.

Diamond Organics ∅∅∅∅
Moss Landing • **888-674-2642**
Order online or call to set up account www.diamondorganics.com
100% organic produce, prepared foods, dairy and meat; organic gift baskets with free shipping. Delivers to greater Los Angeles area.

Farmer's Cart, The ∅∅∅∅
Los Angeles • **213-509-9821**
Daily 9am-7pm; delivers weekly or bi-weekly www.thefarmerscart.org
Field-fresh, certified organic produce delivery to home or office. Serves Echo Park, Downtown Los Angeles, Silverlake, Los Feliz, Pasadena.

Izo Force Energy Products ∅∅∅∅
Hollywood • **310-963-5332**
Order online or call to set up account www.izocleanze.com
Produces and delivers raw organic vegan cleanse program, juices, teas, and supplements. Delivers to greater Los Angeles area.

L.O.V.E. Delivery ∅∅∅∅
Venice • **310-821-5683**
Order online or call to set up account; delivers Wednesdays
www.lovedelivery.com
Delivers organic fruits, vegetables, coffee, flowers. Serves greater Los Angeles area.

Organic Express ∅∅∅∅
Los Angeles • **310-674-2642**
Order online or call Mon-Fri 9am-5pm to set up account
www.organicexpress.com
All certified organic produce, coffee, grocery items, baked goods. Serves greater Los Angeles area.

Papa's Organic ✐✐✐✐
Van Nuys • **818-974-0109**
Mon-Fri 8:30am-9pm Sat by appt. www.papasorganic.com
Organic grocery items, produce boxes, meats, beverages. Gift cards available. Serves greater Los Angeles area.

ParadiseO ✐✐✐✐
Order and contact online only www.paradiseo.com
Delivers organic fruits and vegetables. Serves greater Los Angeles area.

Santa Monica Market Basket Program ✐✐✐✐
Topanga • **310-740-7544**
By appt. www.sfma.net
Seasonal, all-organic or locally grown produce handpicked from the Santa Monica Farmers' Market. Serves the Westside.

Vegin' Out ✐✐✐
Playa Del Rey • **310-574-9405**
Order online or call store to set up account; delivers Mon bet. 11am-5pm
www.veginout.com
Vegan, mostly organic, fully-prepared meals. Delivery throughout Southern California.

Specialty Markets

Businesses in this category vary widely due to the many different product areas they focus on. We looked for stores that are not just specialists in their niche but also offer food and/or beverages that are organic and healthy as well as tasty.

Where there is one primary product area at a given market, we focused on that in awarding our leaves. If a market offers goods in several product categories, we have evaluated all major ones. Specialty markets can be rated in all food areas, depending on what they offer: produce, meat and poultry, fish, dairy products, nondairy beverages, canned and dry goods, and/or prepared foods.

- For produce, we checked the percentage purchased that is certified organic and/or locally grown without pesticides and chemical fertilizers.

- For fresh meat (beef, lamb, pork, and game) and meat alternatives (tofu, soy), we determined the percentage that is certified organic and/or grass fed and produced without the use of hormones and antibiotics.

- For fresh poultry and eggs, we evaluated the percentage purchased that is certified organic, free-range/cage-free and/or locally raised, free-range/cage-free without the use of hormones and antibiotics.

- With fish, we checked into whether it was wild caught or sustainably farm raised and processed without chemical treatment. (We have included a Seafood Guide on page 34 to help you make healthy and sustainable seafood choices.)

- For dairy products, we checked the percentage of certified organic options or ones that were locally produced without hormones and antibiotics.

- We looked into the percentage of certified organic canned and dry goods, and nondairy beverages.

- For prepared foods, we determined the percentage made with certified organic ingredients and/or locally grown ingredients without pesticides and chemical fertilizers.

⊘ at least 25% of products meet the above criteria.

⊘⊘ at least 50% of products meet the above criteria.

⊘⊘⊘ at least 75% of products meet the above criteria.

⊘⊘⊘⊘ at least 90% of products meet the above criteria.

Accent on Health ⊘⊘⊘
18559 Devonshire St. Northridge 91324 • **818-360-1516**
Mon-Fri 9am-8pm Sat 9am-6pm
Offers selection of organic dry and packaged goods, grains, nuts, juices; supplements, vitamins, homeopathics.

All Star Nutrition ⊘⊘⊘
18515 Sherman Way Reseda 91335 • **818-345-6403**
Mon-Fri 9am-8pm Sat 9am-6pm
Selection of organic dry and packaged goods, grains, nuts, juices; supplements, vitamins, homeopathics.

Artisan Cheese Gallery ⊘
12023 Ventura Blvd. Studio City 91604 • **818-505-0207**
Mon-Sat 10:30am-7pm Sun 9am-5pm www.artisancheesegallery.com
Raw and organic artisanal cheeses; sandwiches and salads made with some organic ingredients. Slow Food member.

Blue Table ⊘⊘
4774 Park Granada Unit 4 Calabasas 91302 • **818-222-5195**
Mon-Fri 10am-6:30pm Sat 10am-5pm www.bluetablecalabasas.com
Offers some all natural and organic meats, cheeses, gourmet grocery items; prepared Italian cuisine made with organic ingredients.

Cheese Store of Beverly Hills, The ⊘⊘
419 N. Beverly Dr. Beverly Hills 90210 • **310-278-2855**
Mon-Sat 10am-6pm www.cheesestorebh.com
Gourmet, rare, artisanal, and organic cheeses; some all natural gourmet grocery items.

Cheese Store of Silverlake, The ⊘
3926-28 W. Sunset Blvd. LA 90029 • **323-644-7511**
Mon-Sat 10am-6:45pm Sun 11am-5pm www.cheesestoresl.com
Offers some organic and all natural cheeses; selection of olive oils, honey, preserves.

Daybreak Health Foods 🌿
1565 Colorado Blvd. Ste. A LA 90041 • **323-258-3881**
Tue-Fri 10am-7pm Sat 10am-6pm
Organic baking ingredients: flour, dried fruit, nuts, herbs. Special orders available on request.

Eaturna 🌿🌿🌿
1110 W. Alameda (Pavilions) Burbank 91506 • **818-567-0257**
715 Pier Ave. (Vons) Hermosa Beach 90254 • **310-374-4484**
LAX Airport (Terminal 1) LA 90045
710 Broadway (Vons) Santa Monica 90401 • **310-260-0260**
820 Montana Ave. (Pavilions) Santa Monica 90403 • **310-385-1682**
1311 Wilshire Blvd. (Vons) Santa Monica 90403 • **310-394-1414**
Hours vary by location www.eaturna.com
Prepared foods made with organic and all natural ingredients; compostable containers.

Essential Living Foods 🌿🌿🌿🌿
920 Colorado Ave. Santa Monica 90401 • **310-319-1555**
Sat 9am-2pm www.essentiallivingfoods.com
Organic superfood buyers club specializing in raw cacao, goji berries, goldenberries, agava nectar, tropical fruit slices. Membership required.

Euphoria Loves Rawvolution 🌿🌿🌿🌿
2301 Main St. Santa Monica 90405 • **310-392-9501**
Daily 9am-9:30pm www.euphorialovesrawvolution.com
Raw, organic, vegan food products, snacks, beverages; natural body care products; supplements; raw food deli.

Famima!! 🌿
10704 Venice Blvd. Ste. B Culver City 90232 • **310-836-5600**
134 North Brand Blvd. Glendale 91203 • **818-241-6400**
6759 Hollywood Blvd. Hollywood 90028 • **323-836-0200**
525 W. 6th St. LA 90014 • **213-629-5100**
800 S. Figueroa Street Ste. 101 LA 90017 • **213-624-7700**
621 E. Colorado Blvd. Pasadena 91101 • **626-304-0500**
25 N. Raymond Ave. Pasadena 91103 • **626-578-0545**
1348 3rd St. Santa Monica 90401 • **310-393-2486**
22529 Hawthorne Blvd. Torrance 90505 • **310-378-1984**
8525 Santa Monica Blvd. West Hollywood 90069 • **310-659-2684**
Hours vary by location www.famima-usa.com
Offers some organic and all natural grocery, snack, and deli items. Recycled content paper products.

Food 🌿🌿
10571 W. Pico Blvd. LA 90064 • **310-441-7770**
Mon-Fri 8am-8pm Sat 8am-6pm Sun 8am-3pm www.food-la.com
Selection of organic cheeses, meats, gourmet food items, wine, beer.

Froma on Melrose 🌿
7960 Melrose Ave. LA 90046 • **323-653-3700**
Mon-Sat 10am-8pm Sun 10am-7pm www.fromaonmelrose.com
Offers selection of organic cheeses, olive oil, and gourmet food items. Provides catering.

Global Nutrition 🌿
22323 Sherman Way Ste. 14 Canoga Park 91303 • **818-932-8982**
Mon-Sat 10am-7pm
Carries some organic baking ingredients, whole food supplements, vitamins, minerals, herbs.

Granny's Pantry 🌿🌿
560 S. Arroyo Pkwy. Pasadena 91105 • **626-796-8442**
Mon-Sat 9am-7pm
Organic and all natural bulk items, dry goods.

Little Next Door 🌿🌿
8142 W. 3rd St. LA 90048 • **323-951-1010**
Daily 9am-9:30pm www.thelittledoor.com
French deli and market offering some organic baked goods, pastries, salads, sandwiches, gourmet food items.

Market Gourmet 🌿🌿
1800A Abbot Kinney Blvd. Venice 90291 • **310-305-9800**
Mon-Fri 9am-7pm Sat 10am-7pm Sun 12pm-6pm www.marketgourmet.biz
Gourmet condiments, olive oils, wines; gift and kitchen items.

Mrs. Winston's Green Grocery 🌿🌿
1999 Ave. of the Stars Ste. 120 LA 90067 • **310-553-4100**
2450 Colorado Ave. Ste. 1040W Santa Monica 90404 • **310-315-2777**
2901 Ocean Park Blvd. Ste. 107 Santa Monica 90405 • **310-452-7770**
Hours vary by location
Self-serve salad bar with organic ingredients. Selection of organic dry goods, prepared foods, nondairy beverages.

Nijiya Market 🌿
17869 Colima Rd. City of Industry 91748 • **626-913-9991**
124 Japanese Village Plaza Mall LA 90012 • **213-680-3280**
2130 Sawtelle Blvd. Ste. 105 LA 90025 • **310-575-3300**
2121 W. 182 St. Torrance 90504 • **310-366-7200**
2533B Pacific Coast Hwy. Torrance 90505 • **310-534-3000**
Hours vary by location www.nijiya.com
Carries some organic and all natural Japanese grocery and deli food items.

Oh Happy Days' Healthfood Grocery and Café 🌿🌿🌿🌿
2283 Lake Ave. Altadena 91001 • **626-797-0383**
Mon-Fri 11am-6:30pm Sat 11am-6pm
Organic produce, beverages, prepared vegan meals, herbs, supplements.

Organic To Go 🌿🌿🌿🌿
1880 Century Park East Ste. 103 LA 90067
2040 Century Park East Ste. B4 LA 90067 • **310-556-1895**
2049 Century Park East Ste. ROL14 LA 90067 • **310-552-6995**
350 S. Grand Ave. D6 LA 90071 • **213-628-7144**
555 W. 5th St. Ste. C56 LA 90013 • **213-228-0448**
5757 Wilshire Blvd. Ste. 106 LA 90036 • **323-954-0787**
21820 Burbank Blvd. Ste. 120 Woodland Hills 91367
5780 Canoga Ave. Warner Center Food Court Woodland Hills 91367
818-703-1131
Hours vary by location www.organictogo.com
Grab-n-go, ready-to-eat organic meals packaged in biodegradable containers. Delivery service uses eco-friendly vehicles; employees wear organic cotton uniforms; stores use nontoxic cleaning supplies.

Robins Nest Market 🌿🌿🌿
68 N. Venice Blvd. Venice 90291 • **310-821-7281**
Mon-Fri 7am-8pm Sat-Sun 7am-7pm www.robinsnestmarket.com
Small neighborhood store offering organic grocery items, prepared foods, produce; natural household items. Drive-thru/curbside valet grocery service. Recyles 90% of its trash items.

Santa Monica Seafood 🌿🌿🌿

1205 Colorado Blvd. Santa Monica 90404 • **310-393-5244**
Mon-Fri 9am-7pm Sat 9am-6pm Sun 10am-5pm www.smseafood.com
Family-owned fish market carrying wild-caught and sustainably farmed fish
and seafood.

Sophie's Produce 🌿🌿🌿🌿

8950 W. Olympic Blvd. Ste. 103 Beverly Hills 90211 • **310-860-1071**
Mon-Fri 9am-7pm Sat 9am-6pm Sun 10am-5pm www.sophiesproduce.com
Offers locally grown organic produce and herbs, organic grocery items,
gluten-free products; organic deli.

Catering and Personal Chefs

Catering your events with certified organic food or food that is locally
grown in a sustainable manner is a great way to be healthy and kind to
the planet, and to turn people on to sustainable products. This section
contains caterers and personal chefs whose primary focus is just that.
Readers should also check the *Restaurants and Cafés* section (starting
on page 3) to see if a favorite establishment caters. Look for the "C"
designation next to the restaurant name.

In this category, we identified those services and chefs whose primary
focus is to offer organic food and whose menus feature organic items.
We evaluated eight different food areas and also determined whether or
not reuseable utensils were used.

- For produce, we checked the percentage purchased that is certified organic and/or locally grown without pesticides and chemical fertilizers.

- For fresh meat (beef, lamb, pork, and game) and meat alternatives (tofu,
  soy), we determined the percentage that is certified organic and/or
  grass fed and produced without the use of hormones and antibiotics.

- For fresh poultry and eggs, we evaluated the percentage purchased
  that is certified organic, free-range/cage-free and/or locally raised,
  free-range/cage-free without the use of hormones and antibiotics.

- With fish, we checked into whether it was wild caught or sustainably
  farm raised and processed without chemical treatment. (We have
  included a Seafood Guide on page 34 to help you make healthy and
  sustainable seafood choices.)

- For dairy products, we checked the percentage of certified organic
  options or ones that were locally produced without hormones and
  antibiotics.

- We looked into the percentage of certified organic canned and dry
  goods, and nondairy beverages.

- For prepared foods, we determined the percentage made with certified organic ingredients and/or locally grown ingredients without pesticides and chemical fertilizers.

- For utensils, we checked into what percentage is reuseable.

> To be listed, catering services or personal chefs must use at least 25% of the above products in their menus and services and must promote organic foods and sustainable agriculture to their customers as a regular part of their business.

Bon Mélange Catering
Venice • **310-584-6593**
By appt www.bonmelangecatering.com
Gourmet catering using only organic, local, seasonal ingredients.

Brian Lucas—Chef Be Live
LA • **310-460-9253**
By appt www.belivelight.com
Private chef of gourmet, organic, raw cuisine.

Café Nagomi
LA • **310-923-8515**
Call or check website for truck locations and schedule www.cafenagomi.com
Mobile kitchen and catering company serving organic gourmet Japanese lunches and dinners. Uses organic produce and sustainable seafoods; no dairy, egg, refined sugar, or artificial additives.

Clean Plate
Culver City • **310-908-4753**
By appt www.cleanplate.us
Organic personal chef and catering service specializing in progressive Calicuisine. Delivers farm-to-table, fresh, organic meals. Serves the Westside.

Deuce Events
Glendale • **323-819-9733**
By appt www.deuceevents.com
Provides organic catering featuring culturally diverse cuisines.

Erin Swendeman Organic Catering
Venice • **310-804-1807**
By appt
Provides organic catering, personal chef, and meal delivery services.

Ghalia Organic Desserts
LA • **310-351-7870**
By appt www.ghaliaorganicdesserts.com
Specializes in desserts and bakery items using organic ingredients; accommodates special diets (gluten-free, vegan).

Green Truck
3515 Helms Ave. Culver City 90232 • **310-204-0477**
Call or check website for truck locations and schedule
www.greentruckonthego.com
Catering/commissary trucks serving 100% sustainable, local, and certified organic food. Trucks run on vegetable oil and are solar powered; zero carbon business. Serves greater Los Angeles area.

Heaven-ly Catering Company
Venice • 310-450-9808
By appt. www.heavenlycateringco.com
Specializes in Asian fusion and classic Americana cuisine using organic
ingredients when possible. Serves greater Los Angeles area.

Jam
Malibu • 310-403-5638
By appt. www.jamgourmet.com
In-home private chef/food delivery services, menu planning, and full-service
catering using organic, locally grown produce and meats. Vegetarian
options. Serves San Fernando Valley and the Westside.

Jennie Cook's Catering Company
9806 Washington Blvd. Culver City 90232 • 310-815-8273
By appt. www.jenniecooks.com
Specializes in vegan and healthy traditional cuisine with organic
ingredients. Uses recycled and compostable ware. Serves Beach Cities,
San Fernando Valley, and greater Los Angeles area.

Let's Be Frank Dogs
San Francisco • 415-515-8084
By appt. www.letsbefrankdogs.com
Hot dog cart carrying 100% local, grass-fed beef dogs, heritage pork
bratwurst; organic condiments, juices, and sodas. Available for special
events in Los Angeles.

Lulu Powers Food to Flowers
LA • 323-935-1337
By appt. www.lulupowers.com
Organic chef, caterer, party planner, and lifestyle consultant. Serves greater
Los Angeles area.

Melissa Ward Organic Gourmet
Santa Monica • Contact via website/e-mail
By appt. www.mwardonline.com
Provides organic catering, nutritional counseling, and culinary instruction.
Serves the Westside and Beach Cities.

Orchestration
Venice • 310-450-1233
Mon-Fri 10am-5pm
Full-service event and wedding orchestration. International and comfort
food using organic and locally sourced ingredients. Serves greater Los
Angeles area.

Organic to Go (Catering Department)
LA • 310-837-9944 800-304-4550
Daily 6:30am-7pm www.organictogo.com
Delivers organic meals to homes and businesses. Serves greater Los
Angeles.

Paleta
Venice • 310-396-7820
By appt. www.paleta.com
Provides home delivery of organic and nutritionally balanced meals using
seasonal and locally sourced ingredients. Specializes in California fusion
cuisine. Uses biodegradable and recycled products and packaging. Serves
greater Los Angeles area.

Rasa Foods
Venice • **310-804-9914**
Daily 24 hrs   www.rasafoods.com
Organic, local, seasonal ingredients; bio-fueled delivery vehicles;
specializes in event and personal chef services. Ayurvedic nutrition classes
and workshops. Serves the Westside.

Sweet Debbie's Organic Cupcakes
Sherman Oaks • **818-294-2496**
Daily 9am-5pm and by appt.   www.sweetdebbiesorganiccupcakes.com
Delivers organic desserts and baked goods only. Serves greater Los
Angeles area; free delivery to some areas.

Wine, Beer, and Spirits

In spite of the trend toward organics in the last decade, growers and
producers, as well as consumers, largely ignored organic alcoholic beverages. Many thought organic production methods were incompatible
with quality beer, wine, and spirits.

However, an increasing number of growers and producers are redis-
covering what many brewers, vintners, and distillers have known for
centuries: the joys and challenges of growing and processing beer, wine,
and spirits without the use of artificial ingredients, chemical pesticides
and fertilizers, or synthetic additives.

The shops listed here have made an extra effort to carry an assortment
of organic wines, beers, and spirits. You may also find a selection of
biodynamic wines in these stores.

The owners and managers of these stores are enthusiastic about the
organic and sustainably produced products they carry and possess a
wealth of information they would be happy to share. Ask them about
their products and show your support for their organic selections.

All of the stores listed here meet our threshold for entry into the guide
because of their commitment to quality organic products. Of all the
wine, beer, and spirits they stock, a store must carry a minimum of 15%
organic and/or biodynamic wines, beers, or spirits and demonstrate its
commitment to these items by promoting them in special display areas
and to their customers.

Biodynamic
Begun about seventy years ago, biodynamic farming uses basic
organic practices but adds special plant, animal, and mineral
preparations to the land and uses the rhythm of the sun, moon,
planets, and stars to create a healthy, self-supporting farming
eco-system.

Fireside Cellars 🍃
1421 Montana Ave. Santa Monica 90403 • **310-393-2888**
Mon-Thu 9am-9pm Fri-Sat 9am-10pm Sun 10am-7pm www.firesidecellars.com
Features a small section dedicated to organic wines. Also carries a select number of organic beers and vodka.

WineStyles Pacific Palisades 🍃
1970 Monument Ste. 116 Pacific Palisades 90272 • **310-454-6960**
Mon-Sat 11am-8pm Sun by appt. www.winestyles.net/pacificpalisades
Wine boutique and club offering some organic wines. Conducts tastings and events featuring organic wines.

🍃 GREEN TIP

As interest in organic wine, beer, and spirits has grown, their availability has expanded to include many grocery stores and specialty markets. Check those listings in the *Eating In* section of the guide for merchants that may carry these products.

🍃 GREEN TIP

The next time you're in the market and are deciding which product to buy, think about the following top ten reasons to choose organic. Simple choices can offer big benefits for your own health, your community, and the environment!

TOP 10 REASONS TO BUY ORGANIC

1. Protect the health of future generations.
2. Protect water quality.
3. Nurture soil quality and prevent erosion.
4. Save energy.
5. Keep poisons off your plate.
6. Protect farm worker health.
7. Help small farmers.
8. Promote biodiversity.
9. Expose the hidden environmental and social costs of conventional foods.
10. Enjoy better flavor and greater nourishment.

🍃 WRITE A REVIEW

We've done our best to compile a list of the merchants who offer local, sustainable, and organic products, but we'd like for you to tell us about your experiences—the quality of the service, the value for the price, or whether you would shop there again. Write your review at greenopia.com.

ORGANIC WINE

Made with Organic Grapes—Grapes have been grown in accordance with the strict organic rules set by the USDA National Organic Program. In addition, the wine is produced and bottled in a certified organic facility. Low levels of added sulfites are allowed, up to 100 parts per million (ppm). (Sulfites occur naturally during wine fermentation but are also added as preservatives. Conventional wines may contain from 80 to 350 ppm.)

Organic Wine—Grapes have been grown in accordance with the strict organic rules set by the USDA National Organic Program. In addition, the wine is produced and bottled in a certified organic facility. No added sulfites are allowed. Organic wine may carry the USDA ORGANIC green logo.

Most wines making an organic claim fall into the "Made with Organic Grapes" category because of the USDA's sulfites standard. Therefore, only domestic wines can be found labeled as "Organic Wine."

ORGANIC BEER

Organic beer is made from certified organic malted barley, hops, and yeast. These ingredients are grown without the use of synthetic pesticides, herbicides, and fertilizers. Although there are relatively few bottled organic beers on the market, they are clearly labeled.

To be labeled "Certified Organic," the beer must conform to all standards set by the USDA including the use of organic ingredients. The USDA also specifies which chemicals may be used to clean breweries. If the label reads "made with organic ingredients," the grains used are organic but the beer has not been processed in a certified organic facility. Either way, you are supporting organic farmers and farming methods by purchasing an organic product.

ORGANIC SPIRITS

Organic spirits are made from organic ingredients such as grains or potatoes. In the United States there are only a few producers and distributors of organic spirits but these products are available. You can find vodka, rum, grappa, gin, whiskey, and a variety of liqueurs that are organic. Some spirits are made with some organic ingredients but may not qualify for full organic certification.

Look for the USDA certified organic seal for U.S.-made products, or an internationally recognized organic seal for those made overseas.

Lowest in Pesticides	Highest in Pesticides
Onions	Peaches
Avocados	Apples
Sweet Corn (Frozen)	Sweet Bell Peppers
Pineapples	Celery
Mangos	Nectarines
Sweet Peas (Frozen)	Strawberries
Asparagus	Cherries
Kiwis	Lettuces
Bananas	Grapes (Imported)
Cabbages	Pears
Broccoli	Spinach
Eggplants	Potatoes

WHY SHOULD YOU CARE ABOUT PESTICIDES?

There is a growing consensus in the scientific community that small doses of pesticides and other chemicals can adversely affect people, especially during vulnerable periods of fetal development and childhood when exposures can have long-lasting effects. Because the toxic effects of pesticides are worrisome, not well understood, or in some cases completely unstudied, shoppers are wise to minimize exposure to pesticides whenever possible.

WILL WASHING AND PEELING HELP?

Nearly all of the data used to create these lists already considers how people typically wash and prepare produce (for example, apples are washed before testing, bananas are peeled). While washing and rinsing fresh produce may reduce levels of some pesticides, it does not eliminate them. Peeling also reduces exposures, but valuable nutrients often go down the drain with the peel. The best option is to eat a varied diet, wash all produce, and choose organic when possible to reduce exposure to potentially harmful chemicals.

HOW WAS THIS GUIDE DEVELOPED?

The produce ranking was developed by analysts at the not-for-profit Environmental Working Group (EWG) based on the results of nearly 51,000 tests for pesticides on produce collected by the U.S. Department of Agriculture and the U.S. Food and Drug Administration between 2000 and 2005. A detailed description of the criteria used in developing the rankings, as well as a full list of fresh fruits and vegetables that have been tested, is available at www.foodnews.org.

 **ENVIRONMENTAL WORKING GROUP**

Reprinted with the permission of the Environmental Working Group (EWG). EWG is a not-for-profit environmental research orgaization dedicated to improving public health and protecting the environment by reducing pollution in air, water, and food. For more information, visit www.ewg.org.

Green indicates that a product is available and is being harvested.

	Jan	Feb	Mar	Apr	May	Jun	Jul	Aug	Sep	Oct	Nov	Dec
Artichokes	▲	▲	●	●	●	●				●	●	●
Arugula	●	●	●	●	●	●	●	●	●	●	●	●
Asian Greens	●	●	●	●	●	●	●	●	●	●	●	●
Asparagus	●	●	●	●	●		●	●	●			●
Avocados		●	●	●		●	●	●	●	●		
Basil					●	●	●	●	●			
Beans, Shell							●	●	●			
Beans, Dried	▲	▲	▲	▲	▲	▲	▲	▲	▲	●	●	▲
Beans, Snap						●	●	●	●	●		
Beets	●	●	●	●	●	●				●	●	●
Bok Choy	●	●	●	●	●				●	●	●	●
Broccoli	●	●	●	●					●	●	●	●
Brussels Sprouts	●	●	●							●	●	●
Cabbage	●	●	●	●	●	●	●	●	●	●	●	●
Cactus Pads				●	●	●						
Cardoons		●	●									
Carrots	●	●	●	●	●	●	●	●	●	●	●	●
Cauliflower	●	●	●	●	●	●	▲	▲	●	●	●	●
Celery	▲	▲	▲	●	●	●	●	●	●	●	●	●
Chard	●	●	●	●	●					●	●	●
Collards	●	●	●	●							●	●
Corn						●	●	●	●	●	●	
Cress		●	●	●	▲	▲	●	●	●	●	●	●
Cucumbers					▲	●	●	●	●	●		
Dandelion	●	●	●	●								
Eggplant							●	●	●	●		
Escarole	●	●	●	●	●	●	●	●	●	●	●	●
Fava Beans			●	●	●	●						
Fennel	●	●	●	●								
Garlic	▲	▲	▲	▲	▲	▲	●	●	●	●	●	●
Gourds										●	●	●
Green Garlic			●	●	●							

Orange indicates that it is available but is not within its natural harvest season (possible through storage or hot house production).

	Jan	Feb	Mar	Apr	May	Jun	Jul	Aug	Sep	Oct	Nov	Dec
Green Onions	●	●	●	●	●	●	●	●	●	●	●	●
Herbs, Various	●	●	●	●	●	●	●	●	●	●	●	●
Kale	●	●	●	●	●	●	●	●	●	●	●	●
Kohlrabi	●	●	●	●								●
Leeks	●	●	●	●	●	▲	▲	▲	▲	▲	●	●
Lettuces	▲	●	●	●	●	●	●	●	●	●	●	●
Mushrooms	●	●	●	●	●	●	●	●	●	●	●	●
Nettles	●	●	●	●	●	●	●					
Mustard		●	●	●						●	●	●
Okra							●	●	●	●		
Olives	▲	▲	▲	▲	▲	▲	▲	▲	●	●	●	▲
Onions	▲	▲	●	●	●	●	●	●	●	●	●	▲
Parsnips	●	●	●	●							●	●
Peas					●	●	●	●	●			
Peppers						●	●	●	●	●		
Potatoes	▲	▲	▲	▲	●	●	●	●	●	●	●	●
Purslane						●	●	●	●			
Radicchio				●	●	●	●	●	●	●	●	
Radishes	●	●	●	●	●	●						
Rapini		●	●	●	●					●	●	●
Rhubarb				●	●	●	●	●	●	●		
Rutabagas	●	●								●	●	●
Shallots	▲	▲	▲	▲	▲	▲	●	●	●	●	▲	▲
Spinach		●	●	●	●	●	●	●	●	●	●	
Squash, Summer					●	●	●	●	●			
Squash, Winter	▲	▲						●	●	●	●	●
Sunchokes										●	●	
Sweet Potatoes									●	●	●	●
Tomatillos							●	●	●	●	●	
Tomatoes				▲	▲	●	●	●	●	●	●	
Turnips	●	●	●	●	●							●

Green indicates that a product is available and is being harvested.

	Jan	Feb	Mar	Apr	May	Jun	Jul	Aug	Sep	Oct	Nov	Dec
Almonds	▲	▲	▲	▲	▲	▲	▲	▲	▲	●	●	▲
Apples	▲	▲	▲	▲	▲	▲	▲	●	●	●	●	▲
Apricots					●	●	●					
Asian Pears	▲	▲	▲	▲			●	●	●	●	●	▲
Blackberries					●	●	●	●	●			
Blueberries			▲	▲	●	●	●	●	●	▲	▲	
Boysenberries						●	●					
Cactus Pears					●	●	●	●	●	●		
Cherimoyas	●	●	●	●								
Cherries					●	▲						
Chestnuts										●	●	●
Clementines	●	●	●	●								●
Dates	▲	▲	▲	▲	▲	▲	▲	▲	●	●	●	●
Dried Fruits	●	●	●	●	●	●	●	●	●	●	●	●
Figs							●	●	●			
Grapefruit	●	●	●	●	●	●	●	●	●	●	●	●
Grapes							●	●	●	●	●	
Guavas	●	●	●	●	●					●	●	●
Jujubes										●	●	●
Kiwis	●	●	●							●	●	●
Kumquats	●	●	●	●	●	●	●	●				
Lemons, Eureka	●	●	●	●	●	●	●	●	●	●	●	●
Lemons, Meyer	●	●	●	●								●
Limes, Bearss	●	●	●	●	●			●	●	●	●	●
Limes, Key							●	●	●	●		
Loquats				●	●	●						

Become a member greenopia.com

Orange indicates that it is available but is not within its natural harvest season (possible through storage or hot house production).

	Jan	Feb	Mar	Apr	May	Jun	Jul	Aug	Sep	Oct	Nov	Dec
Mandarins	●	●	●	●								●
Melons						●	●	●	●	●		
Mulberries							●	●				
Nectarines						●	●	●	●	●		
Oranges, Blood	●	●	●	●	●							●
Oranges, Navel	●	●	●	●							●	●
Oranges, Valencia			●	●	●	●	●	●	●	●		
Peaches						●	●	●	●	●		
Pears								●	●	●	●	●
Persimmons									●	●	●	
Pistachios	▲	▲	▲	▲	▲	▲	▲	▲	▲		▲	
Plums						●	●	●	●	●		
Pluots						●	●	●	●			
Pomegranates									●	●	●	●
Pumelos	●	●	●	●								●
Quinces									●	●	●	
Raspberries		▲	▲	▲	●	●	●	●	●	●		
Strawberries			●	●	●	●	●					
Tangelos		●	●	●								
Tangerines						●	●	●	●	●	●	
Tomatillos								●	●	●	●	●
Tomatoes				▲	▲	●	●	●	●			
Walnuts	▲	▲	▲	▲	▲	▲	▲	▲	▲	●	●	

Amelia Saltsman
Amelia Saltsman is a television host, cooking teacher, and writer. She developed the "Eating in Season" chart especially for Greenopia. She is the author of *The Santa Monica Farmers' Market Cookbook: Seasonal Foods, Simple Recipes, and Stories from the Market and Farm* (www.ameliasaltsman.com).

Conscious Beauty

BY JANE KENNEDY

Having sold natural personal care products for more than twenty-five years, I am excited and energized by the rapid changes happening in our environmental awareness and the conscious choices people are making in their overall skin care. We are learning to green our lives. This connection between social consciousness and personal health is vital and inspires healthy choices in how we care for our planet and ourselves.

It wasn't too long ago that finding products that were clean and pure, without harsh chemicals, was not easy and more than confusing. I grew up with allergies and sensitivities to commercially and chemically made products. Traveling through Europe in my early twenties, I remember finding small shops with natural products completely unknown to me. It was a revelation and a thrill. When I moved to Los Angeles soon after, I found a whole new world. But still, the only place you could find natural skin care products was in small health food stores with no one to really guide you. Your choices were very limited. And that's where my story began . . . I had found my "natural niche."

It's been a rewarding journey, helping customers make healthier choices. For me, personal care has always meant personal service. Education is the key. Today, it's not enough to see the word *natural* on a product label. It has been overused and abused. You have to dig deeper. Knowing what to look for is important. Imagine how many more chemicals have been introduced in our lives during the past twenty years. It is daunting. We have to pay attention to the build-up of chemicals in our system, from the air we breathe, the food we eat, and what we put on our skin—our body's largest organ. What goes "on" really goes "in."

It feels good to choose healthy skin care. There are many small companies making products that are better for you and for our environment. More and more high-quality, organic ingredients are being used. Companies are responding to consumer demands by changing formulas, using recycled packaging, and becoming sustainable. Go explore and enjoy your local green beauty businesses. We will continue to offer you the best choices to stay pure, clean, and green. Looking good does come naturally!

JANE KENNEDY

Jane Kennedy is the owner of Palmetto, a store in Santa Monica that has specialized in clean, pure-ingredient personal care products for more than twenty-five years.

Beauty Product Supplies

The cosmetics industry is, in many ways, self-regulating. That means makers of cosmetics do not need approval from the Food and Drug Administration (FDA) for every chemical they use in their products. It's up to us to make sure we're getting products that are natural and nontoxic. That's why it makes sense to shop where you can get help from a knowledgeable staff person.

Organic beauty products, once rare, are now easier to find. Their effectiveness is on par with, and oftentimes superior to, conventional commercial beauty products. If you can't find an organic product that suits you, look for ones that offer organic ingredients combined with all natural ingredients.

We've determined leaf awards based on the percentage of all the beauty product brands sold and/or used by an establishment containing one or more of the following:

- all certified organic ingredients,

- a mix of certified organic ingredients and natural ingredients, and/or

- all natural ingredients, or mostly natural ingredients, and that do not contain any of the following: *mercury, thimerosal, lead acetate, formaldehyde, nickel, toluene, petroleum distillates, acrylonitrile, ethylacrylate, coal tar, dibutyl phthalate, potassium dichromate, methyl cellosolve.*

℘ at least 25% of the products meet the above criteria.

℘℘ at least 50% of the products meet the above criteria.

℘℘℘ at least 75% of the products meet the above criteria.

℘℘℘℘ at least 90% of the products meet the above criteria.

A Touch of Beauty ℘
Northridge Mall 9301 Tampa Ave. Northridge 91324 • **818-718-8386**
Mon-Thu 10am-9pm Fri-Sat 9am-10pm Sun 11am-7pm
Beauty supply store and salon. Offers some organic and natural skin and hair products.

Aveda ℘℘
2117 Glendale Galleria Glendale 91210 • **818-246-3680**
6801 Hollywood Blvd. Ste. 213 Hollywood 90028 • **323-962-1596**
Westfield Century City 10250 Santa Monica Blvd. LA 90067 • **310-203-9946**
Beverly Center 131 N. La Cienega Blvd. LA 90048 • **310-659-5067**
1301 Montana Ave. Santa Monica 90403 • **310-576-0989**
Hours vary by location www.aveda.com
Hair and skin care products, essential oils, and body care products made from plant-based, organic, or sustainable ingredients.

Bare Escentuals ℘℘
Westfield Topanga Plaza 6600 Topanga Canyon Rd. Canoga Park 91303
818-346-1101

Bare Escentuals (cont.)

Westside Pavillion 10800 W. Pico Blvd. LA 90064 • **310-441-2912**
Thousand Oaks Mall 538 West Hillcrest Dr. Thousand Oaks 91360
805-418-1864
Hours vary by location   www.bareescentuals.com
All natural cosmetics and treatments without additives.

Beauty Essentials, Inc. 🌿🌿

Westfield Fashion Square 14006 Riverside Dr. Sherman Oaks 91423
818-990-8989
Mon-Fri 10am-9pm Sat 10am-7pm Sun 11am-6pm
Beauty supply store with some organic products.

Beverly Hills Beauty Center 🌿🌿

350 N. Beverly Dr. Beverly Hills 90210 • **310-278-8815**
Mon-Sat 9:30am-7pm Sun 11am-6pm
Carries several organic and natural beauty lines.

Bey's Garden, The 🌿🌿🌿🌿

2919 Main St. Santa Monica 90405 • **310-399-5420**
Daily 10am-8pm www.beysgarden.com
Aromatherapy boutique carries organic, all natural products, essential oils,
and gift packages. Uses recycled or sustainable products in all aspects of
its business. Day spa services.

Blunda Aromatics 🌿🌿🌿🌿

304 S. Edinburgh Ave. LA 90048 • **323-658-7507**
Mon-Wed by appt. Thu-Sat 11am-7pm www.blundalosangeles.com
Raw materials for making perfumes, makeup, and skin care products. Offers
classes on raw materials, botanical perfumery, aromatherapy, body care,
makeup, incense, and creating your own beauty products.

Body Shop, The 🌿

Westfield Topanga Plaza 6600 Topanga Canyon Rd. Canoga Park 91303
818-704-0604
2148 Glendale Galleria Glendale 91210 • **818-242-4880**
Westfield Century City 10250 Santa Monica Blvd. LA 90067 • **310-203-9221**
Westside Pavillion 10800 W. Pico Blvd. LA 90064 • **310-474-2639**
Beverly Center 8500 Beverly Blvd. LA 90048 • **310-659-7513**
Northridge Fashion Center 9301 Tampa Ave. Northridge 91324 • **818-886-2494**
Westfield Fashion Square 14006 Riverside Dr. Sherman Oaks 94123
818-789-7522
The Oaks Shopping Center 222 W. Hillcrest Dr. Thousand Oaks 91360
805-373-6845
3 Del Amo Fashion Square Torrance 90503 • **310-370-0132**
LAX Airport (Terminal 1) Westchester 90045 • **310-337-3922**
Hours vary by location www.thebodyshop.com
Beauty supplies, skin care, aromatherapy, fragrances and essential oils.
Hair care and bath products. Some all natural items.

Body Suite, The 🌿🌿🌿

316 Manhattan Beach Blvd. Manhattan Beach 90266 • **310-379-3686**
Daily 10am-6pm www.thebodysuite.com
Beauty and aromatherapy products, meditation tools and accessories.

Brentwood Skincare 🌿🌿🌿

1610 Broadway Unit B Santa Monica 90404 • **310-264-9800**
Tue-Sat 9am-5pm www.brentwoodskin.com
Skin care treatments using 100% handmade organic products crafted to
European standards.

Chaz Dean Studio ✐✐✐✐
6444 Fountain Ave. LA 90028 • **323-467-6444**
Tue-Sat 10am-5pm Wed-Fri 12pm-7pm www.chazdean.com
Private label hair care products made with all natural ingredients.

Classic Beauty Center ✐
18100 Chatsworth St. Unit C Granada Hills 91344 • **818-363-9090**
Mon-Sat 9:30am-7pm Sun 10am-5pm
Natural and organic hair, skin, and body care products and cosmetics.

Euphoria Beauty and Wisdom ✐✐✐✐
2307 Main St. Santa Monica 90405 • **310-396-4300**
Daily 11am-7pm www.euphorialovesrawvolution
Eco-conscious, organic, vegan, and raw body products. Books and energy
healing products.

Green Cradle ✐✐✐✐
13344 Ventura Blvd. Sherman Oaks 91423 • **818-728-4305**
Mon-Sat 10am-7pm www.greencradle.com
Organic and all natural health and beauty products for the whole family.

Hair Doc Company, The ✐✐
9136 De Soto Ave. Chatsworth 91311 • **818-882-4247**
Mon-Fri 8am-4:30pm www.thehairdoccompany.com
Line of natural, environmentally-friendly hair brushes and combs; Sisal
loofahs; natural toothbrushes.

Jurlique Concept Stores ✐✐✐✐
358 N. Beverly Dr. Beverly Hills 90210 • **310-285-9820**
1230 Montana Ave. Ste 105 Santa Monica 90403 • **310-899-1923**
Hours vary by location www.jurlique.com
Bath and body care, essential oils. Facial, waxing, and skin care treatments.
Natural- and plant-based products; no chemicals, artificial colors, or
fragrances. Herbs grown organically and biodynamically. Recycled
packaging.

Kiehl's Since 1851 ✐✐✐
100 N. Robertson Blvd. LA 90048 • **310-860-0028**
The Grove 189 The Grove Dr. LA 90036 • **323-965-0569**
1516 Montana Ave. Santa Monica 90403 • **310-255-0055**
Hours vary by location www.kiehls.com
Modern apothecary for the entire family. Skin and hair care formulated with
natural ingredients.

Lavender Natural Beauty ✐✐✐✐
13559 Ventura Blvd. Sherman Oaks 91423 • **818-986-1280**
Mon-Sat 10am-6pm Sun 11am-4pm www.lavendernaturalbeauty.com
Organic and natural boutique specializing in skin and body care, and home
fragrances.

Le Pink & Co. ✐✐
3820 W. Sunset Blvd. LA 90026 • **323-661-7465**
Mon-Fri 12pm-7pm Sat-Sun 11am-6pm www.lepink.net
Beauty apothecary offering some organic skin care and beauty products.

L'Occitane en Provence ✐
367 N. Beverly Dr. Beverly Hills 90210 • **310-205-9107**
4751 Commons Way Calabasas 91302 • **818-222-0169**
Westfield Century City 10250 Santa Monica Blvd. LA 90067 • **310-557-1779**
2106 Glendale Galleria Glendale 91210 • **818-662-9653**
The Grove 189 The Grove Dr. LA 90036 • **323-857-1123**

L'Occitane en Provence (cont.)
Beverly Center 8500 Beverly Blvd. LA 90048 • **310-659-5665**
Westfield Fashion Square 14006 W. Riverside Dr. Sherman Oaks 91423
818-386-2129
Westfield Topanga Plaza 6600 Topanga Canyon Blvd. Canoga Park 91303
818-704-9410
3900 Cross Creek Rd. Unit 4 Malibu 90265 • **310-317-0780**
1239 3rd St. Santa Monica 90401 • **310-451-3845**
Hours vary by location www.loccitane.com
Skin and body care, and home fragrances. Made from pure plant- and
vegetable-based sources. Minimal packaging; Braille on label. No child
labor, animal testing, or animal products.

Lush Fresh Handmade Cosmetics 🌱🌱🌱
312 N. Beverly Dr. Beverly Hills 90210 • **310-271-0880**
24 E. Colorado Blvd. Pasadena 91105 • **626-792-0901**
1404 3rd St. Promenade Santa Monica 90401 • **310-255-0030**
Universal Citywalk Universal City 91608 • **818-487-9800**
Hours vary by location www.lush.com
Fresh and handmade bath, body, hair care, and skin care products.

Mélange Apothecary 🌱🌱🌱
20929 Ventura Blvd. Ste. 15 Woodland Hills 91364 • **818-703-8481**
Mon-Fri 10am-6pm Sat 10am-5pm www.melangeapothecary.com
Natural fragrance, bath, and beauty products.

Michele International 🌱🌱🌱
1016 Swarthmore Ave. Pacific Palisades 90272 • **310-454-1885**
Mon-Sat 9am-6pm
Hair salon with a selection of organic and all natural hair and skin care
products.

Milena's Boutique 🌱🌱🌱🌱
8302 W. 3rd St. LA 90048 • **323-655-9999**
Mon-Sat 11am-6pm Sun 12pm-5pm www.milenasboutique.com
Soy candles, body products, and soaps made from organic, all natural
products.

Naturella Beauty Center 🌱🌱🌱
15220 W. Sunset Blvd. Pacific Palisades 90272 • **310-459-3446**
Daily 9am-6pm
Soaps, hair, makeup, and baby products made with organic and all natural
ingredients.

Origins 🌱🌱🌱
6801 Hollywood Blvd. Hollywood 90028 • **323-460-6970**
Westfield Century City 10250 Santa Monica Blvd. LA 90067 • **310-772-0272**
15 Douglas Alley Pasadena 91103 • **626-564-1790**
Del Amo Shopping Center 3525 Carson St. Torrance 90503 • **310-370-3515**
Hours vary by location www.origins.com
Organic and all natural wellness, beauty, and body care products.

Palisades Hair & Beauty Center 🌱🌱🌱
1043 Swarthmore Ave. Pacific Palisades 90272 • **310-454-8022**
Mon-Sat 9am-6pm Sun 9am-5pm
Natural soaps and bath products, organic shampoos and conditioners,
mineral-based makeup.

Palmetto 🌱🌱🌱🌱
8321 W. Third St. LA 90048 • **323-653-2470**
1034 Montana Ave. Santa Monica 90403 • **310-395-6687**

Palmetto (cont.)
Mon-Sat 10am-6pm Sun 12pm-5pm www.palmettobeauty.com
Large selection of all natural and organic beauty products. Uses recycled packaging.

Planet Blue ✐
2940 Main St. Venice 90405 • **310-396-1767**
3835 Cross Creek Rd. Ste. 15B Malibu 90265 • **310-317-8566**
Daily 10am-6pm www.shopplanetblue.com
Soy candles and vegetable soaps, organic and all natural beauty products.

Rooibos Tea House ✐✐✐✐
401 ½ S. Fairfax Ave. LA 90036 • **323-658-7832**
533 N. Farifax Ave. LA 90036 • **323-658-7832**
Hours vary by location www.africanredtea.com
Organic soap, skin care, and health products all made with tea. Also sells organic tea.

Strange Invisible Perfumes ✐✐✐✐
1138 Abbot Kinney Blvd. Venice 90291 • **310-314-1505**
Tue-Sat 11am-7pm Sun 12am-6pm www.siperfumes.com
Perfumes crafted using essential oils from 100% organic or wild-crafted, sustainably sourced botanical ingredients. Uses solvent-free hydro-distillation method. Product packaging made from post-consumer recycled fibers and plastics.

Studio at Fred Segal ✐
500 Broadway Santa Monica 90401 • **310-394-8509**
Mon-Sat 10am-7pm Sun 12pm-6pm
Organic and all natural beauty and home fragrance products.

Vert ✐✐✐✐
1121 Abbot Kinney Blvd. Venice 90291 • **310-581-6126**
Tue-Sun 11am-7pm www.vertlosangeles.com
Eco-friendly, all natural beauty products, as well as educational seminars, workshops, and makeup sessions.

✐ GREEN TIP

As the beauty product selection has grown, so has their availability. In addition to the above retailers, many grocery stores, specialty markets, and pharmacies that you find in this guide carry a wide selection of organic and all natural beauty products.

✐ WRITE A REVIEW

When it comes to beauty products, it can be really challenging to separate what's good for you and the planet and what the product label says. We've tried to identify the best eco-friendly beauty retailers, but we know your experiences also matter. Visit greenopia.com and tell us about the effectiveness and assortment of the products you've found.

Anyone who has ever been in, or walked near, a conventional hair and nail salon knows that the chemical vapors coming from within can be overwhelming. And many of the chemicals used in the products are potentially hazardous to the health and safety of stylists as well as customers. Improper or poor ventilation can worsen the problems. Environmentally-friendly alternatives for toxic ingredients are increasingly available so it makes sense to choose salons that are healthier for you and the workers inside.

If you already have a favorite salon, ask for the least-toxic treatments and check on sanitation procedures. (The only way to effectively and naturally clean salon equipment is by using an FDA-approved *autoclave,* a device designed to heat solutions and the equipment they contain above their boiling point.) Also, ask your salon to carry beauty products with nontoxic or less-toxic ingredients. Or, don't be shy about asking if you can bring in your own organic shampoo or hair color for them to use or apply.

For hair care, we have determined leaf awards based on the percentage of hair coloring that is nontoxic and whether or not nonsynthetic henna is used.

For nail salons, we checked for phthalate-, toluene-, and formaldehyde-free polish use and whether or not the polish remover used is acetone-free. We also checked for the presence of ventilation systems that allow for outdoor air exchange and for proper sanitation.

For both hair and nail salons, we also reviewed the supplies used on customers and grooming products for sale in the salon. We based our leaf awards on the percentage sold or used that are made with one or more of the following:

- all certified organic ingredients,

- a mix of certified organic ingredients and natural ingredients, and/or

- all natural ingredients, or mostly natural ingredients, and that do not contain *mercury, thimerosal, lead acetate, formaldehyde, nickel, toluene, petroleum distillates, acrylonitrile, ethylacrylate, coal tar, dibutyl phthalate, potassium dichromate, methyl cellosolve.*

Of salon practices, salon supplies used, and products sold:

🍃 at least 25% meet the above criteria

🍃🍃 at least 50% meet the above criteria

🍃🍃🍃 at least 75% meet the above criteria

🍃🍃🍃🍃 at least 90% meet the above criteria

Alyson Powell at The Parlor ✿✿✿✿
8113 W. 3rd St. LA 90048 • **310-402-8989**
By appt.
Holistic personalized hair care consultant and stylist using natural coloring with low and zero ammonia products. Specializes in fine to curly hair.

Amato Hair Salon ✿
9908 Santa Monica Blvd. Beverly Hills 90212 • **310-277-6524**
Tue-Wed 9am-6pm Thu-Fri 9am-8:30pm Sat 8:30am-6pm
www.amatohairstudio.com
Sulfate-free and organic hair care products. Uses vegetable dyes.

Ambiance Salon ✿✿✿✿
2525 Main St. Santa Monica 90405 • **310-392-4866**
Daily 10am-6pm
Organic shampoos and conditioners. Natural products used in hair salon services.

Bernard Halimi at Salon Gonchi ✿✿✿
1547 Westwood Blvd. LA 90024 • **213-924-9175**
Tue-Sat 11am-6pm
Hair services and products using all natural and organic ingredients.

Beyond Hair ✿✿
999 E. Green St. Pasadena 91106 • **626-431-2804**
Tue-Fri 9am-7pm, Sat 9am-5pm
All natural hair color, perms, makeup, skin care, and hair styling.

Blush Salon ✿
404 S. San Vicente Blvd. LA 90048 • **310-657-4336**
Tue-Sat 10am-6pm www.blush-salon.com
Vegetable-based hair coloring. Sells all natural skin care products.

Bokaos ✿✿
134 W. Colorado Blvd. Pasadena 91105 • **626-304-0007**
Mon-Sat 10am-10pm Sun 10am-8pm www.bokaos.com
Aveda day spa and hair salon. Hair color, perms, and styling using all natural products. Complimentary sensory rituals.

Bruno & Soonie Salon ✿
404 N. Canon Dr. Beverly Hills 90210 • **310-275-8152**
Tue-Sat 8am-6pm www.brunoandsoonie.com
Offers vegetable-based hair dyes.

Capelli Lounge ✿
1001 Gayley Ave. LA 90024 • **310-824-2711**
Tue-Fri 11am-7pm Sat-Sun 9am-4pm www.capelilounge.com
All natural nontoxic hair care products.

Chaz Dean Studio ✿✿✿✿
6444 Fountain Ave. LA 90028 • **323-467-6444**
Tue 1pm-5pm Wed-Fri 11am-7pm Sat 1pm-5pm www.chazdeanstudio.com
Hair services include own line of nontoxic cleansing conditioners, low-ammonia hair colorants, and bleach-free color lifts.

Creative Airs Holistic Hair Salon ✿✿✿
5210 Laurel Canyon Blvd. North Hollywood 91604 • **818-769-3666**
Wed-Sat 8am-6pm www.creativeairs.com
Chemical-free perms, styling, and straightening; all natural botanical hair coloring.

Crop Salon ✿✿✿
515 N. Ave. 64 LA 90042 • **323-344-7038**

Crop Salon (cont.)
By appt. Tue-Sat www.cropsalon.com
Natural hair coloring and organic hair products. Also sells some eco-fashion accessories and recycled jewelry.

David Dru Salon 🍃🍃
8950 W. Olympic Blvd. Ste. 214 Beverly Hills 90211 • **310-273-8060**
Wed-Sat 7:30am-6pm www.daviddrusalon.com
All natural hair color, perms, makeup, skin care, and hair styling.

Deja Vu Salon, The 🍃🍃🍃
13028 San Vicente Blvd. LA 90049 • **310-319-9559**
Tue-Sat 9am-6pm www.thedejavusalon.com
Hair services include vegetable dyes, nonsynthetic henna, and environmentally-friendly hair products; Japanese hair straightening.

Élan Vital Hair Salon 🍃🍃
2905 Sepulveda Blvd. Ste. B Manhattan Beach 90266 • **310-546-1431**
Tue-Fri 10am-7pm Sat 9am-5pm www.elanvitalhairsalon.com
Aveda Concept salon. All natural hair color, perms, makeup, and hair styling.

Epitome Salon 🍃🍃
2938 N. Beverly Glen Cir. LA 90077 • **310-441-8800**
Mon Tue Sat 10am-6pm Wed-Fri 10am-8pm Sun 10am-4pm
www.epitomesalon.com
Eco-friendly hair care products sold and used in services.

Fandango Salon 🍃🍃
1601 Griffith Park Blvd. LA 90026 • **323-663-6965**
Tue-Fri 10am-7pm Sat 9:30am-7pm www.fandangosalon.com
All natural hair color, perms, makeup, and hair styling services.

Fringe Hair Salon and Spa 🍃🍃
110 Santa Monica Blvd. Santa Monica 90401 • **310-260-7900**
Daily 9am-9pm
Hair salon and spa offering Aveda products and services.

Glendale SalonSpa 🍃🍃
513 E. Broadway Glendale 91205 • **818-240-6340**
Tue-Fri 9am-8pm Sat 9am-5pm www.glendalesalonspa.com
Aveda Concept salon using Aveda's all natural products. Offers color, texture, and hair styling; massages, facials, and skin care treatments; manicures and pedicures.

Goldhill International 🍃🍃
14060 Ventura Blvd. Sherman Oaks 91423 • **818-907-7770**
Mon-Fri 9am-7pm Sat 9am-6pm Sun 11am-5pm www.goldhillinternational.com
Aveda Concept salon. Beauty products and services that are all natural and organic.

Hair by Ramona at Scissors 🍃🍃🍃
2303 Main St. Santa Monica 90405 • **310-391-2575**
By appt.
Master stylist specializing in organic hair color and color correction.

Hilites 🍃
15328 Antioch St. Pacific Palisades 90272 • **310-230-4010**
Mon-Sat 9am-6pm
Organic and all natural hair and nail products available.

Jolie Coupe ✏✏
1459 Westwood Blvd. LA 90024 • **310-444-0042**
Tue-Fri 10am-7pm Sat 9am-7pm Sun-Mon by appt.
Phyto organic shampoo and conditioners used for services.

Kriza Salon Spa ✏✏
Westfield Fashion Square 14006 Riverside Dr. Sherman Oaks 91423
818-501-1444
12132 Ventura Blvd. Studio City 91604 • **818-506-1220**
Westfield Topanga Plaza 6600 Topanga Canyon Blvd. Canoga Park 91303
818-348-0800
Hours vary by location www.krizasalonspa.com
Aveda Lifestyle salon. All natural and organic hair treatments and services.
Complimentary sensory rituals.

Le Studio ✏✏
875 Via De La Paz Pacific Palisades 90292 • **310-459-0366**
Daily 12pm-9pm
Hair salon specializing in organic hair extensions, products, and coloring.

Linda Kammins ✏✏
848 N. La Cienaga Blvd. Ste. 204 LA 90069 • **310-659-6257**
Thu-Sat 11am-6pm www.lindakammins.com
Natural hair salon and aromatherapy beauty products.

Loft Hair Lounge, The ✏✏
5112 Townsend Ave. LA 90041 • **323-258-2840**
Tue-Sat 9am-7pm
Organic, all natural skin care products and facials. Also offers ammonia-
free hair dye.

M Salon ✏✏
8209 Melrose Ave. LA 90046 • **323-658-6682**
Tue-Sat 10am-6pm
Aveda's all natural hair color, perms, makeup, skin care, and hair styling
products.

Mark Erik's Beauty Lounge ✏✏
18523 Devonshire St. Northridge 91324 • **818-363-4501**
Tue-Sat 9:30am-7pm
Aveda products, some natural hair coloring.

Mark Slicker Salon ✏✏
1107 Gayley Ave. LA 90024 • **310-443-8018**
Mon-Sat 10am-6pm www.markslicker.com
Vegetable-based hair dyes and all natural products such as Korres and
Apivita. Also sells soy candles.

Michele International ✏✏✏
1016 Swarthmore Ave. Pacific Palisades 90272 • **310-454-1885**
Mon-Sat 9am-6pm
Organic hair and skin care products and services; massage and facial.

Mimosa ✏
405 Pier Ave. Hermosa Beach 90254 • **310-372-9411**
Mon 10am-6pm Tue-Fri 10am-8pm Sat 9am-6pm Sun 10am-6pm
www.mimosasalon.com
Selection of all natural and organic hair products and services.

Next Salon ✏
2400 Main St. · Santa Monica 90405 • **310-392-6645**
Daily 9am-6pm www.nextsalon.com

Next Salon (cont.)
Open air, natural light, odor- and ammonia-free hair coloring.

Nori's EcoSalon ✐✐✐✐
15826 Ventura Blvd. Ste. 223 Encino 91436 • **818-995-6571**
Tue-Sat 10am-6pm www.norisecosalon.com
Natural hair care services including nontoxic permanent hair coloring and
100% botanical henna using their own formulations. Interior built using all
eco-friendly and nontoxic materials.

Okie Dokie Kids Salon ✐✐✐✐
20929 Ventura Blvd. Ste. 41 Woodland Hills 91364 • **818-340-7771**
Tue-Sat 10am-6pm Sun 10am-4pm www.okiedokie.tv
Hair products for kids that are organic, gentle, alcohol-free, and
environmentally friendly.

Orpheum Salon ✐✐
610 S. Lake Ave. Pasadena 91106 • **626-304-9903**
Mon 9am-5pm Tue Thu 8:30am-8pm Wed Sat 8:30am-5pm Fri 8:30am-6pm
www.orpheumsalon.com
Aveda Concept salon using all natural hair color, perms, makeup, and hair
styling.

Palisades Hair & Beauty Center ✐✐
1043 Swarthmore Ave. Pacific Palisades 90272 • **310-454-8022**
Mon-Sat 9am-6pm Sun 9am-5pm
Organic and all natural products, including Pureology and Modern Organic
Products.

Planet Salon ✐✐
323 S. Robertson Blvd. Beverly Hills 90211 • **310-659-8789**
Tue 12pm-8pm Wed 10am-5pm Thu 9am-9pm Sat 8am-5pm
www.planetsalon.com
Aveda Concept salon. Provides naturally based hair care services that
are environmentally friendly; all natural hair color and texture; restorative
treatments; makeup and waxing.

Privé ✐✐
7373 Beverly Blvd. LA 90036 • **323-931-5559**
Mon 10am-6pm Tue-Sat 9am-7pm Thu 9am-8pm Sun 11am-6pm
www.privesalon.com
Natural hair products made with herbs and vegetable dyes.

Recess for Your Hands and Feet ✐✐✐✐
8408 Beverly Blvd. Ste. B LA 90048 • **310-782-9919**
Mon-Sat 10am-8pm Sun 10-5 www.recess-la.com
Eco-friendly, nontoxic nail salon using own line of organic, paraben-free
products; uses autoclave for sterilization.

Refuge Salon ✐✐
1837 Hyperion Ave. LA 90027 • **323-644-9740**
Daily 11am-7pm www.refugeforhair.com
Organic hair coloring and natural hair products used in salon services.

Renaissance Hair Studio ✐✐
116 E. Wilson Ave. Glendale 91206 • **818-240-3329**
Mon-Fri 9am-9pm Sat 9am-7pm Sun 11am-6pm
Aveda Concept salon. All natural hair color, perms, and hairstyling; makeup
and waxing.

Rescue Hand & Foot Spa ✐✐✐
8001 Santa Monica Blvd. West Hollywood 90046 • **323-822-1887**
Mon 12pm-6pm Tue-Fri 12pm-8pm Sat-Sun 10am-6pm www.rescuespa.com
Formaldehyde- and phthalate-free nail polish, acetone-free polish remover.
Carries all natural skin care products.

Rumba Hair Studio ✐✐
1830 S. Elena Ave. Redondo Beach 90278 • **310-791-1711**
Mon 10am-5pm Tue-Fri 10am-7pm Sat 9am-5pm www.rumbasalon.com
Aveda Concept salon. All natural hair color, perms, and styling; makeup and
waxing.

Salon Desire ✐✐
1921 N. Bronson Ave. LA 90068 • **323-461-2941**
Mon-Sat 9am-7pm Sun 10am-5pm
Aveda products used in most salon services.

Shades Natural Hair Color Studio ✐✐✐✐
144 S. Doheny Drive Beverly Hills 90211 • **310-275-4882**
Tue-Sat 10am-6pm www.shadesnaturalcolor.com
Natural hair coloring process using 100% ammonia-free hair colorants.

Skin Sense, A Wellness Centre ✐✐
8448 W. 3rd St. LA 90048 • **323-653-4701**
Daily 9am-6:30pm www.skinsensewellness.com
Spa services, manicures, pedicures, massage, waxing, and facials with
mostly organic and all natural ingredients.

Solis Salon ✐✐
1015 Swarthmore Ave. Pacific Palisades 90272 • **310-454-0321**
Mon-Sat 9am-6pm
Vegetable dyes used for hair coloring.

Sumiko ✐✐✐
9119 W. Olympic Blvd. Beverly Hills 90212 • **310-271-8387**
Fri-Sat 9:30am-6pm
Nontoxic hair coloring; organic, all natural hair care products.

Taboo Hair Salon ✐✐✐
8446 W. 3rd St. LA 90048 • **323-655-3770**
Tue Wed Sat 9am-6pm Thu 11am-8pm Fri 10am-7pm Sun 11am-5pm
www.taboohaircare.com
All natural hair care products and vegetable-based hair dyes.

Tiji Beauty Salon ✐✐✐✐
429 N. Western Ave. Ste. 2 LA 90004 • **323-461-8454**
Mon-Sat 10am-7pm
Soy and henna hair dye; nonchemical Japanese hair relaxing system.

Ultima Salon ✐
142 S. Barrington Ave. LA 90049 • **310-476-3008**
Tue-Sat 9am-5pm
Vegetable and nonsynthetic hair dyes.

BEING BEAUTIFUL

There is nothing like indulging yourself with a massage, sauna, or special beauty treatment and the spas listed here can all pamper you. Best of all, you can rest easier knowing that you are nurturing your body in an eco-friendly way.

The day spas we've listed have all created environments that are healthy and restful and have also committed to using and carrying eco-friendly, natural products.

We sought out spas that keep their sauna, bath, and Jacuzzi rooms mold-free without using chlorine bleach or chemicals. We determined whether or not the rooms have exhaust fans and/or allow for outdoor air exchange. We also checked into whether or not they get inspected periodically for proper drainage.

If the spa offers hair salon services, we looked into the percentage of hair coloring that is nontoxic and whether or not the henna used is non-synthetic. Where nail care is concerned, we asked if the polishes were phthalate-, toluene-, and formaldehyde-free and if the polish remover was acetone-free.

We have determined leaf awards based on the criteria outlined above, as well as the percentage of beauty and spa products that the spa sells and uses in-house that contain one or more of the following:

- all certified organic ingredients,

- a mix of certified organic ingredients and natural ingredients, and/or

- all natural ingredients, or mostly natural ingredients, and that do not contain *mercury, thimerosal, lead acetate, formaldehyde, nickel, toluene, petroleum distillates, acrylonitrile, ethylacrylate, coal tar, dibutyl phthalate, potassium dichromate, methyl cellosolve.*

Of spa treatments and practices, and salon products used and sold:

✑	at least 25% meet the above criteria
✑✑	at least 50% meet the above criteria
✑✑✑	at least 75% meet the above criteria
✑✑✑✑	at least 90% meet the above criteria

Arcona Studio, The ✑✑✑
425 Broadway Santa Monica 90401 • **310-458-3800**
Mon-Sat 9am-6pm www.arcona.com
Natural customized facial treatments using Arcona products.

Being in LA Wellness Boutique ✑✑✑✑
2016 Hillhurst Ave. LA 90027 • **323-665-9355**

Being in LA Wellness Boutique (cont.)

www.beinginla.com
Day spa with holistic, pure, and natural product lines for skin and body.
Offers nutritional counseling.

Bey's Garden, The ✑✑✑✑

2919 Main St. Santa Monica 90405 • **310-399-5420**
Mon-Sun 11am-8pm www.beysgarden.com
Day spa and aromatherapy boutique offering organic facials, soy-based
waxing, and nontoxic nail services. Uses organic and all natural products.

Body in Balance Health Center & Spa ✑✑✑✑

808 Manhattan Ave. Manhattan Beach 90266 • **310-406-1910**
Mon-Thu 10am-8pm Fri-Sat 10am-7pm www.bodyinbalancedayspa.com
Organic and nontoxic well-being center and spa. Organic facials and
skin care, massage, chiropractic care, Reiki energy balance, detox and
rejuvenation programs, nutrition, and life coaching.

Bokaos ✑✑

134 W. Colorado Blvd. Pasadena 91105 • **626-304-0007**
Mon-Fri 10am-9pm Sat 9am-8pm Sun 11am-6pm www.bokaos.com
Day spa and hair salon using all natural Aveda products. Offers massage,
body wraps, makeup, skin care, and waxing. Complimentary sensory rituals.

Chocolate Sun ✑✑✑✑

204 Bicknell Ave. Santa Monica 90405 • **310-450-3075**
By appt. www.chocolatesun.net
Sunless tanning company. Uses products made from organically grown
wild-crafted botanicals and herbs, essential oils, vitamins, and minerals.
Call for additional locations.

Dancing Shiva Yoga & Ayurveda ✑✑✑✑

The Grove 7466 Beverly Blvd. 2nd Flr. LA 90036 • **323-934-8332**
By appt. www.dancingshiva.com
Ayurvedic natural, organic spa treatments.

Dtox Day Spa ✑✑✑✑

3206 Los Feliz Blvd. LA 90039 • **323-665-3869**
Mon-Fri 10am-8pm Sat-Sun 10am-6pm www.dtoxdayspa.com
Body treatments featuring organic products. Offers own line of botanical
skin care products.

Faith Valentine For Beauty ✑✑✑✑

22333 Pacific Coast Hwy. Ste. 204 Malibu 90265 • **310-456-6405**
Tue-Sat 10am-4:30pm
Organic skin and body care.

Fringe Hair Salon and Spa ✑✑

110 Santa Monica Blvd. Santa Monica 90401 • **310-260-7900**
Daily 9am-9pm
Hair salon and spa offering Aveda products and services.

Garden Spa't, The ✑✑✑✑

2511 Colorado Blvd. LA 90041 • **323-344-8259**
By appt. www.thegardenspat.com
Organic and natural skin care with a complete line of organic products.
More than 75% of the products are locally produced.

Get Waxed ◁◁◁◁
304 Westminster Ave. Venice 90291 • **310-396-2929**
Mon-Fri 11-9 Sat-Sun 11-7 (Seasonal hours) www.getwaxedvenice.com
Eco-friendly private studio waxing salon. Also sells a selection of eco-friendly gifts and body care products.

Glendale SalonSpa ◁◁
513 E. Broadway Glendale 91205 • **818-240-6340**
Tue-Fri 9am-8pm Sat 9am-5pm www.glendalesalonspa.com
Aveda Concept salon. Uses Aveda's all natural products. Offers color, texture, and hair styling; massages, facials, and skin care treatments; manicures and pedicures.

GreenBliss EcoSpa ◁◁◁◁
323-630-4537
Daily 8am-10pm www.greenblissecospa.com
Luxury, eco-friendly mobile spa service for home appointments, parties, and special events. Body products and nail services use only organic or all natural ingredients.

Kristine's Day Spa ◁◁◁◁
223 S. Robertson Blvd. Beverly Hills 90211 • **310-652-4078**
By appt.
Custom-made body treatments using a holistic line of products.

La Blush Spa ◁◁
11670 San Vicente Blvd. LA 90049 • **310-820-2950**
Mon-Fri 9am-7pm Sat 10am-6pm
Mineral-based cosmetics and spa treatments.

Le Spa at Sofitel ◁◁◁
8555 Beverly Blvd. LA 90048 • **310-228-6777**
Daily 8am-9pm www.sofitella.com
All natural, holistic, and ritualistic therapies.

Lilese Skin Care ◁
861 Via de la Paz Pacific Palisades 90272 • **310-459-7921**
Tue-Sat 9am-5:30pm Sun-Mon by appt.
Skin care services using organic and natural products.

Mila Skin Care Salon ◁◁◁◁
831 Via de la Paz Pacific Palisades 90272 • **310-573-7551**
Mon-Sat 9am-6pm
Some organic and all natural skin care treatments, facials, waxes, and exfoliation therapy.

Mobile Spa Los Angeles ◁◁◁
888-685-0885
By appt. www.mobilespalosangeles.com
Mobile spa using organic products for skin, hair, beauty treatments, massage, and nails. Features a variety of treatments and services, including parties for adults and children of all ages.

Natural Face Place, The ◁◁◁◁
8230 Beverly Blvd. Studio 18 LA 90048 • **323-702-4279**
By appt. www.thenaturalfaceplace.com
Holistic and organic skin care services and products.

Nitespa ◁◁◁◁
1303 Abbot Kinney Blvd. Ste. 33 Venice 90291 • **310-396-5122**

Nitespa (cont.)

Tue-Sun 12pm-12am www.nitespa.com
Custom designed treatments using organic products for spa and nail services.

Ona Spa ✐✐

7373 Beverly Blvd. LA 90036 • **323-931-4442**
Mon 10am-6pm Tue-Sat 10am-8pm Sun 10am-7pm www.onaspa.com
Organic and all natural body products made on the premises daily.

Petite Spa ✐✐

723 Broadway Santa Monica 90401 • **310-393-3105**
Mon 11am-7pm Tue-Sat 11am-8pm Sun 11am-7pm www.petitespa.net
Day spa offering organic and chemical-free treatments.

Piel Skin Care ✐✐✐✐

223 S. Beverly Dr. Ste. 211 Beverly Hills 90212 • **310-247-1321**
Mon-Sat 10am-6pm www.pielskincare.com
Facial treatments using organic and natural products.

Ra Organic Spa ✐✐✐

119 N. San Fernando Blvd. Burbank 91502 • **818-848-4772**
Daily 10am-10pm www.raorganicspa.com
Organic oils, herbs, and spices along with organic products for treatments
such as body wraps, scrubs, and massages.

Renaissance Hair Studio and Day Spa ✐✐

116 E. Wilson Ave. Glendale 91206 • **818-240-3329**
Mon-Thu 9am-8pm Fri 9am-9pm Sat 9am-7pm Sun 11am-6pm
All natural hair color, perms, makeup, skin care, and hairstyling.

Salon Carabella ✐✐✐✐

21220 Ventura Blvd. Woodland Hills 91364 • **818-340-4034**
Tue-Fri 10am-7pm Sat 9am-4pm www.saloncarabella.com
Skin and body salon using organic products. Wraps and body polishes done
in a dry room with hand removal of products using hot towels.

Skin Haven ✐✐✐✐

300 N. Crescent Heights Blvd. LA 90048 • **323-658-7546**
Mon Tue Thu 11:30am-8:30pm Wed by appt. Fri 10am-5:30pm Sat-Sun 10am-7pm
www.skinhaven.com
Face, body, and nontoxic nail services using organic products. Also sells
organic products.

Skin Sense, A Wellness Centre ✐✐✐

8448 W. 3rd St. LA 90048 • **323-653-4701**
Daily 9am-6:30pm www.skinsensewellness.com
Spa services, manicures, pedicures, massage, waxing, and facials with
mostly organic and all natural ingredients.

Spa d'Marie ✐✐✐✐

1515 Palisades Dr. Pacific Palisades 90272 • **310-454-5302**
Wed-Fri 10am-6pm Sat 9am-5pm www.spadmarie.net
All natural skin care. Uses and sells organic products for adults and babies.

Thibiant ✐

449 N. Canon Dr. Beverly Hills 90210 • **800-825-2517**
Mon-Wed 8am-7pm Thu 8am-8pm Fri-Sun 8am-7pm www.thibiantspa.com
Offers a host of facial treatments using its own locally formulated and
produced organic skin care products.

Tola Life Spa ✿✿
23755 Malibu Rd. Ste. 700 Malibu 90265 • **310-456-9504**
Mon-Fri 10am-7pm Sat 10am-6pm Sun 11am-5pm www.tolaspa.com
Organic detox programs, facials, hair and nail services, massage, and body treatments.

TreeHouse, The ✿✿✿
1629½ Abbot Kinney Blvd. Venice 90291 • **310-664-1378**
Daily 9am-9pm www.thetreehouseinvenice.com
Organic facials, natural skin care, and waxing. Creative visualization and relaxation.

Veda ✿✿
1301 Montana Ave. Santa Monica 90403 • **310-576-0989**
Mon 12pm-5pm Tue-Sat 10am-6pm Sun 12pm-5pm www.aveda.com
All natural hair color, perms, makeup, skin care, and hairstyling. Aveda concept salon.

Veda Organic Spa ✿✿✿✿
310-729-7189
Daily 8am-8pm www.vedaorganicspa.com
Mobile day spa offering organic spa treatments in your home or business; parties for all ages.

Wellness Spa, The ✿
9707 Washington Blvd. Culver City 90232 • **310-202-8133**
Mon-Wed 10am-9pm Thu-Fri 9am-9pm Sat 9am-7pm Sun 11am-7pm
www.thewellnessspa.com
Spa services feature some organic and all natural skin care products.

Zen Spa ✿✿✿
23975 Park Sorrento Dr. Ste. 120 Calabasas 91302 • **818-591-0046**
Mon-Thu 10am-8pm Fri-Sun 9am-8pm www.zenspa.biz
Organic and all natural products and spa services.

Ziba Beauty ✿✿
17832 Pioneer Blvd. Artesia 90701 • **562-402-5131**
Mon-Fri 10am-8pm Sat 10am-7pm Sun 11am-6pm www.zibabeauty.com
Offers the art of Threading and waxing using water-based, all natural wax; henna tattoos; natural henna powder for hair dye. Skin care treatments using all natural ingredients.

ABOUT FRAGRANCE

Try to look for products that contain natural fragrance rather than synthetic fragrance. The latter is by far more common so you'll have to be on the lookout.

For the past fifty years, 80-90% of fragrances have been synthesized from petroleum, not from natural sources, as advertisers might like us to believe. A few of the commonly found harmful chemicals in fragranced products are acetone, benzene, phenol, toluene, benzyl acetate, and limonene. Stay away from these!

Harmful health effects of fragrance are caused not only by the chemicals mentioned above and a few thousand other individual chemicals, but each fragrance may well contain hundreds of different chemical combinations.

Since fragrance ingredients are protected under trade secret laws, the consumer is kept in the dark about many of the harmful chemicals that make up synthetic fragrances. When the label says "fragrance," watch out!

Synthetic fragrances are also harmful to marine life, and are a source of pollution. One of the EPA's top ten reasons for poor indoor air quality is the presence of artificial fragrances. Fragrance is increasingly cited as a trigger in health conditions such as asthma, allergies, and migraine headaches.

CHECK THE *SKIN DEEP* DATABASE

Looking for the words *natural* or *safe* won't guarantee that the beauty products you buy really are safe. But some companies are making safer products today and are striving to make even less harmful products in the future.

Choose products that are healthier for you now. Visit the Environmental Working Group's Skin Deep database (www.ewg.org/reports/skindeep), the world's largest searchable database of ingredients in cosmetics. Find out if your favorite products contain hazardous chemicals and find safer alternatives at this site. Also check out www.safecosmetics.org for more information about what's being done to encourage manufacturers to make their products safer.

Tell your cosmetics companies you want safe products. Call them, write them, or e-mail them to let them know where you stand. Look on product packaging for a customer service hotline or check the company's website.

ORGANIC
COTTON

Nature Is the Original Punk

BY LINDA LOUDERMILK

Style has the power to express who we are and how we live in the world. Choosing what you wear is not simply a decorative decision, but also a choice that reflects your inner passion and values. It can be a conscious choice imbued with a commitment to activism—to saving our planet Earth.

Five years ago something major happened to me. As a couture designer, I had made it to the Paris runways and the top of high fashion. In that moment I should have been rejoicing in the accolades. Instead, I felt empty. I was creating beauty, but beauty without soul. I realized then that I wanted to make a difference in the world, to shift the way people think about the Earth. But how was I going to do that? I began researching products that are sustainable and seeking out companies that create fibers without pesticides. I developed relationships with manufacturers that do not poison the water supply with high impact dyes, because they have a consciousness about their effect on the Earth.

What I discovered is a world of design that can be blended with eco-responsibility in an exciting way. I began using organic textiles that are woven from natural sources like bamboo, SeaCell® (seaweed) and Ingeo™ (corn). I collected scraps of lace and other fine fabric remnants from European sources and started weaving them into my fashions. I found a way to personalize the beauty of the Earth through my designs by honoring the edge that nature presents.

I challenge you to embrace your style with a fierce heart. You can express your sense of fashion while also helping the Earth. It's about making bold, intelligent choices.

Let's make a statement! Change is inevitable. We are redefining sustainability in a way that is hip, fun, edgy, and most importantly, here to stay. It's not a trend. In five to ten years from now, our collective force will transform the world. We can save the planet. There's no doubt about it.

Together we are pioneers in this shift in consciousness. Join me in supporting other like-minded retail businesses and designers who are building a new framework and offering more sustainable options.

LINDA LOUDERMILK

Linda Loudermilk studied Shakespeare and costume design at Oxford University in England. After honoring her design skills as a sculptor and on the Paris runway, she returned to Los Angeles to launch Linda Loudermilk and with it, the luxury eco-movement (www.lindaloudermilk.com).

Clothing and Shoes

A significant percentage of the world's pesticides, herbicides, and water is used in growing and processing the fibers that are made into our clothing. So buying clothes made with organically grown, natural, or recycled fibers is by far a better choice.

We are seeing more and more eco-friendly fibers used in some very fashionable ways these days. You will find soy shirts, hemp scarves, recycled cashmere sweaters, and bamboo blouses. Organic wool might make your winter wardrobe, and organic cotton could signal your new summer style. And some of us are even sporting used soda bottles in the form of fleece.

Choosing clothing conscientiously could also mean checking for fair trade certification, whether it is Union Made, made by local artisans, or sweatshop-free. Ask about these things so proprietors know you care.

Try to find clothes that are unbleached or bleached with hydrogen peroxide only, and that use natural or low-impact dyes and no wrinkle-free treatments (these can be toxic).

A note: We love vintage clothing stores and resale shops as they are inherently positive on the reduce/reuse/recycle level, and we encourage you to put these stores on your regular shopping route. However, because there are many local resale shops—more than we can list—and since individual items come from a variety of unknown resources and labels may be unreadable or even removed making them difficult to evaluate, we have not included these stores in this category.

Sustainable clothing and shoes are areas with still emerging standards, but at this point, we're evaluating our stores based on the percentage of goods sold that are made with recycled content, organic, natural fibers, or a blend. We also looked at, as we do for all businesses listed in the guide, the store's use of recycled packaging, its own recycling and energy efficiency programs, and other areas, all of which demonstrate its commitment to environmentally-friendly practices.

Of the clothing and shoes sold:

      🍃 at least 25% is made from recycled content, organic or natural fibers, or a blend thereof.

      🍃🍃 at least 50% is made from the materials listed above.

      🍃🍃🍃 at least 75% is made from the materials listed above.

      🍃🍃🍃🍃 at least 90% is made from the materials listed above.

Type of clothing, shoes and/or gear:

      M Men's

      W Women's

      C Children's

      B Baby

All Shades of Green ⌒⌒⌒⌒ M W C B
3038 Rowena Ave. LA 90039 • 323-665-7454
Mon-Sat 11am-7pm Sun 11am-6pm www.allshadesofgreen.net
Clothing and shoes for the whole family made from hemp, organic cotton,
wool, recycled fibers, and eco-fleece. Many lines are made locally and/or
are fair trade and sweatshop-free.

Apartment #9 ⌒ M
225 26th St. Santa Monica 90402 • 310-394-9440
Mon-Sat 10am-6pm Sun 12am-5pm
Men's clothing made from organic and natural fibers.

Arbor ⌒⌒⌒⌒ M W
102 Washington Blvd. Venice 90292 • 310-577-1131
Daily 11am-7pm www.arborsports.com
Organic cotton and bamboo clothing. Also carries eco-friendly skateboards
and snowboards made from bamboo.

Avita Co-op ⌒⌒⌒⌒ W
8213 W. 3rd St. LA 90048 • 323-852-1716
Mon-Sat 11am-7pm Sun 12pm-6pm www.avitastyle.com
Eco-friendly women's boutique offering apparel and accessories made from
organic cotton, bamboo, recycled cashmere, soy, and hemp.

Bhutan Shop ⌒⌒ M W
415 S. Topanga Canyon Blvd. Topanga 90290 • 310-455-0731
Mon-Fri 9am-5pm Sat-Sun 10am-6pm www.bhutanshop.com
Handmade clothing produced with hemp and hemp/cotton blends.

Carol Young Undesigned Boutique ⌒⌒⌒ W
1953½ Hillhurst Ave. LA 90027 • 323-663-0088
Tue-Sat 12pm-6pm Sun 12pm-5pm www.carolyoung.com
Women's collection made from organic and recycled cotton, bamboo,
recycled fleece, wool, and linen. Member of 1% For The Planet.

Clothing of the American Mind ⌒⌒ M W
1284 W. Sunset Blvd. LA 90026 • 213-481-2004
Mon-Fri 11am-5pm or by appt. www.cotam.org
Eco-conscious clothing with a political perspective for men and women.
Uses some organic cotton.

Clover ⌒ M W
2756 Rowena Ave. LA 90039 • 323-661-4142
Mon-Sat 10am-7pm Sun 12pm-6pm www.cloversilverlake.com
Small department-type store offering some organic cotton, bamboo, recycled
canvas clothing and accessories for men and women. Specializes in gift baskets
with local artisan jewelry, organic teas, cards, candles, and wooden toys.

CP Shades ⌒ M W
2937 Main St. Santa Monica 90405 • 310-392-0949
Mon-Sat 11am-7pm Sat 12pm-6pm www.cpshades.com
Selection of men's and women's clothing made from Tencel-processed pulp,
hemp-silk, recycled fabrics, organic cotton, and bamboo. Vegetable-dyed
purses.

El Naturalista ✐✐✐✐ M W
1230 Montana Ave. Ste. 104 Santa Monica 90403 • **310-230-5688**
Mon-Fri 11am-7pm Sat 10am-7pm Sun 11am-6pm www.elnaturalista.com
Shoes made with vegetable-dyed leather, recycled rubber soles, nontoxic adhesives.

Fred Segal Fun ✐ M W
500 Broadway Ste. G Santa Monica 90401 • **310-394-9814**
Mon-Sat 10am-7pm Sun 12pm-6pm www.fredsegalfun.com
Organic cotton and bamboo clothing lines for men and women.

Golden Bridge ✐✐ M W B
6322 De Longpre Hollywood 90028 • **323-936-4172**
Mon-Fri 9am-9pm Sat-Sun 9am-8pm www.goldenbridgeyoga.com
Men's, women's, and baby clothing made from eco-friendly fabrics; Organic Café in studio; also offers eco-workshops.

Green Cradle ✐✐✐✐ M W C B
13344 Ventura Blvd. Sherman Oaks 91423 • **818-728-4305**
Mon-Sat 10am-6pm www.greencradle.com
Specializes in organic and all natural clothing for kids, pregnancy, and the whole family.

Green for Baby ✐✐✐✐ B
2989 E. Thousand Oaks Blvd. Thousand Oaks 91362 • **805-230-2201**
Tue-Fri 10am-6pm Sat 11am-6pm www.greenforbaby.com
Organic cribs, baby clothing, linens, and accessories. Also sells adult organic mattresses.

GreenRohini ✐✐✐✐ M W
13327 Ventura Blvd. Sherman Oaks 91423 • **818-981-0023**
Mon-Fri 10am-6pm Sat-Sun 11am-5pm greenrohini.com
Eco-friendly clothing boutique for women and men. Member of 1% For The Planet.

Hoity Toity ✐✐✐✐ W
4381 Tujunga Ave. Studio City 91604 • **818-766-2503**
Mon, Wed, Thu-Sat 11am-6pm Sun 12pm-5pm
Local designer clothes for women made with vintage fabrics and hemp. Also offers many all natural and organic body care products.

Ivy Greene for Kids ✐ C B
1020 Swarthmore Ave. Pacific Palisades 90272 • **310-230-0301**
Mon-Sat 10am-6pm Sun 11am-4pm
Some baby clothes and accessories made from bamboo, organic cotton, and soy.

J. Gerard Design Studio & Peace Gallery ✐✐✐ M W C B
8575 Melrose Ave. West Hollywood 90069 • **800-543-7273**
Mon-Fri 10am-6pm www.jgerarddesignstudio.com
Bamboo and recycled fabric clothing; all natural fiber yogawear.

Kate ✐ M W
515 S. Fairfax Ave. LA 90036 • **323-938-7311**
Mon-Sat 12pm-7pm Sun 12pm-5pm
Selection of organic and natural fiber sweaters, shoes, and clothing.

Koi ✐ W
1007 S. Fair Oaks Ave. South Pasadena 91030 • **626-441-3254**
Mon-Sat 11am-7pm Sun 12pm-5pm

Koi (cont.)

Women's clothing from environmentally conscious designers; unique item sales support various causes.

Lululemon Athletica ✿ M W

334 N. Beverly Dr. Beverly Hills 90210 • **310-858-8339**
4719 Commons Way Ste. R9 Calabasas 91302 • **818-225-1417**
2008 East Park Pl. Ste. A El Segundo 90245 • **310-640-9476**
110 W. Colorado Blvd. Pasadena 91105 • **626-792-0791**
331 Santa Monica Blvd. Santa Monica 90401 • **310-319-9900**
Hours vary by location www.lululemon.com
Organic cotton, bamboo, modal, soy, seaweed tanks, shirts, pants, dresses, and skirts. Also offers PVC-free, recyclable, and biodegradable yoga mats and bamboo yoga bricks.

Menemsha ✿✿✿✿ M W B

12524 Ventura Blvd. Studio City 91604 • **818-505-8900**
Mon 11am-4pm Tue-Sat 11am-7pm www.menemshastyle.com
Eco-friendly fashion boutique specializing in organic and sustainable clothing, shoes, and accessories.

Modern Child ✿✿ C B

610 Hampton Dr. Venice 90291 • **310-452-6961**
Tue-Sat 12pm-6pm www.modernchild.net
Sustainably designed clothing, furniture, and décor items for child, baby, and home.

Monkie ✿ W

2665 Main St. Santa Monica 90405 • **310-450-4512**
Mon-Sat 11am-7pm Sun 11am-6pm www.monkieboutique.com
Women's clothing, shoes, and accessories made from organic cotton, bamboo, soy, and hemp.

Natural High Lifestyle ✿✿✿✿ M W C B

2900 Main St. Santa Monica 90405 • **310-450-5837**
Daily 11am-7pm www.naturalhighlifestyle.com
Locally made hemp, bamboo, Tencel, and organic cotton clothing.

Organic Rush ✿✿✿✿ B

962 Mission St. South Pasadena 91030 • **626-799-8099**
Tue-Sat 11am-6pm Sun 12pm-5pm www.organicrush.com
Organic cotton clothing for babies.

Pancia Maternity & Baby Boutique ✿ W B

1316½ Abbot Kinney Blvd. Venice 90291 • **310-392-2867**
Mon-Sat 11am-6pm Sun 12pm-5pm www.panciamaternity.com
One-stop boutique for baby and maternity clothes made from organic fibers and fabrics.

Papillon Baby ✿✿ C B

2717 Main St. Santa Monica 90405 • **310-452-0969**
Mon-Wed 11am-6pm Thu-Sat 11am-8pm Sun 9am-5pm www.papillonbaby.com
Carry numerous lines of 100% organic cotton clothing for children and babies. Also carries fair trade goods.

Patagonia ✿✿✿✿ M W C B

47 N. Fair Oaks Ave. Pasadena 91103 • **626-795-0319**
2936 Main St. Santa Monica 90405 • **310-314-1776**
Mon-Sat 11am-7pm Sun 11pm-6pm www.patagonia.com
Clothing and technical wear made from recycled fibers, organic cotton, hemp, and organic wool for everyone in the family. Member of 1% For The Planet.

Pebbles 🍃 C B
2400 Main St. Santa Monica 90405 • **310-314-6472**
Mon-Fri 10:30am-7pm Sat 10am-6pm Sun 10am-4pm
Organic cotton, bamboo, recycled fabrics, and vintage fabrics for kids and baby.

Petit Ami 🍃 C B
15301 Antioch St. Pacific Palisades 90272 • **310-459-0011**
Mon-Sat 10am-6pm Sun 11am-5pm
Organic cotton baby and kids' clothes.

Planet Blue 🍃 M W
409 N. Beverly Dr. Beverly Hills 90210 • **310-385-0557**
3835 Cross Creek Rd. Ste. 13A Malibu 90265 • **310-317-9975**
800 14th St. Santa Monica 90403 • **310-394-0135**
2940 Main St. Santa Monica 90405 • **310-396-1767**
Hours vary by location www.shopplanetblue.com
Organic cotton line of shirts and sweaters, jeans made of pulp mixture, and bamboo shirts.

Regeneration 🍃🍃🍃🍃 W B
1649 Colorado Blvd. Eagle Rock 90041 • **323-344-0430**
Tue-Sun 12pm-6pm www.shopregeneration.com
Bamboo, organic cotton, soy, hemp, wool, corn, and recycled fabrics for women and babies. Fair trade, locally made, and sweatshop-free.

REI 🍃 M W
214 N. Santa Anita Ave. Arcadia 91006 • **626-447-1062**
1800 Rosecrans Ave. Manhattan Beach 90266 • **310-727-0728**
18605 Devonshire St. Northridge 91324 • **818-831-5555**
402 Santa Monica Blvd. Santa Monica 90401 • **310-458-4370**
Hours vary by location www.rei.com
Eco-friendly outdoor apparel and gear made from hemp, recycled fabrics, organic cotton, and bamboo.

Sporteve 🍃 W
3849 Main St. Culver City 90232 • **310-838-6588**
Daily 10am-7pm www.sporteve.com
Activewear created with hemp fabric, bamboo fiber, organic cotton, and organic dyes. PVC-free yoga mats and organic dog treats.

Stella McCartney 🍃 W
8823 Beverly Blvd. West Hollywood 90048 • **310-273-7051**
Mon-Sat 11am-7pm www.stellamccartney.com
Line of women's organic cotton jeans; 100% organic skin care products.

Tianello 🍃🍃🍃🍃 M W
38 Washington Blvd. Marina Del Rey 90292 • **310-821-9203**
Mon-Sat 9:30am-9pm Sun 10am-8pm www.tianello.com
Men's and women's clothing made from Tencel fiber; designed and tailored in the United States.

Topo Ranch 🍃🍃 M W
1219 Abbot Kinney Blvd. Venice 90291 • **310-294-1034**
Mon-Fri 11am-8pm Sat-Sun 11am-6pm www.toporanch.com
Organic cotton clothing for men and women.

Vital Hemptations 🍃🍃🍃🍃 M W
Merchants Mart 2411 Main St. Santa Monica 90405 • **310-390-0507**
Daily 11am-6pm www.vitalhemp.com
Hemp and hemp-blend clothing; custom hemp products for men and women.

Wolf 🍃 M
1405 Abbot Kinney Blvd. Venice 90291 • **310-392-8551**
Daily 11am-7pm
Men's clothing made from organic cotton, hemp, and recycled polyester.

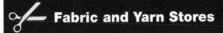

Fabric and Yarn Stores

Making your own clothing out of sustainably produced fabrics and knitting your own sweaters out of low-impact yarns may be the greenest way to dress of all. Fabric and yarn stores are beginning to carry more materials grown without the use of synthetic chemicals, dyed with natural or low-impact dyes, and processed without huge amounts of chemical inputs.

Although the runway red carpet just may be going green, specific standards as to what constitutes sustainability in fabrics haven't, as yet, been developed—so too with yarns. We'd like to help move things in the right direction by supporting businesses that are making an effort to carry natural fibers so we have awarded leaves based on the following criteria:

- the percentage of fabric that is organic or natural fiber,
- the percentage of yarn that is organic or natural fiber, and
- the percentage of materials that is produced with natural or low-impact dyes.

We also checked into whether the store carried stock made by local artisans, union-made items, fair trade-identified and sweatshop-free merchandise, and/or goods made in the USA.

🍃	at least 25% of fabrics and/or yarns meet the above criteria.
🍃🍃	at least 50% of fabrics and/or yarns meet the above criteria.
🍃🍃🍃	at least 75% of fabrics and/or yarns meet the above criteria.
🍃🍃🍃🍃	at least 90% of fabrics and/or yarns meet the above criteria.

A Mano Yarn Center 🍃🍃
12808 Venice Blvd. LA 90066 • **310-397-7170**
Mon, Tue-Fri 11am-7pm Wed 12pm-8pm Sat 10am-6pm Sun 12pm-5pm
www.amanoyarn.com
Bamboo, soy, corn, cotton, alpaca, and hemp yarns; bamboo needles.
Classes in crochet, knitting, and spinning.

Knit Café 🍃
8441 Melrose Ave. West Hollywood 90069 • **323-658-5648**
Mon-Sat 10am-6pm Thu 10am-8:30pm Sun 11am-3pm   www.knitcafe.com
Some organic yarn, knitting materials, and bamboo knitting needles. Knitting and crochet classes; Kids Club classes for children eight years and older.

La Knitterie Parisienne

12642 Ventura Blvd. Studio City 91604 • **818-766-1515**
Tue 10am-6pm Wed 12pm-8:30pm Thu-Sat 10am-6pm
www.laknitterieparisienne.com
Offers some organic yarn. Free knitting classes.

Needlepoints West ✐✐

6227 W. 87th St. Los Angeles 90045 • **310-670-4847**
Tue-Fri 10:30am-5:30pm Sat 10am-4pm Sun 12pm-4pm
www.needlepointswest.com
All natural and organic yarn, fabric, beads, and materials; hand-painted
needlepoint canvasses. Offers finishing services.

Sit 'n Stitch ✐

10154 Riverside Dr. Toluca Lake 91602 • **818-760-9330**
Mon, Fri 10am-9pm Tue-Thu 10am-5pm Sat 10am-4pm www.sitnstitch.com
Organic yarn, wool, soy, bamboo, and cotton material. Classes and online
store available.

Gifts, Accessories, and Baby Products

Before you make your next gift purchase, think about all aspects of the
item: where it came from, how it was made, who made it, and its impact
on the environment and human health.

The shops listed here, offering items such as toys, candles, crafts,
jewelry, fashion accessories, picture frames, baby products, and much
more, do take these considerations into account.

We have determined leaf awards based on the percentage of items that is
made from or use:

• organic materials,

• natural, renewable, or recycled materials,

• fair trade or conflict-free criteria and be certified as such, and/or

• nontoxic or less toxic glues, paints, and finishes (where applicable).

Although it's a bonus if the items are also made by local artisans, this
was not part of our criteria.

> ✐ at least 25% of items for sale meet the above criteria.
>
> ✐✐ at least 50% of items for sale meet the above criteria.
>
> ✐✐✐ at least 75% of items for sale meet the above criteria.
>
> ✐✐✐✐ at least 90% of items for sale meet the above criteria.

Acorn Store, The ✐✐✐✐

1220 5th St. Santa Monica 90404 • **310-451-5845**
Mon-Sat 10am-6pm Sun 11am-4pm
Natural toys and gifts, many made from wood and natural materials;
lead-free.

All Shades of Green ✐✐✐✐
3038 Rowena Ave. LA 90039 • **323-665-7454**
Mon-Sat 11am-7pm Sun 11am-6pm www.allshadesofgreen.net
Baby clothing and accessories, lead-free and wooden toys, organic candy;
locally made beeswax candles; handbags, scarves, and gloves.

Artists' Web, The ✐✐
2806 Main St. Santa Monica 90405 • **310-399-2736**
Tue-Thu 10am-7pm Fri-Sat 10am-8pm Sun 10am-6pm
www.theartistswebstore.com
Original art and unique gifts handmade by local artisans using some
recycled and natural materials.

Aura Visions ✐✐
20929 Ventura Blvd. Ste. 37 Woodland Hills 91364 • **818-992-6178**
Tue-Sat 10am-6pm
Variety of stationery, organic lotions, candles, and other products geared
toward healing.

Bellamie Children's Boutique ✐
6220 W. 87th St. LA 90045 • **310-641-2787**
Mon-Fri 10am-6pm Sat 10am-5:30pm www.bellamieboutique.com
Organic cotton baby clothes, nontoxic wood toys, and soy candles.

Candle Delirium ✐✐✐
7980 Santa Monica Blvd. West Hollywood 90046 • **323-656-3900**
Mon-Sat 11am-7:30pm Sun 12pm-6pm www.candledelirium.com
Offers selection of soy, palm, and beeswax candles.

Clouds ✐
2719 Main St. Santa Monica 90405 • **310-399-2059**
Mon-Sat 11am-9pm Sun 11am-6pm www.cloudsonmain.com
Soy candles, natural soaps, and lotions.

Clover ✐✐
2756 Rowena Ave. Ste. A LA 90039 • **323-661-4142**
Mon-Sat 10am-7pm Sun 12pm-6pm www.cloversilverlake.com
Small department-type store offering organic cotton, bamboo, and recycled
canvas clothes and accessories; local artisan jewelry, organic teas, cards,
candles, and wood toys.

Dove's Bodies ✐✐✐✐
4010 Colfax Ave. Studio City 91604 • **818-980-7866**
Call for retail hours or class schedule www.dovesbodies.com
Organic fitness studio selling natural and organic personal care products,
organic yoga clothing, organic soy candles, perfumes/oils, organic
Teeccino, and elixir products.

Dragonfly DuLou ✐✐✐✐
2066 Hillhurst Ave. LA 90027 • **323-665-8448**
Mon-Sat 10am-6pm Sun 10am-4pm www.dragonflydulou.com
Eco-friendly children's clothing, toys, baby products; skin care products and
accessories.

Ebba Los Angeles ✐✐
8164 Melrose Ave. LA 90046 • **323-651-5337**
Mon-Wed, Fri 10:30am-6:30pm Thu 10:30am-7:30pm Sat 12pm-5pm
www.ebbalosangeles.com
Soy candles made by local artists. Also sells vintage jewelry and
furnishings.

Edna Hart Boutique 𝒫𝒫𝒫

2941 Rowena Ave. LA 80027 • **323-661-4070**
Wed-Sun 1pm-6pm www.ednahartboutique.blogspot.com
Local artisan jewelry; non-leather handbags and wallets.

Firefly 𝒫

1413 Abbot Kinney Blvd. Venice 90291 • **310-450-6288**
Mon-Sat 11am-7pm Sun 11am-5pm (seasonal hours) www.shopfirefly.com
Fair trade, locally crafted, and recycled-content products; soy candles,
organic bath accessories, organic clothing line.

Green Cradle 𝒫𝒫𝒫𝒫

13344 Ventura Blvd. Sherman Oaks 91423 • **818-728-4305**
Mon-Sat 10am-6pm www.greencradle.com
Specializes in organic and all natural clothing, toys, gifts, bedding, and
mattresses. Health and beauty products for kids, pregnancy, and the whole
family.

Green for Baby 𝒫𝒫𝒫

2989 E. Thousand Oaks Blvd. Thousand Oaks 91362 • **805-230-2201**
Tue-Fri 10am-6pm Sat 11am-6pm www.greenforbaby.com
Organic cribs, baby clothing, linens, and accessories. Also sells adult
organic mattresses.

Harmony Works 𝒫𝒫𝒫𝒫

1705 South Catalina Ave. Redondo Beach 90277 • **310-791-7104**
Mon-Sat 10am-7pm Sun 11am-5pm www.harmony-works.com
Organic baby clothes, soy candles, garden accessories, books, and jewelry.

Hoity Toity 𝒫𝒫

4381 Tujunga Ave. Studio City 91604 • **818-766-2503**
Mon, Wed-Sat 11am-6pm Sun 12pm-5pm
Clothes made by local designers using vintage fabrics and hemp. All natural
and organic body care products.

J. Gerard Design Studio & Peace Gallery 𝒫𝒫𝒫

8575 Melrose Ave. West Hollywood 90069 • **800-543-7273**
Mon-Fri 10am-6pm www.jgerarddesignstudio.com
Accessories, clothing, and jewelry made from natural, renewable, or
recycled materials.

Kinara 𝒫

656 N. Robertson Blvd. West Hollywood 90069 • **310-657-9188**
Tue-Fri 9am-9pm Sat 10am-7pm Sun 10am-6pm www.kinaraspa.com
Bamboo robes, baby accessories; organic cotton blankets.

Lemon Tree Bungalow 𝒫𝒫𝒫𝒫

8727 Santa Monica Blvd. West Hollywood 90069 • **310-657-0211**
Mon-Sat 11am-9pm Sun 12pm-7pm www.lemontreebungalow.com
Natural bath and body products; recycled-content gifts.

Little Seed 𝒫𝒫𝒫𝒫

219 N. Larchmont Blvd. LA 90004 • **323-462-4441**
Daily 9:30am-6:30pm www.thelittleseed.com
Children's specialty boutique carrying eco-friendly and organic baby
products: skin care, clothing and bedding, toys. FSC-certified wood
furniture. Nontoxic environment with no-VOC paints; uses recycled
packaging. Classes for kids and parents.

GETTING GOODS

Mission Street Yoga 🌿🌿🌿
1017 Mission St. South Pasadena 91030 • **626-441-1144**
Daily 8am-9pm www.missionstreetyoga.com
Yoga studio with massage treatment, retail shop, and green café.

Moonlight Candles 🌿🌿🌿🌿
8500 Beverly Blvd. Ste. 761 LA 90048 • **310-659-0582**
Mon-Fri 10am-9pm Sat 10am-8pm Sun 11am-6pm www.moonlightcandles.com
Large assortment of eco-friendly candles and jewelry.

M'pressions 🌿🌿🌿
1700 South Catalina Ave. Ste. 104 Redondo Beach 90277 • **310-540-6115**
Mon 11am-6pm Tue-Sat 11am-7pm Sun 11am-6pm
Fair trade gifts, organic cotton clothes, décor made from recycled
billboards, all natural beauty products, and eco-friendly candles.

Natural High Lifestyle 🌿🌿🌿🌿
2400 Main St. Santa Monica 90405 • **310-450-5837**
Daily 11am-7pm www.naturalhighlifestyle.com
Locally made organic cotton, hemp, bamboo, and Tencel products.

OK 🌿
8303 W. 3rd St. LA 90048 • **323-653-3501**
Mon-Sat 11am-6:30pm Sun 12pm-6pm
Crafts and jewelry made locally with some organic and reclaimed materials.

Organic Rush 🌿🌿🌿
962 Mission St. South Pasadena 91030 • **626-799-8099**
Tue-Sat 11am-6pm Sun 12pm-5pm www.organicrush.com
Natural, organic, and eco-friendly products for home, body, baby, and pet.

Pergolina 🌿
10139 Riverside Dr. Toluca Lake 91602 • **818-508-7708**
Mon-Fri 10:30am-6pm Sat 11am-5pm www.pergolina.com
Organic cotton baby clothes, recycled paper cards, regenerated leather,
organic lotions, reclaimed FEIT bags, newspaper placemats, and purses.

Pulp and Hide 🌿
13020 San Vicente Blvd. LA 90049 • **310-394-0700**
Mon-Sat 10am-6pm
Cards and stationery, hemp bags, beeswax candles, and personal
accessories.

Pump Station, The 🌿🌿
1248 Vine St. Hollywood 90038 • **323-469-5300**
2415 Wilshire Blvd. Santa Monica 90403 • **323-469-5300**
Mon-Sat 10am-5pm Sun 11am-5pm www.pumpstation.com
Organic cotton slings, unbleached diapers, washable cotton bra pads. Baby
shower gifts. Offers classes on toxins and herbal remedies.

ReForm School 🌿🌿🌿
4014 Santa Monica Blvd. LA 90029 • **323-906-8660**
Mon-Fri 12pm-7pm Sat 11am-7pm Sun 11am-6pm www.reformschoolrules.com
Eco-conscious gift boutique with organic T-shirts, recycled gift cards, and
local artwork using recycled material. Organic body care products and
handmade items by independent artists.

Soaptopia 🌿🌿🌿🌿
12228½ Venice Blvd. LA 90066 • **310-398-8333**
Daily 11am-7pm www.soaptopia.com

Soaptopia (cont.)
All natural soaps made on premises using wild-crafted and organic ingredients; bath accessories; gift wrapping.

Soolip 𝒫𝒫
8646 Melrose Ave. West Hollywood 90069 • **310-360-0545**
Mon-Sat 10am-6pm Sun 12pm-5pm www.soolip.com
Soolip's Paperie and Press and Bungalow stores carry extensive line of handmade papers, journals, and letterpress cards; tree-free desk accessories; candles, organic bath products, home décor, gift items.

Soothe Your Soul 𝒫𝒫
415 N. Pacific Coast Hwy. Redondo Beach 90277 • **310-798-8445**
Daily 9am-10pm www.sootheyoursoul.com
Beads, books, soaps, crystals, jewelry, lamps, and fountains.

Sosa's Jewelers 𝒫
6235 W. 87th St. Westchester 90045 • **310-216-6720**
Tue-Fri 10am-6pm Sat 10am-5pm
Jewelry made by local artisans from recycled gold and silver.

Splash Bath & Body 𝒫𝒫𝒫
132 Pier Ave. Hermosa Beach 90254 • **310-376-7270**
Mon-Fri 11am-7pm Sat 10am-7pm Sun 11am-7pm www.splashbathandbody.com
Soy candles, natural soaps, lotions, shampoos, conditioners, body oils, and scrubs.

Sugar Paper 𝒫
1749 Ensley Ave. LA 90024 • **310-277-7804**
225 26th St. Ste. 27 Santa Monica 90402 • **310-451-7870**
Mon-Fri 10am-6pm Sat 10am-5pm Sun 11am-5pm www.sugarpaper.com
Organic cotton baby clothes and handmade letterpress stationery.

Ten Thousand Villages 𝒫𝒫𝒫
496 S. Lake Ave. Pasadena 91101 • **626-229-9892**
Mon-Sat 10am-7pm Sun 12pm-7pm www.tenthousandvillages.com
Handcrafted fair trade home décor, personal accessories, and gift items made by more than 110 artisan groups in 35 countries. Nonprofit store run by volunteers.

Ten Women Gallery 𝒫𝒫
2651 Main St. Santa Monica 90405 • **310-314-9152**
1237 Abbot Kinney Blvd. Venice 90291 • **310-452-2256**
Hours vary by location www.tenwomengallery.com
Community cooperative of local women artists offering handmade crafts and fine art.

Teraine 𝒫𝒫𝒫
15320 Antioch St. Pacific Palisades 90272 • **310-230-2782**
Mon-Sat 10am-6pm Sun 12pm-5pm www.teraine.com
Offers organic cotton linens, candles, soaps, lotions, fair trade artisan jewelry, and toys.

Tinker 𝒫𝒫
4337 Woodman Ave. Sherman Oaks 91423 • **818-784-7991**
Mon-Fri 10am-6pm Sat 12pm-6pm www.tinkertinker.com
Make your own gifts at this community arts and crafts drop-in studio, using recycled materials. Classes, workshops, and parties for children and adults.

Under the Table ✐✐
3139 Glendale Ave. LA 90039 • **323-660-9393**
Tue-Sat 12pm-6pm www.underthetablestore.com
Selection of organic and natural gifts, toys, and clothing made by local artisans.

Urbanic Paper Boutique ✐
1644 Abbot Kinney Blvd. Venice 90291 • **310-401-0427**
Mon-Sat 11am-7pm Sun 11am-6pm www.urbanicdesigns.com
Eco-friendly stationery and paper products; soy candles; recycled-content gift items.

✐ GREEN TIP

Traces of lead are found in some candles, decorative ceramic dishes, and crystal stemware. Be sure to read the packaging or ask about this when buying plates, bowls, and other tableware. Serve wine in lead-free glasses. Choose clean-burning candles made of pure beeswax, soy, or other vegetable-based waxes. Select ones without metal wicks as these can contain small amounts of lead.

Florists

Purchasing flowers may seem like a wonderful way to bring the beauty of nature into our homes or the perfect way to acknowledge our loved ones, but often, flowers are not quite what they appear to be.

The truth is the flower industry is one of the heaviest users of agricultural chemicals. More than 60% of the fresh-cut flowers sold in the United States are imported from countries whose environmental standards are less stringent than our own.

In some cases, chemicals banned in the United States are used in other countries and find their way back here through imported agricultural goods—on all those flowers, for instance. Luckily, local, organically grown flowers are increasingly available, just as beautiful, and better for you and the planet.

To be included, at least 15% of a florist's total flower stock must be organically grown, and of the organic flowers purchased, at least 15% must be grown within 500 miles. Note, however, that some of the florists listed performed substantially higher than the required minimum.

Jasmine Blue Flower Shop
13607 Ventura Blvd. Sherman Oaks 91423 • **818-986-0333**
Mon-Sat 9am-5pm www.jasmineblue.com
Sustainably grown flowers with many organic options.

Sada's Flowers

10612 Culver Blvd. Culver City 90232 • **310-839-2434**
Mon-Fri 9am-6pm Sat 10am-5pm www.sadasflowers.com
Established in 1927. Locally grown, organic bouquets. Delivery to Westside areas.

Trellis Flowers

11977 San Vicente Blvd. LA 90049 • **310-472-6063**
Mon-Fri 9am-6pm Sat 9am-4:30pm www.trellisflorist.com
Organic and locally grown flowers; uses organic flower food. Also sells recycled glassware and environmentally-friendly gifts. Hold your next event in the "Jungle" in the back of the store.

Wisteria Lane

22776 Ventura Blvd. Ste. A Woodland Hills 91364 • **888-345-6101**
Mon-Sat 9:30am-5:30pm www.wisterialaneflowershop.com
Uses organic and Veriflora-certified flowers and products that are sustainably grown. Arrangements made with recycled glass vases and wax paper for floral wrapping.

 ## Office, Paper, and Party Supplies

Most of us recycle our paper, try to use both sides, and read as much as we can online. But when we do need to buy paper and office supplies, what about closing the loop and buying recycled materials? By purchasing paper and paper goods with recycled content we can affect the choices that paper mills eventually make as investors in new technology and processes, thereby saving our forests and protecting our watersheds.

You'll find different levels of recycled content in paper and other supplies—from 10% to 30%, and sometimes up to 100% post-consumer waste. Look for the recycled symbol (chasing arrows), and a minimum of 30% post-consumer recycled content, also known as post-consumer waste. Dedicated recyclers can find three-ring binders made of recycled corrugated cardboard and pocket portfolios and dividers made from 100% recycled paperboard (the majority post-consumer). For those whose CD jewel cases weigh heavily on their minds, there are CD cases made from recycled paper, complete with recycled-paper labels.

Planning a party? Be sure to invite the Earth as an honored guest. Use disposable dinnerware made from the pulp from sugar cane processing, a perfectly useful material that would otherwise go to waste. Other non-paper options include party plates and utensils made from completely biodegradable corn-based materials. For a real celebration, there's even biodegradable confetti and balloons. Party on!

As you sort through your eco-friendly options, remember also that paper products bleached without chlorine are safer all around. Making sound choices relies on understanding definitions (see the following page), enforced federal standards, and accurate labeling.

To encourage increased availability and sales of recycled and/or biode-gradable paper products in all office and paper supply stores, we urge you to speak up as you shop.

Our listings reflect the percentage of office, paper, and party supplies sustainably made and produced, and made from recycled or reclaimed resources.

> 🍃 at least 25% of the items for sale meet the above criteria.
>
> 🍃🍃 at least 50% of the items for sale meet the above criteria.
>
> 🍃🍃🍃 at least 75% of the items for sale meet the above criteria.
>
> 🍃🍃🍃🍃 at least 90% of the items for sale meet the above criteria.

Post-Consumer Material/Fiber

End products generated by consumers that have been separated or diverted from the solid waste stream (garbage).

Recovered Material/Fiber

Paper materials that have been separated, diverted, or removed from the solid waste stream for the purpose of use, reuse, or recycling.

Totally Chlorine-Free (TCF)

Virgin paper produced without chlorine or chlorine derivatives (the bleaching process uses oxygen-based compounds).

Processed Chlorine-Free (PCF)

Recycled paper in which the recycled content is unbleached or bleached without chlorine derivatives. Any virgin material portion of the paper must be TCF. Must contain at least 30% post consumer content.

Balloon Celebrations 🍃
1059 Gayley Ave. LA 90024 • **310-208-1180**
Mon-Sat 9am-6pm Sun 9am-1pm www.ballooncelebrations.com
Party supplies, including recycled paper goods and biodegradable balloons.

Epoxy Green 🍃🍃🍃🍃
602 Venice Blvd. Venice 90291 • **310-578-2123**
Mon-Sat 10am-6pm
Biodegradable and bamboo picnic plates, utensils, and cups.

GETTING GOODS

Invitations by Ferial 🌿🌿🌿🌿
1559 Westwood Blvd. LA 90024 • **310-996-7576**
Mon-Fri 11am-6pm By appt. www.invitationsbyferial.com
Custom invitations printed on recycled paper.

Jonathan Wright and Company 🌿🌿
7404 Beverly Blvd. LA 90036 • **323-931-1710**
Mon-Sat 10am-6pm www.jonathanwright.com
Gifts and paper are 50% recycled; soy-based dyes. Manufactured in the U.S.

Kelly Paper 🌿
9640 Telstar Ave. El Monte 91731 • **626-575-0116**
844 N. La Brea Ave. Hollywood 90038 • **323-957-1176**
1611 E. 15th St. LA 90021 • **213-749-1310**
12641 Saticoy St. North Hollywood 91605 • **818-764-0854**
56 Waverly Dr. Pasadena 91105 • **626-683-9695**
Hours vary by location www.kellypaper.com
Wide selection of recycled copy and fine papers. Paper available for purchase by the sheet, ream, or pallet.

Real Earth, Inc., The 🌿🌿🌿🌿
Malibu • **310-455-7010**
Daily 9am-5pm www.treeco.com
Large selection of nontoxic, recycled, and eco-friendly paper and office supply products; environmentally-friendly janitorial and cleaning supplies. Delivers to greater Los Angeles area. Received City of Santa Monica Sustainable Quality Award.

Soolip Papier & Press 🌿🌿
8646 Melrose Ave. West Hollywood 90069 • **310-360-0545**
Mon-Sat 10am-6pm Sun 12pm-5pm www.soolip.com
Paper boutique offering handmade and tree-free papers; custom stationery, invitations, handmade greeting cards, and gift wrap supplies. Letterpressed designs.

Xpedx Paper and Graphics 🌿
21720 Marilla St. Chatsworth 91311 • **818-718-9606**
9620 Flair Dr. El Monte 91731 • **626-443-2241**
1611 W. 190th St. Gardena 90248 • **310-532-2497**
2101 S. Barrington Ave. LA 90025 • **310-478-3775**
6947 Hayvenhurst Ave. Van Nuys 91406 • **818-785-4237**
Hours vary by location www.xpedxstores.com
Recycled copy and fine papers; various office and paper supplies in bulk or by the ream.

Low-Impact Fabrics and Fibers

Most people think natural fibers are better for the environment than synthetic fibers. This isn't necessarily true. When considering the sustainability of fibers, it's necessary to look at the whole lifecycle: from the growing or extraction, through the processing and dyeing, to the cutting and sewing of fabric to clothing. Further, the shipping from place of manufacture to point of purchase, the washing, drying, dry cleaning and other care requirements, and ultimately the garment's disposal must also be taken into consideration. Each fiber has a different impact at each stage of its lifecycle.

FABRICS

Cotton When it comes to cotton, look for organically grown without pesticides, biologically produced, with low-impact dyes. Selecting cotton with these characteristics will help minimize this fabric's traditionally chemically intensive production. Biological production refers to how the cotton fibers are purified and prepared for spinning. It is water-based and results in no environmental pollution. Similarly, the use of natural or vegetable-based dyes minimizes the negative impacts of the dyeing process.

Wool Look for organic, naturally sourced, undyed or dyed without the use of heavy metals.

Linen and Hemp Ask for dew-retted (this is the means by which the fibers are extracted to make the fabric), organic, non-chlorine bleached.

Bamboo A natural textile made from the pulp of the bamboo grass that is naturally antibacterial. Look for unbleached fabric, since many manufacturers use extensive bleaching processes.

Polyester Look for recycled content and recyclable options. Virgin polyester is petrochemical-based exclusively and its production is greenhouse-gas intensive. A small but growing alternative to standard polyester is a hybrid of recycled polyester and cornstarch, sometimes referred to as "corn-based polyester." There are socks, shirts, and a growing number of other items made from this material.

Tencel or Lyocell A man-made nonsynthetic fiber made from the natural cellulose found in wood pulp harvested from tree-farm trees and produced without chlorine.

FIBERS

Natural All natural fibers are renewable and biodegradable, as long as the dyes and dye treatments are nontoxic.

Synthetic Synthetic fibers are petroleum based and made from a nonrenewable resource. They are not biodegradable but are readily recyclable if not blended with natural fibers.

Fair trade certification strives to ensure that farmers in the developing world get a fair price for their crops and good conditions under which to work. Fair trade helps guarantee freedom of association, prohibits forced child labor, and preserves agricultural traditions by keeping farming profitable, especially for small-scale and family farmers. Developing-world farmers often lack market access and pay high premiums to dealers. By forming cooperatives, cutting out intermediaries, guaranteeing a set floor price for crops (including a bonus for organics), and setting labor and environmental standards, it is the goal of the fair trade model to create market opportunities for disadvantaged producers.

TransFair, a leading fair trade certifier, currently offers certification in the United States for coffee, tea and herbs, cocoa and chocolate, fresh fruit, sugar, rice, and vanilla.

Although it is not widely recognized, fair trade certification also has strong ecological benefits. TransFair enforces strict environmental guidelines created by Fairtrade Labelling Organizations International (FLO), the world's main association of fair trade groups based in Bonn, Germany. Through detailed integrated farm-management practices, these standards serve to protect watersheds, virgin forests and wildlife, prevent erosion, promote natural soil fertility, conserve water, and prohibit the use of genetically modified organisms.

TransFair's long list of prohibited agro-chemicals also helps protect workers and reduce fossil fuel dependence. TransFair claims that its environmental standards are the most stringent in the industry, second only to the USDA's organic label. Since TransFair guarantees growers a premium for organic crops, this also creates an incentive to go organic and helps pay for ongoing certification fees.

The Rainforest Alliance is another third-party certifier of sustainable agricultural products and also has programs for sustainable forestry and tourism. Through their labeling program, a product can be certified if it meets their high standards of land conservation, integrated farm management practices, and fair labor conditions. The Rainforest Alliance's agricultural program currently covers bananas, citrus, cocoa, coffee, and flowers.

For more information, visit www.transfairusa.org and www.rainforest-alliance.org.

Training Ourselves

BY TODD WARNER

Our pets seem to know what they like to eat and what is good for them. But they have a hard time convincing us sometimes. Take their food, for instance. Back in the 1940s, dogs and cats ate table scraps, that is, the same stuff their owners ate—good, wholesome food. At that time, cancer was virtually nonexistent in pets. But with the advent of mass-produced, filler-filled pet food, disease at some point is almost a given.

What was once considered "unfit for consumption" is often what you'll find in conventional brands of pet food, the kind every supermarket across the country stocks in vast quantities. This "food" is not adequately regulated and is full of byproducts, most of which are indigestible and some of which are downright bad.

It's really important to read the list of ingredients on the back of any bag or can of pet food. A good rule of thumb—if you can't pronounce it, don't serve it. Check for things like carrots, peas, cranberries, and other fruits and vegetables. Yes, your animals need these things.

Look for a company that just makes pet food. Avoid those whose pet lines are just a piece of their business. Good companies were started by pet lovers who wanted something better for their animals. Seek out organic lines. They may cost more because organic certification is a significant expense, but they are worth it. You will be paid back over time because your pet will have fewer health issues, which means lower vet bills.

Good pet care doesn't stop with proper food selection. Natural, nontoxic grooming and flea and tick control products are just as important. Choose all natural shampoos that are tearless and safe. You'll find them as effective as their chemical-rich counterparts and much better for your pets. And if you drop off your pet at the groomer, before you depart, be sure to ask about the ingredients in the products that will be used. Often a groomer will use the cheapest shampoo available—good for the groomer maybe but not so for your pet.

The more of us that start asking for the kind of products that are good for our pets, the more the stores will get the message. Good pet care requires retraining ourselves as pet owners—and retraining stores and suppliers to offer the natural, nontoxic, and green options that are best for pets and their people alike.

TODD WARNER

Todd Warner founded Tailwaggers Pet Food and Supplies and Tailwashers Grooming in 2003 in Hollywood. Tailwaggers and Tailwashers are committed to supplying customers with healthy and eco-friendly pet care products and services (www.twaggers.com).

As with humans, natural, organic food, free from unnecessary additives, is best for pets. All too often, commercial pet food is chockfull of ingredients that may not be conducive to optimal health for dogs, cats, and other friends.

We have evaluated pet food purveyors based on the percentage of products sold that contain all certified organic, a mix of certified organic and natural, or all natural ingredients.

When it comes to pet care and grooming, we feel it is best to minimize the use of products containing harsh chemicals and potentially toxic treatments. Not only is your pet exposed, you and other household members are as well every time you touch, scratch, pat, or hold your animal. In fact, some pet treatments can be very harmful, so it is important to know what you are purchasing.

We took a look at pet care products (such as flea/tick treatments, shampoos, and other grooming supplies) with an eye toward their content. Our listings reflect the percentage of products sold and, in the case of grooming, day/overnight care establishments or other services, the percentage of products used that contain nontoxic, natural, and/or organic ingredients.

To be included in the guide, businesses must meet our minimum requirement that 25% of their products used or sold comply with the standards outlined above.

$\mathscr{D}$ at least 25% of products meet the above criteria.

$\mathscr{D}\mathscr{D}$ at least 50% of products meet the above criteria.

$\mathscr{D}\mathscr{D}\mathscr{D}$ at least 75% of products meet the above criteria.

$\mathscr{D}\mathscr{D}\mathscr{D}\mathscr{D}$ at least 90% of products meet the above criteria.

Type of services available:

FS Pet food and supplies

G Grooming

B Boarding or daycare

O Other services as described

A Paw-fect World $\mathscr{D}\mathscr{D}\mathscr{D}\mathscr{D}$ FS G
23916 Crenshaw Blvd. Torrance 90505 • **310-326-8881**
Tue-Sat 8am-6pm
Almost all products sold and used in grooming services are 100% natural or organic.

Animal Crackers $\mathscr{D}\mathscr{D}$ FS
8023 Beverly Blvd. LA 90048 • **323-658-1919**
Mon-Sat 9am-7pm Sun 10am-6pm

Animal Crackers (cont.)
Natural and organic pet shampoo, conditioners, flea treatments, food, and treats.

Animal World ✿✿✿ FS
11360 Ventura Blvd. Studio City 91604 • **818-505-9315**
Mon-Fri 10am-5pm www.animalworldnetwork.com
Variety of organic and all natural pet food and treats. Mostly order online; customers can pick up at Studio City warehouse.

Aquarium Pet Center ✿ FS
826 Wilshire Blvd. Santa Monica 90401 • **310-395-1009**
Mon-Fri 10:30am-7pm Sun 10am-6pm
Offers some organic and natural pet and fish supplies.

Bark Williams ✿✿✿ FS G
2901 Ocean Park Blvd. Ste. 118 Santa Monica 90405 • **866-333-2275**
Mon-Tue, Fri 10am-7pm Sat 8:30am-7pm Sun 2pm-7pm
www.bark-williams.com
Self-service dog wash; gifts and supplies.

Barks & Bubbles ✿✿✿ G
8320 Lincoln Blvd. Westchester 90045 • **310-649-1585**
Tue-Sat 8am-5pm Thu 7am-5pm
Grooming services using organic products.

Behr's Pet Depot ✿✿ FS G
2256 Tapo St. Simi Valley 93063 • **805-582-1340**
Mon-Sat 9am-8pm Sun 11am-7pm www.petdepot.net/behrs.html
Carries organic pet food and supplies.

Biju Pet Spa ✿✿✿ FS G
4528 Saugus Ave. Sherman Oaks 91403 • **818-990-7387**
Mon-Sat 10am-5pm www.bijupetspa.com
Pet spa using all natural products.

Burbank Pet Plaza ✿✿ FS
1080 W. Alameda Ave. Burbank 91506 • **818-557-0144**
Mon-Fri 9am-8pm Sat 9am-7pm Sun 10am-6pm
Offers wide selection of organic and all natural pet food; holistic and nontoxic pet care products.

C & C Pet Food and Grooming ✿✿✿ FS G
21720 Sherman Way Canoga Park 91303 • **818-348-3018**
Mon-Fri 9am-7pm Sat 9am-6pm Sun 9am-5pm
Large selection of organic pet food; all natural grooming services.

California Groomin' ✿✿✿ FS G
4308 Overland Ave. Culver City 90230 • **310-398-0227**
Mon-Sat 9am-5:30pm Sun 9:30am-5pm www.californiagroomin.com
All natural and organic pet supplies and grooming.

Catt's and Dogg's Pet Supplies ✿✿✿ FS G
2833 Hyperion Ave. LA 90027 • **323-953-8383**
Mon 10am-6pm Tue-Fri 8am-7pm Sat 8am-6:30pm Sun 10am-6pm
Organic pet food; all natural supplies and grooming services.

Centinela Feed & Pet Supplies ✿ FS G
331 N. Robertson Blvd. Beverly Hills 90211 • **310-246-0367**
5299 Sepulveda Blvd. Culver City 90230 • **310-572-6107**

Centinela Feed & Pet Supplies (cont.)

3860 Centinela Ave. LA 90066 • **310-398-2134**
11055 Pico Blvd. LA 90064 • **310-473-5099**
7600 S. Sepulveda Blvd. LA 90045 • **310-216-9261**
28901 S. Western Ave. Rancho Palos Verdes 90275 • **310-547-3008**
413 N. Pacific Coast Hwy. Redondo Beach 90277 • **310-318-2653**
1448 Lincoln Blvd. Santa Monica 90401 • **310-451-7140**
22840 Hawthorne Blvd. Torrance 90505 • **310-373-4437**
Hours vary by location www.centinelafeed.com
Organic pet food, pet toys, and products; grooming available.

Chow Bella Pet Spa ✐✐✐ FS G B

11939 Ventura Blvd. Studio City 91604 • **818-763-0300**
Mon-Sat 7am-7pm Sun 9am-6pm www.chowbellapetspa.com
Pet supplies, grooming, and boarding; natural flea and hypoallergenic
shampoos; organic and human-grade pet food; organic fiber pet clothing.

Classicut Dog Grooming ✐✐ FS G

1202 Montana Ave. Santa Monica 90403 • **310-451-4478**
Tue-Fri 7:30am-5pm Sat 7:30-3pm
Some organic pet products and dog grooming services.

Collar & Leash ✐✐ FS

8555 Santa Monica Blvd. West Hollywood 90069 • **310-657-6638**
Daily 9am-9pm
Some organic, vegetarian pet food and treats. Carries all natural flea
treatments, grooming products, pet supplies, and biodegradable dog bags.

Darla's Dogwash ✐✐✐ G

3163 Los Feliz Blvd. LA 90039 • **323-664-0622**
Mon-Sat 9am-5pm Sun 9am-4pm
All natural, organic grooming service with self-serve stations.

Denise's Pet Grooming & Supplies ✐✐✐ FS G

21701 Devonshire St. Ste. H Chatsworth 91311 • **818-709-9744**
Tue-Fri 9:30am-4:30pm Sat 8:30am-5:30pm
Uses and sells all natural pet care and grooming products.

Doggie Styles ✐✐✐ FS

9467 Charleville Blvd. Beverly Hills 90212 • **310-278-0031**
Mon-Sat 10am-6pm Sun 11am-4pm www.doggiestylesonline.com
Focuses on pet accessories: natural grooming products, frozen raw food,
and biodegradable dog bags.

Dogromat ✐✐✐ FS G

12926 Venice Blvd. LA 90066 • **310-306-8885**
Tue-Sun 8:30am-5:30pm Self Service 8am-4:30pm
All natural and organic shampoos; self-service grooming stations.

Eco-Pet ✐✐✐ FS G

6955 La Tijera Blvd. LA 90045 • **310-645-8892**
Mon-Tue 10am-7pm Wed-Sat 8am-7pm www.ecopetla.com
Wide selection of natural, healthy pet food and treats; herbal grooming
services using all natural shampoos and therapeutic HydroSurge bathing.

Elaine's Pet Depot ✐✐ FS G O

2919 Wilshire Blvd. Santa Monica 90403 • **310-823-4545**
Mon-Fri 9am-7:30pm Sat 9am-7pm Sun 10am-6pm
www.petdepot.net/elaines.html
All natural and organic pet products, grooming services; anesthesia-free
dental services.

Euphuria Pet Salon ✐✐✐ FS G
10538 Magnolia Blvd. North Hollywood 91601 • **818-760-2110**
Tue-Sat 9am-6pm Sun 10am-6pm
Grooming service using all natural shampoos; carries all natural food and supplies.

Fifi & Romeo ✐✐✐ FS
7282 Beverly Blvd. LA 90036 • **323-857-7215**
Mon-Fri 11am-7pm Sat 11am-6pm Sun 12pm-5pm www.fifiandromeo.com
Creates recycled cashmere fashions for humans, babies, pets, and home.

George ✐✐✐ FS
1111 Montana Ave. Santa Monica 90403 • **310-393-8737**
Daily 10:30am-6pm www.georgesf.com
Pet supplies and organic food for dogs and cats.

Healthy Pet ✐ FS
5881 Kanan Rd. Agoura Hills 91301 • **818-706-0360**
1775 E. Thousand Oaks Thousand Oaks 91362 • **805-494-3524**
Mon-Fri 9am-7pm Sat 9am-6pm Sun 10am-5pm
Carries some all natural and organic pet supplies.

Helen's Pet Depot ✐✐ FS G
10531 W. Pico Blvd. LA 90064 • **310-470-2922**
Mon-Sat 9am-7:30pm Sun 10am-6pm www.petdepot.net/helens.html
Some organic and mostly all natural options: pet food, supplies, accessories, and grooming.

Judy's Pet Depot ✐ FS G
1278 Westwood Blvd. LA 90024 • **310-441-4122**
Mon-Sat 9am-7:30pm Sun 10am-6pm www.petdepot.net/judys.html
Organic and natural food and treats for fresh, frozen, and raw pet diets. Carries all natural grooming supplies and flea treatments.

K9 Loft ✐✐✐ FS G B
2170 W. Sunset Blvd. LA 90026 • **213-484-6006**
Mon-Fri 7am-7pm Sat 10am-6pm Sun 11am-5pm www.k9loft.com
Dog spa offering raw, organic, and all natural pet food, treats; pet care products and organic shampoo. Indoor and outdoor facility with filtered air/water.

Kahoots Pet Store ✐✐ FS
10360 Mason Ave. Chatsworth 91311 • **818-718-9850**
Mon-Sat 8am-9pm Sun 10am-6pm www.kahootspet.com
Pet store offering some organic products.

Kirby's Pet Depot ✐✐ FS G B
12112 Venice Blvd. LA 90066 • **310-313-1801**
Mon-Fri 9am-8pm Sun 10am-6pm
Offers natural and organic pet food, supplies, and grooming; boarding available.

L.A. Doggie Style ✐✐✐✐ FS G
1639 Silverlake Blvd. LA 90026 • **323-664-3647**
Tue-Sat 10am-6pm Sun 11am-5pm www.ladoggiestyle.com
Organic grooming, food, wellness, and pampering products.

LA Dogworks ✐✐✐ FS G B
1014 N. Highland Ave. LA 90038 • **323-461-5151**
Daily 7am-7pm

LA Dogworks (cont.)
Organic and all natural pet food and treats. Grooming using all natural shampoos and conditioners. Indoor dog park; day care and boarding.

Laundered Beast ✐✐✐ G
Venice • **323-893-3647**
Mon-Fri 9am-5pm
Mobile, natural grooming service. Serves the Westside.

Mabel's Dog Grooming ✐✐✐ G
641 N. Sepulveda Blvd. LA 90049 • **310-440-9495**
Tue-Sat 8am-4pm www.mabelsdoggrooming.com
Grooming service using all natural shampoos and flea treatments.

Mary's Pet Salon ✐✐✐ FS G
2681 Thousand Oaks Blvd. Thousand Oaks 91362 • **805-496-3400**
Mon-Sat 9:30am-close
Grooming and pet supply services with mostly organic and all natural products.

My Pet Naturally ✐✐✐✐ FS
12001 W. Pico Blvd. LA 90064 • **310-477-3030**
Mon-Sat 10am-7pm Sun 12pm-5pm www.mypetnaturally.com
Specializes in holistic, organic, raw, and natural pet food; baked treats; apothecary; eco-friendly hemp toys and beds.

Natural Touch 4 Paws ✐✐✐✐ FS
21789 Ventura Blvd. Woodland Hills 91604 • **818-594-7297**
Mon-Thu 10am-6pm Fri 10am-6:30pm Sat 10am-6pm
Offers natural, chemical-free, and homeopathic pet goods.

Nature's Grooming & Boutique ✐✐✐✐ FS G
3110 Main St. Ste. 104 Santa Monica 90405 • **310-392-8758**
Tue-Fri 7:30am-6pm Sat 7:30am-4pm www.naturesgrooming.com
Offers all natural pet food, supplies, and grooming services.

New Age Pet Supply ✐✐ FS
19315 Saticoy St. Unit C Reseda 91335 • **818-886-7387**
Mon-Sat 9am-8pm Sun 10am-7pm www.newagepetsupplies.com
Sells all natural and holistic pet food, toys, grooming tools, and supplies.

Pacific Palisades Veterinary Center ✐✐✐ G B
853 Via de la Paz Pacific Palisades 90272 • **310-573-7707**
Mon-Fri 8am-6pm Sat 8am-4pm
Nontoxic, botanical grooming products; provides day and overnight care.

Paws N' Claws ✐✐✐ FS G
16634 Marquez Ave. Pacific Palisades 90272 • **310-459-2009**
Tue-Fri 7:45am-4:30pm Sat 7:45am-3:30pm
All natural pet supplies and grooming services.

Pet Adventure ✐ FS
11130 Balboa Blvd. Ste. A Granada Hills 91344 • **818-368-0269**
Mon-Fri 10am-8pm Sat 9am-7pm Sun 10am-6pm
Carries some all natural and organic pet supplies.

Pet Haven All Natural Pet Boutique ✐✐ FS O
626 N. Glenoaks Blvd. Burbank 91502 • **818-260-0511**
Mon-Sat 11am-7pm Sun 12pm-5pm www.pethavenonline.com
All natural and organic pet food; holistic and natural flea treatments; health products.

Pet Life FS

23367 Mulholland Dr. Woodland Hills 91364 • **818-222-9119**
Mon-Sat 9am-7pm Sun 10am-7pm
Carries some all natural and organic pet supplies.

Pet Salon G

12243 Santa Monica Blvd. LA 90025 • **310-207-0838**
By appt.
Grooming services using organic and all natural shampoo; nontoxic flea
treatments for cats and dogs.

Pet Stuff FS

13400 W. Washington Blvd. Marina Del Rey 90292 • **310-306-5175**
Mon-Fri 10am-7pm Sat 10am-6pm Sun 11am-5pm
Offers organic and natural pet food, treats, and cleaning supplies.

Pet Wash FS G

7357 W. Sunset Blvd. Hollywood 90046 • **323-882-6855**
Daily 9am-6:30pm www.hollywoodpetwash.com
Offers all natural, hypoallergenic, nontoxic grooming. Self-serve pet
washing service using organic shampoos; all natural pet food.

PetEx FS G

18955 Ventura Blvd. Tarzana 91356 • **818-705-3333**
Mon-Fri 9am-8pm Sat-Sun 9am-6pm www.petexusa.com
Offers organic and natural pet food, treats, and shampoos. Grooming
service with pickup and free delivery services within five-mile radius.

Pets Naturally FS

13459 Ventura Blvd. Sherman Oaks 91423 • **818-784-1233**
Mon-Thu 10am-6pm Fri 11am-4pm Sat 10am-7pm Sun 11am-4pm
Specializes in natural and raw food, homeopathics, flower essences, and
supplements.

Pets Plus FS

17440 Crenshaw Blvd. Torrance 90504 • **310-719-7088**
Mon-Fri 9:30am-8pm Sat-Sun 10am-7pm
Holistic pet food and natural pet products. Frozen raw pet food, natural pet
stain remover, and toys made from natural materials.

Pour La Pooch FS G

7617 Beverly Blvd. LA 90036 • **323-934-0940**
Tue-Sat 8am-6pm
Organic, nontoxic, and hypoallergenic shampoo and flea treatments. Also
sells all natural cleaning products.

Prestige Pet Supply FS

18425 Nordhoff St. Unit A1 Northridge 91325 • **818-772-6611**
Mon-Fri 10am-8pm Sat 10am-7pm Sun 10am-6pm www.prestigepetsupply.com
Natural and organic pet food and treats.

Puppy Palace, The G

11156 Balboa Blvd. Granada Hills 91344 • **818-366-9069**
Mon-Sat 8am-5pm
Cat and dog grooming using all natural, nontoxic, and biodegradable
products.

Red Barn Feed and Saddlery FS

18601 Oxnard St. Tarzana 91356 • **818-345-2510**
8393 Topanga Canyon Rd. West Hills 91356 • **818-887-7388**

Red Barn Feed and Saddlery (cont.)

Hours vary by location
Offers some organic and all natural pet supplies.

Sparky's Pet Salon 🌿🌿🌿 FS G

9221 W. Olympic Blvd. Beverly Hills 90210 • **310-274-3647**
617 N. La Brea Ave. LA 90036 • **323-936-3647**
11960 Wilshire Blvd. LA 90025 • **310-571-3191**
Mon-Sat 8am-4pm www.sparkysgrooming.com
Products used and sold are 100% natural and chemical free, including all
flea treatments.

Spot 🌿🌿🌿 FS

456 S. Robertson Blvd. LA 90048 • **310-275-2820**
Mon-Sat 10am-7pm Sun 12pm-5pm (seasonal hours) www.spotlosangeles.com
Offers organic beds, hemp collars, organic and all natural food, nontoxic
shampoos, and organic dog clothes.

Symply Grooming 🌿🌿🌿 G

4353 Sepulveda Blvd. Culver City 90230 • **310-390-1400**
Tue-Sat 9am-5pm
Offers full or self-service pet grooming using chemical-free products.

Tails of Santa Monica 🌿🌿🌿 FS

2912 Main St. Santa Monica 90405 • **310-392-4300**
Mon-Sat 11am-7pm Sun 11am-6pm www.tailsofsantamonica.com
Natural dog and cat boutique that offers organic food, treats, collars, bedding.

Tailwaggers/Tailwashers 🌿🌿🌿🌿 FS G

1929 N. Bronson Ave. Hollywood 90068 • **323-464-9600**
Store: Mon-Fri 8am-8pm Sat 10am-7pm Sun 10am-6pm
Grooming: Mon-Fri 8am-7pm Sat-Sun 10am-6pm www.twaggers.com
Organic, holistic, and premium pet food, treats, supplies. Tailwashers uses
all natural pet grooming products.

Three Dog Bakery 🌿🌿🌿 FS

6333 W. Third St. Ste. 710 LA 90036 • **323-935-7512**
24 Smith Alley Pasadena 91103 • **626-440-0443**
411 Santa Monica Blvd. Santa Monica 90401 • **310-260-9604**
14545 Ventura Blvd. Sherman Oaks 91403 • **818-304-0440**
Hours vary by location www.threedog.com
Pet food and supply store; makes its own all natural dog food and treats.
Also carries natural shampoo and grooming products.

Top Dog Grooming 🌿🌿🌿 G

9000 Reseda Blvd. Unit C Northridge 91325 • **818-701-1813**
Every other Mon, Thu-Sun 9am-7pm
Grooming for dogs and puppies only; uses all natural grooming products.

UrbanTails 🌿🌿🌿 FS O

7515 Beverly Blvd. LA 90036 • **323-933-2100**
Mon-Fri 9am-8pm Sat 10am-7pm Sun 9am-6pm www.urbantails.net
Organic, holistic, and premium pet food, treats, and products: beds, toys,
leashes, collars, and shampoos. Offers training.

Ushampooch 🌿🌿🌿 FS G

1218A Beryl St. Redondo Beach 90277 • **310-798-7300**
Mon-Wed, Fri 10:30am-6pm Thu 10:30am-7:30pm Sat-Sun 9:30am-5pm
www.ushampooch.com
Self-serve pet wash and boutique with all natural products, foods for raw
and organic diets, holistic remedies, and accessories.

Valley Pet ⊘ **FS**
10218 Mason Ave. Chatsworth 91311 • **818-349-5520**
Mon-Fri 9am-7pm Sat 9am-6pm Sun 10am-5pm
Carries some natural and organic pet supplies.

Wagging Tail, The ⊘⊘ **FS**
1123 Montana Ave. Santa Monica 90403 • **310-656-9663**
Mon-Sat 10am-6pm Sun 12pm-5pm www.wagwagwag.com
Carries some all natural pet foods, treats, and grooming products.

Wagville ⊘⊘⊘⊘ **FS G B O**
2400 San Fernando Rd. LA 90065 • **323-222-4442**
Mon-Fri 7am-9pm Sat-Sun 9am-9pm www.wagville.com
All natural and organic pet food, holistic treatments, boarding, and
massage.

Woof Dog Boutique ⊘⊘⊘ **FS**
3172 Glendale Blvd. LA 90039 • **323-661-7722**
Tue-Fri 11:30am-7pm Sat 9am-6pm Sun 10am-4pm www.woofdogboutique.com
Organic dog food, supplies, and bakery. Carries biodegradable dog bags,
dog beer, organic soaps, and all natural birthday cakes.

⊘ GREEN TIP

Clay-based cat litters are produced by strip mining. The clay,
known as *bentonite*, is found under several layers of soil, which
are removed in the mining process. The first few inches of clay are
discarded, and the final clay is removed and processed into cat
litter. Look for a sustainable alternative for your feline friend at any
of the pet stores listed here.

⊘ WRITE A REVIEW

We were excited to find many local merchants and service
providers with eco-friendly options. Have you discovered ones
we haven't listed? Share your findings with other pet owners on
greenopia.com: How was the grooming? Did your pets like the
food? Did the flea treatment work? How was the staff's rapport
with your pet?

For many people, pets make life better. Some basic "green" knowledge can help make for a happier pet, a healthier household, and a greener world.

Look for natural and organic pet food. This will not only be good for your pet's health, but buying organic products helps support good land management and sustainable practices.

Kids benefit from having a pet in the family. Certain studies have shown that children who grow up with at least two pets are more than 75% less likely to develop allergies later in life.

Pesticides aren't good for pets or the people who pet them. Be very cautious with pet products that include toxic pesticides. The chemicals they contain are potentially harmful to your pet, you, and especially children. But this doesn't mean you need to live in fear of fleas in your home and on your pets. There are nontoxic alternatives to traditional pesticides. They work equally well and won't cause unnecessary harm to people or pets.

Prevention is always preferable to treatment so it is important to keep bugs in check. Ticks can carry Lyme disease, a serious and poorly understood illness that attacks the nervous system. If you live in an area where Lyme disease is a risk, be very cautious and seek sound advice on keeping ticks off you and your furry friends.

Pet waste doesn't just smell bad, it can represent a major source of bacterial pollution when rain washes it into waterways and onto beaches. ALWAYS clean up after your pet. Try to use biodegradable, non-petroleum-based bags for this purpose. They are widely available. Put the waste in the trash. Dog waste may be put in the toilet but cat waste must not be. Water treatment systems are not able to remove all the microorganisms in cat waste.

Finally, if you are ready to add a new family member, remember that a shelter or rescue organization is the best place to adopt.

Natural Evolution

BY DEIRDRE WALLACE

When I first became interested in environmentally responsible hotel development, the choices for guests were limited. I realized that to provide travelers with a truly green hospitality experience, I would need to create one. In 1998, I began development of The Ambrose as a health-minded hotel, so the decision to go green was a natural progression. What started with a few sustainable practices grew into a company-wide dedication to minimize our negative environmental impact on the world around us.

The Ambrose initially implemented basic environmental programs including recycling and towel reuse. We enrolled in Santa Monica's Sustainable Works Green Business Certification Program to learn more about environmentally friendly business operation, and as the first hotel to participate, we creatively applied our knowledge in ways meaningful to the hospitality industry. Our efforts encompass waste management, energy and water conservation, and sustainable purchasing practices. Our rooms are outfitted with low-flow toilets and showerheads. We use compact fluorescent light bulbs. More than 75% of our paper, plastic, glass, and aluminum is recycled. Our in-room appliances are all Energy Star-rated. We employ nontoxic housekeeping practices and use water-based paints and sealants.

In addition, we have built partnerships with local eco-conscious vendors, including Urth Caffé, who provides our catering using organic, locally grown ingredients. I encourage other hotels to do as we have done and find ways to establish green practices. Start small with basic projects. Take advantage of local resources. Partner with like-minded companies. You'll find that once you take the initial steps toward a greener hotel, the response will be overwhelmingly positive.

Recently, The Ambrose took its environmental pledge to the highest level by registering for Leadership in Energy and Environmental Design Certification for Existing Buildings from the US Green Building Council. Slated to be the first LEED®-EB rated hotel in Southern California, we are setting standards for green hotels and offering guests a unique green lifestyle experience. We strive to inspire other hotel developers, managers, and guests to follow our example. The industry is learning, but there are still opportunities for improvement, and I'm excited to be a part of this evolution. It makes sense to go green, for business and for the benefit of future generations.

DEIRDRE WALLACE

Deirdre Wallace launched The Ambrose Group LLC, a green hotel development and management company, and is developing sustainable hotels across the U.S. Ms. Wallace is owner of The Ambrose, Santa Monica's award-winning green hotel.

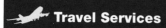

We live in a world in which travel has become increasingly essential and complex. We, as travelers, are faced with a myriad of choices—the form of transport, the type of accommodation, or the planning of an itinerary.

Eco-tourism offers some exciting new opportunities to experience the world without leaving a heavy footprint. Work with an agency or service that specializes in that kind of travel if you'd like to see faraway places in an environmentally friendly way. *Bon voyage!*

> This is a changing area so this category has not yet been leaf awarded. However, to be listed here, businesses must be very familiar with, focus primarily on, and actively promote eco-travel.

Better World Club Travel Service
Portland OR • **866-238-1137**
Mon-Fri 8:30am-5:30pm www.betterworldclub.com
Auto club and insurance company offering online database of eco-friendly hotels, eco-tourism packages, and travel agent consultation. Discounts for members.

Earth Routes
Penobscot ME • **207-326-8635**
Mon-Sat 9am-6pm www.earthroutes.net
Green travel planning service; focuses especially on transportation.

Ecoclub.com (International Ecotourism Club)
Online service only www.ecoclub.com
Worldwide network promoting eco-conscious tourism; features ecotourism-related information for all levels of research and application.

Ecotravel.com
Online service only www.ecotravel.com
Online magazine and directory listing ecotourism information and resources: search engine, articles, and online community.

Global Exchange Reality Tours
2017 Mission St. Ste. 303 San Francisco CA 94110 • **800-497-1994**
Daily 9am-5pm www.globalexchange.org
Socially responsible, community-oriented, education- and service- based travel to more than 30 countries.

Green Earth Travel, LLC
7 Froude Circle Cabin John MD 20818 • **888-246-8343**
Daily 9am-5:30pm www.greenearthtravel.com
Travel agency catering to clients with eco-friendly, vegetarian, sustainable lifestyles. Offers package trips, adventure travel, cooking tours, and more.

Solikai
Santa Monica CA • **310-455-6900**
Mon-Fri 9am-6pm www.solikai.com
Adventure sports destination club using low-impact, sustainable housing around the globe. Members granted full use of surfing, biking, skiing, and snowboarding equipment.

Travel Specialists, The

120 Beacon St. Somerville MA 02143 • **800-370-7400 x51**
By appt. www.thetravelspecialists.biz
Full-service travel agency devoted to responsible travel and the
preservation of natural places. Co-op America resource.

 Hotels and Lodging

Whether you are planning a family vacation, welcoming family or friends
into town, or going away on business, the hotel you choose matters.
Next time, when selecting a hotel, take into account factors that will affect your personal health and the health of the planet.

We have evaluated hotels in a number of key areas, all of which directly
impact both the hotel guest and/or the environment. Some of the hotels
listed below have an official environmental policy to which they aspire
to adhere. Others are making a concerted effort to be better planetary
citizens. The actions they take are reflected in the evaluations that follow.

Our criteria is extensive and includes the following:

- Extent of recycling program (paper, plastic, glass, aluminum).

- Efficient resource management including energy, water, and waste
  systems (low-flow toilets and showerheads; compact fluorescent
  lights and LED exit signs; Energy Star rated room appliances; alternative energy use, etc.).

- Good ventilation and fresh air exchange (operable windows, wall- or
  window-mounted air handling units) for healthy indoor air.

- Use of nontoxic or low-toxic maintenance and cleaning products and
  practices (linen reuse program; cleaning and laundry products that are
  chemical- or phosphate-free and/or readily biodegradable; low-toxic
  pest control; chlorine-free pool and spa maintenance; nonsmoking
  areas).

- Environmentally sound purchasing practices (bulk purchases; recycled-
  content, chlorine-free paper products; reusable glasses, napkins,
  flatware; refillable soap, shampoo, and conditioner containers; natural
  guest amenities).

- "Green" landscaping (drought-resistant and/or native plants; organic
  fertilizer use; alternative or less-toxic pesticide use; water conservation or reclamation program).

- Sustainable restaurant services (organic, locally grown produce; com-
  posted kitchen waste; meat, poultry, and eggs raised organically and/
  or hormone/antibiotic-free; sustainably caught or raised fish, etc.).

- Eco-friendly building materials (low VOC paints, sustainable woods
  and materials).

- Beds, bedding, towels, and other linens made of organic and/or natural fibers; mattresses made of mostly organic, chemical-free, and/or natural materials.

⌁ Performed at an overall average of at least 25% in the areas listed above.

⌁⌁ Performed at an overall average of at least 50% in the areas listed above.

⌁⌁⌁ Performed at an overall average of at least 75% in the areas listed above.

⌁⌁⌁⌁ Performed at an overall average of at least 90% in the areas listed above.

Average room price:

$ $175 or less

$$ $176 - $250

$$$ $251 - $325

$$$$ $326 and up

SEEING THE WORLD

Ambrose, The ⌁⌁⌁⌁ $$$
1255 20th St. Santa Monica 90404 • **310-315-1555**
www.ambrosehotel.com
Green boutique hotel committed to providing upscale amenities sustainably with low-impact living practices: recycles graywater, composts, offers guests natural bath products and organic continental breakfast. LEED-EB registered project with U.S. Green Building Council.

Belamar Hotel, The ⌁⌁ $$
3501 N. Sepulveda Blvd. Manhattan Beach 90266 • **310-750-0300**
www.thebelamar.com
Luxury boutique hotel. Smoke free, pet friendly; complimentary valet service and Internet service. Strong recycling program.

Fairmont Miramar Hotel, The ⌁ $$$
101 Wilshire Blvd. Santa Monica 90401 • **310-576-7777**
www.fairmont.com/santamonica
Luxury hotel atop Santa Monica bluffs, overlooking the beach. Eco-friendly practices include organic menu items, free valet parking for guests driving hybrid vehicles.

Hollywood Pensione ⌁⌁⌁ $
1845 N. Wilton Pl. LA 90028 • **323-369-2411**
www.hollywoodpensione.com
Sustainably renovated 1915 house transformed into upscale inn catering to the arts and entertainment industry for short- and long- term stays. Organic bedding; air purifiers in each room; reclaimed teak and bamboo furnishings.

Venice Beach Eco-Cottages ⌁⌁⌁⌁ $$
447 Grand Blvd. Venice 90291 • **866-802-3110**
www.venicebeachecocottages.com
Three 1920s vacation cottages restored and renovated using all sustainable, eco-friendly materials; solar powered; all-organic bedding and nontoxic interior décor.

Putting Your Money Where Your Pollution Is

BY NANCY SUTLEY

The service sector is one where cities, counties, businesses, and individuals can all make a difference. At the macro level, cities and counties are taking significant steps to address environmental problems and climate change.

The City of Los Angeles has made large capital investments in combating water pollution, has pioneered advanced recycling methods and collection, has embarked upon a massive tree planting project as the most economically-efficient means of reducing greenhouse gasses in the LA basin, and has shown its commitment to conservation and energy efficiency though its green power program, its green building incentives, and its fleet of fuel cell-powered vehicles.

When it comes to water pollution (what we like to call "urban slobber"), although our City is addressing it, it is individuals and businesses that are generating that "slobber." Runoff from excess landscape watering; toxins from fertilizers and pesticides; and paint and oil poured into storm drains pollute the ground water and eventually the ocean. The best way to attack this problem is to keep these products out of the waste stream to begin with. Consumers should hire operators who are familiar with and use less-toxic means of pest control. Selecting dry cleaners that use nontoxic or low-toxic methods also prevents pollution at the source. Finding landscaping professionals who use Integrated Pest Management (IPM) and nontoxic fertilizers, installing smart irrigation systems that apply only the amount of water needed, and even picking up after your dog are also important steps individuals can take.

The best way to build markets for sustainable goods and services is to seek them out and support them. If you can't find the green services, recycled goods, or knowledgeable providers you are looking for, ask traditional businesses to begin supplying what you need. Educate your providers and share your insights with your neighbors. We are exposed to many things in our urban environments. If everyone did one thing to reduce their use of toxic chemicals, we could really begin to remove some of the ingredients in our toxic soup.

NANCY SUTLEY

Nancy Sutley serves as the Deputy Mayor for Energy and Environment for the City of Los Angeles and is also Mayor Villaraigosa's appointee to the Board of Directors for the Metropolitan Water District of Southern California. From 2003 to 2005, Ms. Sutley served on the California State Water Resources Control Board.

Pharmacies

Pharmacies are where we go to meet health needs and sometimes to seek professional guidance. Traditionally, pharmacists mixed and dispensed medications on the orders of physicians. However, more recently, pharmacies have come to include other services related to preventative care as well as illness treatment.

When our quest is for good health, how we treat ourselves becomes paramount. Many of us consider natural remedies first, and the pharmacies listed here offer the most extensive selection of alternative medications, including homeopathic remedies, herbal tinctures, powders, medications, creams, and other holistic preparations.

A few stores are solely holistic pharmacies, and others, like some larger health food stores and grocery stores, have an extensive holistic remedy and personal care department.

In determining which pharmacies to include, we looked at the percentage of homeopathic remedies, natural remedies, and the presence of organic ingredients in these remedies. Where vitamins were concerned, we checked for plant-based (vs. synthetic), natural, organic, and/or herbal ingredients.

We also evaluated a pharmacy's stock of natural alternatives to traditional personal care products and medications (for example, cough medicines, sleep aids, cold and flu treatments, skin creams, shampoos, deodorants, makeup, and soap) and the availability of health books and books on alternative medicine.

To be in the guide, at least 25% of a given store's pharmacy stock must include the type of products outlined above.

Apothecary Pharmacy
11700 National Blvd. LA 90064 · **310-737-7277**
Mon-Fri 9am-7pm Sat 9am-5pm www.apothecarypharmacy.com
Specializes in vitamins and herbal supplements, homeopathic remedies.
Also provides prescription medication and conventional over-the-counter products.

Capitol Drugs
4454 Van Nuys Blvd. Ste. J Sherman Oaks 91403 · **818-905-8338**
8578 Santa Monica Blvd. West Hollywood 90069 · **310-289-1125**
Hours vary by location www.capitoldrugs.com
Pharmacy offering some organic, natural, and homeopathic medicines.

Montana Natural
930 Montana Ave. Santa Monica 90403 · **310-395-2059**
Mon-Sat 10am-6pm www.montananatural.com
Carries many homeopathic and natural remedies, some organic snacks.

Natural Path Nutrition & Wellness Center
8916 Pico Blvd. LA 90035 • **310-858-7661**
Mon-Thu 10am-5:30pm Fri 10-2 Sun by appt.
Large selection of natural remedies and homeopathic items.

Pharmaca Integrative Pharmacy
15150 Sunset Blvd. Pacific Palisades 90272 • **310-454-1345**
Mon-Fri 8am-8pm Sat 9am-6pm Sun 10am-6pm www.pharmaca.com
Offers wide selection of organic and all natural homeopathic remedies. Also
carries pet food, gifts, and clothes.

Santa Monica Homeopathic Pharmacy
629 Broadway Santa Monica 90401 • **310-395-1131**
Mon-Sat 9:30am-5:15pm www.smhomeopathic.com
Offers a variety of homeopathic and herbal remedies. Free consultations.

 GREEN TIP

Many grocery stores and specialty markets also have extensive
alternative pharmacy and personal care sections. Check those
listings in the Eating In section of the guide for merchants that
may carry these products, such as Whole Foods, Erewhon Natural
Foods Market, Pacific Coast Greens, and others.

 ## Personal Services

Wanting to "go green" and learning how is one thing; finding green
service providers is another. When you need help from a specialist who
is well versed in green living, you've got to do some digging.

We've uncovered some entrepreneurial service providers who can help
you move along a greener path—in your home, your lifestyle, and even
in your personal career choices.

To be included, providers must have a primary focus on sustainable
living. In addition, 15% or more of their projects or client base must be
dedicated to sustainable living and at least 15% of the products they use
or sell in their practice need to be green or sustainable. We didn't award
leaves in this category because there aren't objective measurements
across these varied services that we could reasonably apply. But we
encourage you to check references and give these groundbreakers a try.

All Shades of Green
3038 Rowena Ave. LA 90039 • **323-665-7454**
Mon-Sat 11am-7pm Sun 11am-6pm www.allshadesofgreen.net
Sustainable living coaching and consultation; green decision-making
workshops.

Creative Green Sustainability Coaching
LA • **323-935-1214**
By appt.

Creative Green Sustainability Coaching (cont.)

Phone or in-person consultation on greening home, business, and lifestyle. Offers sustainable living workshops.

DkkEvents
LA • **818-519-2074**
Mon-Fri 9am-6pm Sat-Sun by appt. www.dkkevents.com
Corporate and private event planning utilizing reusable, recyclable, and repurposed products; sources caterers working with local, organic food. Supports 1% For The Planet and CarbonFund.

Drivers Ed Direct
9121 Oakdale Ave. Ste. 120 Chatsworth 91311 • **800-728-1048**
Mon-Fri 8am-6pm Sat 10am-4pm www.driverseddirect.com
Driving school offering behind-the-wheel driver training exclusively with hybrid vehicles; offers online education course. California DMV licensed; serves Los Angeles, the Westside and San Fernando Valley.

EarthFriendlyMoving
Costa Mesa • **888-900-7225**
By appt. www.earthfriendlymoving.com
Rents reusable RecoPack moving boxes made from hard-to-recycle salvaged plastic, delivered direct to customer's door. Serves greater Los Angeles area.

Eco I Consulting LA
149 S. Barrington Ave. Ste. 142 LA 90049 • **310-795-3138**
Mon-Fri 8am-6pm www.ecoconsultingla.com
Helps clients find eco-friendly, healthy options for building and renovating their homes, planning events, and improving their lives. Build It Green Certified.

Eco Organizer, The
6420 Balboa Blvd. Ste. 207 Lake Balboa 91406 • **818-279-8167**
By appt. www.eco-organizer.com
Professional home organization services using nontoxic and recycled products; offers personalized energy conservation, waste reduction, and sustainability coaching. Serves the Westside, Hollywood, San Fernando Valley, South Beach.

Green Lotus Events
2221 Tenth St. Unit A Santa Monica 90405 • **805-798-4806**
By appt. www.greenlotusevents.com
Eco-friendly event planning utilizing sustainable yet stylish production and design.

Green Weddings & Events
LA • **323-953-0453**
By appt. www.greenweddings.net
Planning, design, and production of eco-friendly weddings and events since 2004.

MeanGreen Trucking & Transport
5443 Aura Ave. Tarzana 91356 • **818-392-8436**
By appt. www.meangreentrucking.com
Residential and commercial moving and delivery services using solar power and biofuel. Serves nationwide.

Orchestration
55 Navy St. Venice 90291 • **310-450-1233**
Mon-Fri 10am-5pm
Full-service green event and wedding orchestration. Serves greater Los Angeles area.

Pink Cloud Events
LA • **310-415-3998**
Daily 7am-7pm   www.pinkcloudevents.com
Event styling, wedding, and production company dedicated to practices
yielding minimal environmental impact.

Privilege Lifestyle Management
264 S. La Cienega Blvd. Ste. 1423 Beverly Hills 90211 • **310-424-5058**
By appt. www.privilegelm.com
Lifestyle managers teach clients how to become more environmentally and
socially responsible in all daily activities. Emphasis on eco-luxury.

Serene Star Productions
13547 Ventura Blvd. Ste. 248 Sherman Oaks 91423 • **310-270-6327**
By appt. www.serenestar.com
Offers Green Star Events, utilizing environmentally-friendly products
applicable to any event.

Simply Mumtaz Events
20929 Venutra Blvd. Ste. 47-492 Woodland Hills 91364 • **818-996-1109**
By appt. www.simplymumtaz.com
Eco-chic services, from invitations to décor, to make any event green.

Soirée Verde
501 W. Glenoaks Blvd. Ste. 558 Glendale 91202 • **818-919-0052**
Mon-Fri 9am-6pm Sat-Sun by appt.   www.soireeverde.com
Event planning providing options to conserve energy, minimize
consumption, reuse resources, and employ earth-friendly products. Serves
greater Los Angeles area.

UsedCardboardBoxes.com
1453 Third St. Ste. 370 Santa Monica 90401 • **888-269-3788**
Call or order online www.usedcardboardboxes.com
Provides quality used boxes for packing, moving, shipping, and storage.
Serves nationwide.

Zencierge
4230 Stansbury Ave. Ste. 102 Sherman Oaks 91423 • **310-848-3969**
By appt. www.zencierge.com
Lifestyle consulting services guiding and educating clients toward choices that
are healithier for the planet and for themselves. Serves Los Angeles County.

✐ WRITE A REVIEW

We've done our best to establish how green the providers are for
the services we've identified. Now, we would like your feedback:
How was your experience? How effective was the service? Was
the price right? Was the provider on time and available when
you needed her/him? How was the customer service? Would
you recommend them to a friend or use them again? Share your
findings and experiences at greenopia.com.

Conventional "dry" cleaning actually involves washing clothes in a liquid chemical solvent to remove stains. In about 85% of dry cleaning businesses this solvent is *perchloroethylene* (or *perc*). Perc is a dangerous chemical that harms workers, brings toxins into the home, and damages the environment. Perc has been identified as a "probable" human carcinogen by California's Proposition 65, and by the Environmental Protection Agency (EPA) as a health and environmental hazard.

By state law, ALL dry cleaners must replace their "perc" machines with one of four EPA-approved methods. However, not all of the alternatives are equally healthy for you and the environment, so here's what we recommend (in order of preference):

1. Before taking your garment to be cleaned, decide if it could be hand washed instead. Many garments can be safely washed at home rather than professionally dry cleaned. Clothing manufacturers often put on the "dry clean only" label to play it safe. Wash these garments by hand or use your washing machine's delicate cycle.

2. If you decide you still need to have the items cleaned professionally, we highly recommend either of the following two methods as your first choice:

   Wet Cleaning. Uses water as a solvent. Free of volatile organic compounds (VOCs). No health and safety or environmental risks. Saves water and is energy efficient. Washer and dryer are computer-controlled so cleaning can be tailored to type of fabric. Sophisticated machines and trained operators ensure wet cleaning quality is equal to that of dry cleaning.

   CO2 Cleaning. Uses pressurized liquid CO_2 in combination with other cleaning agents in a machine emptied of air. The liquid CO_2 can often be reused and no new CO_2 is generated. Although the liquid CO_2 is recycled and recyclable, thereby keeping its cost low, the price of the machine itself is very high, limiting conversion to this method by existing dry cleaners.

3. If neither of the above methods are available in your area, then your next best choices are the following two methods:

   Hydrocarbon dry cleaning. Uses a petroleum-based solvent. Not as toxic as perc but produces significant quantities of greenhouse gases.

   Silicone-based solvent dry cleaning. Is known by the brand GreenEarth or by the chemical name, siloxane or D-5 (created by Dow Corning). No chemicals mix with the clothing but GreenEarth's manufacture requires chlorine, which, when manufactured itself, releases dioxin, a potent carcinogen.

SORTING THROUGH SERVICES

Lately, you may have seen some dry cleaning establishments advertising "environmentally-friendly cleaning" or "organic dry cleaning." Unfortunately, this signage is often misleading since most of these businesses are just switching to hydrocarbon or silicone-based solvents, which, as we've mentioned, are not the best choices.

However, some of these dry cleaners offer the choice to have your clothes safely wet cleaned. We urge you to seek out cleaners from our list or ask your neighborhood cleaners (even if they still use perc) to specifically wet clean your garments. Many cleaners offer this alternative but may not use it unless you request it.

Only those cleaners that meet our strict requirement of offering wet cleaning and/or liquid CO2 cleaning exclusively qualify for a four-leaf award. Those that offer hydrocarbon/silicone-based solvent cleaning in addition to wet or liquid CO2 cleaning qualify for a two-leaf award.

WET AND/OR CO2 CLEANERS

We recommend using any of the following wet and/or CO2 cleaners as your first choice before using a chemical method:

Brentwood Royal Cleaners ✐✐✐✐
256 26th St. Ste. 100 Santa Monica 90402 • **310-451-3663**
Mon-Fri 7am-6pm Sat 7am-1pm www.royalcleaner.com
Provides CO2 and wet cleaning services.

Colony Cleaners ✐✐✐✐
3872 Cross Creek Rd. Malibu 90265 • **310-456-6202**
Mon-Fri 7am-7pm Sat 9am-5pm
Provides wet cleaning services exclusively.

Del Mar Natural Cleaners ✐✐✐✐
701 Washington Blvd. Marina Del Rey 90292 • **310-482-0060**
Mon-Fri 7am-8pm Sat 8am-6pm Sun 10am-3pm
Wet cleaning services used exclusively.

Filo Cleaners ✐✐✐✐
432 N. Cañon Dr. Beverly Hills 90210 • **310-275-2303**
Mon-Fri 8:30am-5pm Sat 9am-2pm
Provides CO2 and wet cleaning.

Forever Treasured ✐✐✐✐
10049 Rubio Ave. North Hills 91343 • **818-360-9943**
Mon-Fri 9am-8pm Sat 10am-5pm
Dedicated wet cleaning and stain removal.

Nature's Touch Cleaners ✐✐✐✐
2041 Palos Verdes Dr. N. Lomita 90717 • **310-530-3973**
Mon-Fri 7am-7pm Sat 8am-6pm www.naturestouchcleaners.com
Provides wet cleaning exclusively.

SORTING THROUGH SERVICES

Nick's Dry Cleaners ✿✿✿✿
923 Montana Ave. Santa Monica 90403 • **310-395-7317**
Mon-Fri 7am-7pm Sat 8am-6pm
Provides wet cleaning services exclusively.

Plaza Cleaners ✿✿✿✿
1730 Ave. De Los Arboles Thousand Oaks 91362 • **805-493-2715**
Mon-Thu 7am-7pm Fri 7am-6:30pm Sat 8am-5pm
Dedicated wet cleaners.

Restor Cleaners ✿✿✿✿
8846 Foothill Blvd. LA 91040 • **818-352-5288**
10501 Sunland Blvd. LA 91040 • **818-353-1808**
Mon-Fri 7:30am-7pm Sat 9am-5pm
Provides wet cleaning services exclusively.

Rosali Cleaners ✿✿✿✿
11335 Magnolia Blvd. North Hollywood 91601 • **818-506-6206**
Mon-Fri 7:30am-6pm Sat 9am-4pm
Offers CO2 cleaning only.

Sunny Brite Natural Cleaners ✿✿✿✿
3756 W. Avenue 40 Ste. J LA 90065 • **323-258-9222**
Mon-Fri 7:30am-7pm Sat 9am-5pm
Dedicated wet cleaners.

Sunset Blvd. Cleaners & Laundry ✿✿✿✿
7223 W. Sunset Blvd. LA 90046 • **323-874-5627**
Mon-Sat 8am-6:30pm
Provides wet cleaning services exclusively.

WET OR CO2 AND HYDROCARBON/ SILICONE-BASED SOLVENT CLEANERS

If establishments that offer exclusively wet or CO2 cleaning are not available in your area, then we suggest the following cleaners as your next best choice. These cleaners offer the hydrocarbon/silicone-based solvent methods, along with wet or CO2 cleaning. We have not listed cleaners that provide only the hydrocarbon and/or silicone-based solvent methods.

Bella Cleaners ✿✿
4760 Admiralty Way Marina Del Rey 90292 • **310-823-4018**
Mon-Fri 6:30am-8pm Sat 7am-6pm Sun 9am-5pm
Offers hydrocarbon and wet cleaning.

Burwood Laundry & Cleaners ✿✿
5550 Woodman Ave. Sherman Oaks 91401 • **818-787-5000**
Mon-Fri 8am-6pm Sat 9am-5pm
Wet and hydrocarbon cleaning.

Clean Living ✿✿
10350 San Vicente Ste. 102 LA 90049 • **310-393-7202**
Mon-Fri 7am-7pm Sat 9am-6pm
Offers hydrocarbon and wet cleaning.

Cleaner By Nature ✿✿
5530 White Oak Ave. Encino 91316 • **818-345-0171**
11919 Wilshire Blvd. LA 90025 • **310-914-4504**
2407 Wilshire Blvd. Santa Monica 90403 • **310-315-1520**
Mon-Fri 7:30am-7pm Sat 9am-5:30pm
Offers wet cleaning and silicone-based dry cleaning.

Door to Door Valet Cleaners ✐✐

310 E. Grand Ave. Ste. 107 El Segundo 90245 • **310-640-3456**
519 Pier Ave. Hermosa Beach 90254 • **310-376-8383**
901 Manhattan Ave. Manhattan Beach 90266 • **310-318-8047**
1830 Manhattan Beach Blvd. Manhattan Beach 90266 • **310-318-3183**
903 N. Sepulveda Blvd. Manhattan Beach 90266 • **310-374-9928**
2118 Highland Ave. Manhattan Beach 90266 • **310-545-7505**
Mon-Fri 7am-7pm Sat 8am-6pm www.doortodoorcleaners.com
Offers hydrocarbon and wet cleaning services.

Dry Clean Express ✐✐

11915 Santa Monica Blvd. LA 90025 • **310-312-1277**
1936 Westwood Blvd. LA 90025 • **310-470-0579**
Mon-Thu 8am-7:30pm Fri 8am-5pm Sun 11am-6pm
Offers hydrocarbon and wet cleaning.

Emerson LaMay Cleaners ✐✐

15333 Sunset Blvd. Pacific Palisades 90272 • **310-454-4015**
Mon-Fri 7:30am-6pm Sat 8:30am-5pm
Offers hydrocarbon and wet cleaning.

Fame Cleaners ✐✐

1232 S. La Cienega Blvd. LA 90035 • **310-659-9311**
5772 Lindero Canyon Rd. Westlake Village 91362 • **818-707-9110**
Mon-Sat 7am-8pm Sun 9am-5pm www.famecleaners.com
Offers hydrocarbon and wet cleaning.

Family Cleaners ✐✐

113 E. Manchester Blvd. Inglewood 90301 • **310-674-8850**
Mon-Fri 7am-7pm Sat 8am-6pm
Offers hydrocarbon and wet cleaning.

Fazio Cleaners ✐✐

9260 W. Olympic Blvd. Beverly Hills 90212 • **310-273-5030**
4732 Commons Way Calabasas 91302 • **818-223-8006**
11702 San Vicente Blvd. LA 90039 • **310-820-0469**
14715 Ventura Blvd. Sherman Oaks 91403 • **818-784-5575**
140 Promenade Way Thousand Oaks 91362 • **805-370-0088**
23383 Mulholland Dr. Woodland Hills 91364 • **818-222-8441**
Hours vary by location www.faziocleaners.com
Hydrocarbon and wet cleaning.

5 Star Quality Cleaners ✐✐

4356 Laurel Canyon Blvd. Studio City 91604 • **818-506-8960**
Mon-Fri 7am-7pm Sat 8am-4pm
Offers hydrocarbon and wet cleaning.

Green Cleaners ✐✐

8887 W. Pico Blvd. LA 90035 • **310-273-8523**
Mon-Fri 7am-6pm Sat 9am-4:30pm
Hydrocarbon and wet cleaning.

Hanger's Cleaners ✐✐

800 Washington Blvd. Marina Del Rey 90292 • **310-827-9565**
Mon-Fri 7am-8pm Sat 8am-6pm Sun 10am-3pm
Wet and hydrocarbon cleaning.

Hollywood Cleaners ✐✐

13020 Pacific Promenade Ste. 4 Playa Vista 90094 • **310-862-5790**
Mon-Sat 7am-7pm Sun 9am-5pm
Offers hydrocarbon and wet cleaning.

Imperial Dry Cleaners & Laundry ✑✑
502 S. Western Ave. LA 90020 • **213-487-5470**
Mon-Fri 6am-9pm Sat 6am-7pm
Offers hydrocarbon and wet cleaning.

Nu Way Cleaners ✑✑
328 Ave. I Redondo Beach 90277 • **310-375-7302**
Mon-Fri 7am-7pm Sat 8am-5pm
Offers hydrocarbon and wet cleaning.

Ogden's Cleaners ✑✑
15317 W. Sunset Blvd. Pacific Palisades 90272 • **310-459-3881**
926 Montana Ave. Santa Monica 90403 • **310-393-3314**
Mon-Fri 7:30am-7:30pm Sat 8am-5pm
Hydrocarbon and wet cleaning.

Olive Cleaners ✑✑
1728 W. Verdugo Ave. Burbank 91506 • **818-842-7786**
Mon-Fri 7am-7pm Sat 8am-5:30pm
Wet and hydrocarbon cleaning.

Patterson Cleaners ✑✑
1904 N. Sepulveda Blvd. Manhattan Beach 90266 • **310-546-1904**
Mon-Fri 6am-7pm Sat 7am-6pm Sun 9am-5pm
Offers hydrocarbon and wet cleaning.

Philip's French Cleaners ✑✑
15224 Sunset Blvd. Pacific Palisades 90272 • **310-454-7244**
Mon-Fri 7:30am-6pm Sat 8am-5pm
Hydrocarbon and wet cleaning services.

Pico Cleaners ✑✑
9150 W. Pico Blvd. LA 90035 • **310-274-2431**
Mon-Fri 7am-8pm Sat 8am-6:30pm Sun 9am-5pm www.picocleaners.com
Offers hydrocarbon and wet cleaning.

Porteranch Cleaners ✑✑
19450 Rinaldi St. Northridge 91326 • **818-368-7474**
Mon-Sat 6am-7pm
Offers hydrocarbon and wet cleaning.

Presto Cleaners ✑✑
1555 N. Verdugo Rd. Unit 103 Glendale 91208 • **866-582-6456**
Mon-Fri 7am-8pm Sat 10am-5pm www.prestocleaners.com
Hydrocarbon and wet cleaning.

Rocket Cleaners ✑✑
15450 S. Normandie Ave. Gardena 90247 • **310-515-9325**
2403 Marine Ave. Gardena 90249 • **310-532-1202**
Hours vary by location
Offers hydrocarbon and wet cleaning.

Sooz and Son Cleaners ✑✑
21314 Ventura Blvd. Woodland Hills 91364 • **818-598-0410**
Mon-Fri 6:30am-8pm Sat 8:30am-6pm Sun 11am-3pm
Offers hydrocarbon and wet cleaning.

Spring Cleaners ✑✑
8611 Sepulveda Blvd. Westchester 90045 • **310-670-8867**
Mon-Fri 7am-7pm Sat 8am-6pm
Offers hydrocarbon and wet cleaning.

Sterling Fine Cleaning 🌿🌿

1600 Westwood Blvd. LA 90024 • **310-474-8525**
3405 Overland Ave. LA 90034 • **310-287-2341**
Hours vary by location www.sterlingcleaners.com
Hydrocarbon and wet cleaning.

Triangle Cleaners 🌿🌿

6242 W. 87th St. Westchester 90045 • **310-670-9351**
Mon-Fri 7am-6:30pm Sat 8am-6pm
Offers hydrocarbon and wet cleaning.

Unique Cleaners 🌿🌿

758 Silver Spur Rd. Rolling Hills Estates 90274 • **310-541-3898**
Mon-Fri 7am-7pm Sat 8am-6pm
Wet cleaning and organic solvent dry cleaning.

Wetherly Cleaners 🌿🌿

8764 Beverly Blvd. West Hollywood 90048 • **310-360-0854**
Mon-Fri 7am-7pm Sat 9am-5pm
Hydrocarbon and wet cleaning.

🌿 GREEN TIP

California has committed to phasing out perc by 2023 and offers grant money to cleaners that switch from perc to one of the four EPA-approved cleaning methods: wet, CO_2, hydrocarbon, or approved silicone-based solvents. Do your part to accelerate this change by urging your local dry cleaner to switch sooner rather than later and to select wet or CO_2 cleaning as the best of the four approved options.

🌿 GREEN TIP

Our suggestions for healthier dry cleaning:

- If you're just after that fresh-pressed look, wash your clothing at home and take it to the cleaners for ironing.

- If something you have has been dry cleaned conventionally, remove it from its bag and hang it outdoors for two days to reduce the amount of perc vapor you bring into your home.

- No matter which cleaners you choose, try bringing your own reusable garment bag to reduce your use of plastic and return your unused hangers for recycling or reuse.

Cleaning Services

The products used by house cleaning services are generally not the same as those you might find in a supermarket. They are typically stronger and more concentrated, and potentially more toxic. When hiring a cleaning company, ask for the brand names or a list of ingredients in all products they use.

Select companies that use Green Seal™ certified products or ask for Material Safety Data Sheets on the products they use. Workers must be trained in the proper use and application of the products and equipment.

SORTING THROUGH SERVICES

You may also want to determine if the service uses vacuum cleaners with HEPA filters and how they dispose of their wastewater.

Because professional cleaning products may be different from those found in stores, and because much depends upon the proper use of even nontoxic cleaning materials, it is difficult to establish firm criteria for granting leaf awards. But the companies listed here meet a minimum requirement of using natural or mostly chemical-free cleaning supplies.

At least 25% of the products used regularly by the following cleaning services are natural and mostly chemical free or are certified by Green Seal™. Note, however, that many of the cleaning services listed below significantly out-performed this threshold requirement.

Green Seal™ Certification

Ensures that a product meets rigorous, science-based environmental leadership standards. Allows manufacturers to back up their claims and gives consumers confidence that certified products are better for human health and the environment.

Big Time Global Services, Ltd.
Redondo Beach • **310-372-8121**
Mon-Sat 8am-6pm www.bigtimecarpetcleaners.com
Provides hypoallergenic, eco-safe, odorless, nonhazardous carpet, oriental rug, tile, and furniture cleaning using Green Seal™ products. Specializes in serving those with chemical sensitivities.

Cool Earth Cleaning
5909 Eucalyptus Ln. Los Angeles 90042 • **310-961-6347**
Mon-Fri 9am-5pm www.coolearthcleaning.com
Eco-friendly maid and carpet cleaning services for residential and commercial establishments; uses mostly Green Seal™ certified products. Also offers consulting on green cleaning.

Eco-Maid House Cleaners
234 Fair Oaks Ave. Ste. F South Pasadena 91030 • **626-794-9201**
By appt.
Environmentally friendly residential cleaning service; waste water reused as graywater. Serves San Gabriel Valley, Glendale, La Canada, La Crescenta.

Environmental Services Solutions
8335 Winnetka Ave. Ste. 105 Winnetka 91306 • **818-772-7694**
Mon-Fri 9am-5pm www.esscleans.com
Cleaning and janitorial service using sustainable, environmentally-friendly, health-conscious products; residential, commercial, and industrial projects.

Green Clean LA
1680 N. Vine St. Ste. 620 Hollywood 90028 • **866-476-4736**
Mon-Sat 8am-6pm www.greencleanla.com
Uses only natural, nontoxic, and environmentally-friendly techniques and Green Seal™ certified products for home and office cleaning; offers education and consulting.

SORTING THROUGH SERVICES

Green Clean Maid Services
912 California Ave. Venice 90291 • **310-383-6309**
Daily 9am-5pm www.greencleanmaidservices.com
Cleaning company using Green Seal™ products for the eco-minded, health-conscious, and chemically sensitive; recycles used water as graywater. Serves homes, offices, schools.

Green Sweep
Venice • **310-396-7340**
Mon-Fri 9am-5pm www.greensweep.us
Uses only environmentally friendly and nontoxic products in cleaning services; used water recycled as graywater. Serves the Westside.

Heaven's Best Carpet Cleaning
23852 Pacific Coast Hwy. Unit 224 Malibu 90265 • **310-456-0820**
Mon-Sat 8am-6pm www.heavensbest.com
Carpet cleaning company using nontoxic, citrus-based products and solutions; no water used in process.

Host Carpet Dry Cleaners
800 S. Flower St. Burbank 91502 • **818-843-6886**
By appt.
Residential carpet and upholstery cleaning using Green Seal™ certified products.

KisClean Environmental Services and Products
287 S. Robertson Blvd. Ste. 413 Beverly Hills 90211 • **310-498-1227**
Mon-Sat 8am-5pm www.kisclean.com
Nontoxic cleaning service for homes and offices, including carpets and windows; sells natural cleaning products.

Organic-b-Natural Cleaning
12357 Magnolia Blvd. Ste. 11 Valley Village 91607 • **818-669-9034**
Mon-Fri 6am-9pm Sat by appt. www.organic-b-natural.info
Home and office cleaning service using 100% organic, biodegradable, nontoxic, Green Seal™ certified products and solutions.

Right Away Carpet Dry Cleaning
787 W. Woodbury Rd. Ste. 3 Altadena 91001 • **877-607-4448**
Mon-Fri 8am-6pm Sat 8am-3pm www.rightawaydrycarpet.com
Provides in-home carpet cleaning service and do-it-yourself rental equipment. Green Seal™ certified Host® distributor.

Spiegel Certified Restoration
Montclair • **800-266-8988**
Mon-Fri 8am-4:30pm www.specialtydeepcleaning.com
Property damage restoration due to mold, water, fire, and other causes; carpet, rug, upholstery, drapery cleaning; forensic, consultation, and inspection services. Over 40 years experience.

Total Domestic Care
Manhattan Beach • **310-447-2229**
Mon-Sat 7am-10pm www.totaldomestic.com
Maid service using natural cleaning methods and nontoxic products.

Wilkins Host Dry Carpet Cleaners
LA • **323-938-2323**
By appt.
Carpet cleaning service using Green Seal™ certified Host® method.

XoomDry Carpet Care

26910 The Old Rd. Ste. 17 Valencia 91381 • **661-253-9794**
Mon-Fri 9am-6pm www.xoomdry.com
Carpet, area rug, upholstery, and air duct cleaning using organic cleaning
products; uses Green Seal™ certified Host® method. Serves greater Los
Angeles area.

Zen Casa

835 4th St. Ste. 204 Santa Monica 90403 • **310-663-2788**
By appt. www.zencasa.org
Cleaning service using aroma therapeutic and Green Seal™ certified
products. City of Santa Monica Green Business certified.

 Pest Control

Pesticides are toxic and although often considered effective against
pests, can be dangerous for people and pets. Outdoors, sprayed pesticides often drift, dusting nearby gardens and yards. Indoors, pesticides
remain in the air, exposing inhabitants to harmful chemicals.

Your first line of attack when it comes to pests is prevention. When that fails,
look for pest control services that use nontoxic or least-toxic methods,
an approach referred to as Integrated Pest Management or IPM. Despite
what you might hear from mainstream providers, alternative, nontoxic pest
control can be as effective as traditional methods, if not more so. Be very
specific about how you want your home or garden treated.

Because we cannot truly measure the efficacy of the various alternative pest control methods, we have chosen not to assign leaf awards
to these businesses. They do, however, meet our minimum requirement
of promoting and using IPM techniques and offering or using nontoxic
or less-toxic alternatives to traditional pest control practices to at least
25% of their customer base.

Integrated Pest Management (IPM)

A pest management strategy that includes using traps to monitor
infestations, using better sanitation practices and beneficial
insects to control the identified pests, and applying pesticides so
that they pose the least possible hazard, and are used only as a
last resort when other control methods have failed.

Borite Termite and Pest Treatment

Sherman Oaks • **866-905-7378**
By appt. www.borite.com
Low-toxicity pest treatments, qualified for EPA environmental stewardship
program. Serving West Los Angeles, San Fernando Valley, San Gabriel Valley.

Bug Central

14742 Beach Blvd. Ste. 408 La Mirada 90638 • **800-398-3764**
By appt. www.naturaltermitecontrol.com

Bug Central (cont.)

Termite and other pest control using Orange Oil™, Bora-Care®, and Termidor®. Serves greater Los Angeles area.

Center Termite Control, Inc.

Lynwood • 866-548-2847
By appt. www.centertermite.com
Earth-friendly termite and pest control treatment methods utilizing Bora-Care®; offers botanically based do-it-yourself pest control products. Serves greater Los Angeles area.

EcoLA Termite and Pest Management

Mission Hills • 818-920-7301
By appt. www.ecolatermite.com
Provides several nontoxic, nonchemical pest control choices. Serves greater Los Angeles area.

Greenleaf Organic Pest Management, Inc.

North Hollywood • 818-752-9989
Mon-Fri 7am-5pm www.greenleafpest.com
Organic pest and termite control company. Certified CleanSpace Crawl Space Encapsulation System installer.

Home Saving Termite Control, Inc.

P.O. Box 661129 LA 90066 • 800-300-0256
Mon-Fri 7:30am-4:30pm www.drywoodtermitecontrol.com
Uses amorphous silica treatment and Dri-Out Dehydration System, for termite control. Serves Southern California.

Jeff Hiatt, Inc. Termite Professionals

456 E. Ave. K-4 Lancaster 93535 • 800-672-6437
By appt. www.jeffhiatttermite.com
Residential and commercial termite control using Orange Oil™ and Termidor®. Serves Southern California region.

Loran's Pest Services

11040 Lorne St. Ste. 227 Sun Valley 91352 • 818-771-0985
By appt.
Nontoxic pest control services serving Hollywood, Pasadena, Glendale, San Fernando Valley.

Pacific Coast Termite Inc.

2600 Walnut Ave. Unit A Tustin 92780 • 714-669-1730
Mon-Fri 8am-5pm Sat 8am-2pm www.pacificcoasttermite.com
Eco-friendly termite control methods, including Orange Oil (XT 2000®) and BoraCare®. Serves all of Southern California.

Precision Environmental, Inc.

Ventura • 800-375-7786
By appt. www.precisionenv.com
Offers heat-based, nonchemical pest and mold management. Serves Los Angeles, Ventura, and Orange Counties.

Banking and Finance

Most people do not connect banking and finance with environmentalism, but direct links can be made through investment and lending practices. For example, an investment firm may offer ways in which potential investors can screen companies on both financial and environmental criteria. These realms are not mutually exclusive. There are companies that respect the environment and are robust financial performers.

You have the right to know if a bank's lending practices require potential clients to meet certain environmental standards or if they are directly providing funding for green projects. Dig into your financial institution's fine print. Find out what your dollars are being used for.

There are financial institutions that are making a concerted effort toward making the world greener by ensuring that, for example, their larger-scale lending practices support sustainable projects (through initiatives such as the Equator Principles), or that they offer clients the option of making socially responsible investments (SRIs) or investments in green funds.

Furthermore, some banks now offer what is called an EEM or Energy Efficient Mortgage. EEMs can be used to purchase homes that are already energy efficient or to refinance ones needing energy upgrades. Monthly energy savings are factored into interest rates, making them more favorable.

Listed below are firms that meet our minimum threshold to be included by offering EEMs, "green" banking options, SRIs with an environmental focus, and/or green funds. We expect the number of banking and financial institutions providing these services to continue to grow. We will continue to seek out new ones and add them to our list.

Equator Principles

A financial industry benchmark for determining, assessing, and managing social and environmental risk in project financing. See www.equator-principles.com/principles.shtml for more information.

Arbor Financial Services
500 E. Cordova St. Pasadena 91101 • **626-578-0022**
By appt. www.arborfin.com
Financial advising firm specializing in Socially Responsible Investing.

Barefoot Investments, LLC
LA • **310-928-3514**
By appt. www.barefootinvestments.com
Creates, markets, and manages investments in eco-friendly resort communities. Utilizes socially responsible, carbon-neutral practices.

CMM Green
21405 Califa St. Ste. 100 Woodland Hills 91367 • See website for list of brokers and phone numbers

CMM Green (cont.)

Mon-Fri 8:30am-5pm www.cmmgreen.com
Full-service insurance agency. Created "The Green Risk Guide" to help
clients understand the benefits of reducing environmental-related risk.

Community Financial Resource Center

4060 S. Figueroa St. LA 90037 • **323-235-1900**
By appt. www.cfrc.net
Nonprofit community development and financial institution providing low-
cost financial services and counseling for residents and businesses in
underserved Los Angeles neighborhoods.

Enright Premier Wealth Advisors, Inc. (Gregory Wendt, CFP)

11400 W. Olympic Blvd. Ste. 200 LA 90064 • **310-543-4559**
By appt. www.gregwendt.com
Registered investment advisory firm with expertise in SRI's. Works with
businesses, individuals, and nonprofits.

Green Bankers Group

4322 Wilshire Blvd. Ste. 200 LA 90010 • **310-709-1125**
By appt. www.greenbankersgroup.com
Provides financing for green projects, green homes, and other green
investment needs.

Greenleaf Financial Group LLC

5900 Wilshire Blvd. Ste. 2600 LA 90036 • **323-330-0579**
By appt. www.greenleaf-fg.com
Financial planning and investment management group specializing in
Socially Responsible Investing. Requires no minimum investment.

Lander Advisory/Progressive Asset Management (Ann-Marja Lander, CFP)

1827 Ximeno Ave. Ste. 361 Long Beach 90815 • **877-952-6337**
By appt. www.landeradvisory.com
Financial planner specializing in socially and environmentally responsible
investing.

Longboard Capital Advisors

1312 Cedar St. Santa Moncia 90405 • **310-450-2151**
By appt. www.longboardcapital.com
Special focus on investment in clean energy technologies. Clean Energy
registered investment advisor.

Modern Earth Finance, Inc.

15821 Ventura Blvd. Ste. 500 Encino 91436 • **818-933-2913**
Mon-Fri 9am-5pm www.modernearth.com
Applies green ethos to building and real estate finance. Member of 1% for
the Planet; LEED accredited staff.

New Resource Bank

405 Howard St. Ste. 110 San Francisco 94105 • **415-995-8100**
Mon-Thu 9-5 Fri 9-6 www.newresourcebank.com
Community-oriented, full-service bank focused on sustainable investments
and lending to green businesses.

ReDirect Guide Visa Credit Card

Apply online www.redirectguide.com
Card offered through ShoreBank Pacific, with portion of proceeds from
every purchase used to offset carbon emissions through Sustainable Travel,
Int'l.

Salmon Nation Visa Credit Card

Apply online www.salmonnation.com
Offered through ShoreBank Pacific; a percentage of the income derived
from the card goes directly to Ecotrust to support building Salmon Nation, a
network dedicated to improving neighborhoods and watersheds.

ShoreBank Pacific

P.O. Box 400 Ilwaco WA 98624 • **877-326-4326**
Mon-Fri 8am-5pm www.eco-bank.com
Full-service bank committed to environmentally sustainable community
development; works with individuals, commercial businesses, and nonprofit
groups.

Working Assets Visa Signature Credit Card
866-438-6262

Call or apply online www.workingassets.com
Consumer credit card donating 10¢ per customer purchase to
environmental and other nonprofit groups. Card issued by MBNA.

 Real Estate

It is becoming more common for real estate agents to obtain training
in the features of eco-friendly properties. More agents are beginning to
understand the real value of energy efficiency, healthy materials, and
sustainable design and construction in the homes they sell. And more
buyers are looking for these features when searching for a new home.
To meet this burgeoning need, Ecobroker.com offers online courses for
brokers to earn the EcoBroker Certified® designation (www.ecobroker.com)
to accompany their real estate license.

Ask at your favorite real estate office if they have a green-certified agent who
can help buyers and sellers find and sell green, sustainably designed homes.

Coldwell Banker (Abigail Dotson)

450 Washington Blvd. Marina Del Rey 90292 • **310-305-4759**
By appt. www.abigaildotson.com
Greater Los Angeles area realtor focusing on creating safe and healthy
homes by identifying and remedying areas of toxicity. Donates portion of
every sale to community-serving nonprofits.

Coldwell Banker (Gillian Caine)
166 N. Cañon Dr. Beverly Hills 90210 • **310-281-3649**
By appt. www.ecoagent.com
Dedicated to helping customers find, buy, and sell green homes. Provides green home renovation services.

Darcy and Associates Real Estate Services
818-326-1069
By appt. www.darcyandassociates.com
Helps eco-conscious customers find, sell, and renovate homes. Certified EcoBroker®. Serves Claremont, Los Angeles, San Gabriel Valley, San Fernando Valley, Santa Monica, and South Bay areas.

Ewing & Associates Sotheby's International Realty (Ron and Tammy Schwolsky)
13501 Ventura Blvd. Sherman Oaks 91423 • **818-640-3400**
By appt. www.greenestateagent.com
Real estate professionals helping clients buy, sell, build, and remodel green homes. Certified EcoBroker® and Green Building Professional. Serves greater Los Angeles area.

Gary Dannenbaum
137 N. Topanga Canyon Blvd. Topanga Canyon 90290 • **310-508-8800**
By appt. www.topangarealtor.com
Realtor emphasizing energy-efficient and health-focused design features in homes. Certified EcoBroker®. Serves Topanga, Malibu, Pacific Palisades, Calabasas.

Green Planet Realty
Santa Monica • **310-902-2667**
Mon-Fri 8:30am-8:30pm www.greenplanet-realty.com
Eco-friendly discount broker. Donates 5% of net income to environmental causes determined by buyers and sellers.

HomeGirl, Inc. Eco-Realtors, Keller Williams Realty (Colleen McLean)
4644 Admiralty Way Marina Del Rey 90292 • **310-301-5400**
By appt. www.homegirl.ws
Works with clients interested in buying, selling, and developing sustainable, energy-efficient, healthy homes. Serves the Westside and beach areas to Echo Park.

Innovative Realtors (Jeffrey J. Fritz)
124 Washington Blvd. Marina Del Rey 90292 • **310-754-8148**
By appt. www.greencityvision.com
Certified EcoBroker® focusing on buying and selling sustainable homes.

JMT Realty
530 S. Lake Ave. Ste. 414 Pasadena 91101 • **626-376-3231**
By appt. www.jmtrealty.com
Green realtor helping clients make choices for healthier and more valuable homes. Serves Pasadena and greater Los Angeles area.

Keller Williams Realty (Shawn Lin)
4465 Wilshire Blvd. Ste. 201 LA 90010 • **310-968-5392**
By appt.
Environmentally-responsible real estate broker helping clients create and buy healthier homes. Certified EcoBroker®. Serves greater Los Angeles area.

KJM Real Estate (KJ Marmon, Marvilyn Wright, Michelle Mathews, Anthony Malveto, and Ryan Flegal)

5455 Wilshire Blvd. Ste. 2010 LA 90036 • **323-634-5500**
Mon-Fri 9am-6pm www.kjmrealestate.com
Boutique green real estate company for residential and commercial properties helping clients buy, sell, build, and renovate green properties.

RealEstateArchitect.com (Erik Lerner, AIA)

345 N. Maple Dr. Ste. 105 Beverly Hills 90210 • **800-775-5582**
By appt. www.realestatearchitect.com
Certified EcoBroker® offering real estate services in the greater Los Angeles area.

Sotheby's International Realty (Jodi Sommers)

233 Wilshire Blvd. Ste. 100 Santa Monica 90401 • **310-260-8269**
By appt. www.santamonicapropertyblog.com
Green real estate broker with a strong knowledge of the rebates, rules, benefits, and financial incentives related to green development.

Sotheby's International Realty (Melinda and Scott Tamkin)

11911 San Vicente Blvd. Ste. 200 LA 90049 • **310-493-4141**
Daily 8am-8pm www.thetamkins.com
Represents buyers and sellers of eco-friendly homes and income properties. Serves the Westside to Pasadena.

South Collection, The

408 W. 11th St. LA 90015 • **213-622-5400**
Daily 11am-6pm or by appt. www.southcollection.com
A three-building, high-rise community developed with eco-smart urban planning principles. Building Elleven is the first LEED Gold certified project in California. The project's other buildings, Luma and Evo, are also seeking LEED certification.

Sustainable Real Estate Services

3206 Washington Blvd. Marina Del Rey 90292 • **310-403-3078**
By appt. www.greenhomesforsaleonline.com
Sustainable real estate services help consumers with green renovation and construction using a network of eco-friendly contractors. Serves the Westside and greater Los Angeles area.

"The cost of a thing is the amount of what I will call life which is required to be exchanged for it, immediately or in the long run."

—*Henry David Thoreau*

Telecommunications

No, there is nothing particular in the telecommunications industry that makes it more or less green, except how the companies choose to allocate their revenues or profits. Just as you choose where to make charitable donations, so too do phone and internet service providers. Since they all offer substantially the same services, why not support a company that puts your money to work for the environment?

Because this isn't an appropriate area in which to award leaves, we offer this list as a reference only. But we thought you might want to help support those businesses that are, in turn, helping support the planet. The telecommunications companies listed below have chosen to donate a part of their profits or a percentage of their revenues to environmental causes.

Note: Some companies identify their donations as a percentage of total revenue, in other cases as a percentage of profit, so the actual amounts and percentages donated will vary considerably. Look carefully when comparing plans and companies.

Better World Telecom
Reston VA • **866-567-2273**
Mon-Fri 9am-5pm www.betterworldtelecom.com
Provides toll-free, long distance and conference call tools. Primarily serves businesses and organizations, though residential service is available. Donates 3% of revenue to causes supporting social justice and the environment.

Come From The Heart, LLC
798 Verdun St. Clarksburg WV 26301 • **888-622-0957**
www.comefromtheheart.com
Provides internet, long distance, and mobile phone services. Donates some profits to environmental and other nonprofit organizations.

Credo Long Distance (formerly Working Assets Long Distance)
101 Market St. Ste. 700 San Francisco • **877-762-7336**
Mon-Fri 5am-8pm Sat-Sun 7am-5pm www.credolongdistance.com
Donates 1% of long distance charges to environmental and other progressive nonprofit groups.

Credo Mobile (formerly Working Assets Wireless)
101 Market St. Ste. 700 San Francisco • **877-762-7336**
Mon-Fri 5am-8pm Sat-Sun 7am-5pm www.credomobile.com
Donates 1% of mobile charges to environmental and other progressive nonprofit groups.

Earth Tones
1536 Wynkoop St. Ste. 100 Denver CO • **888-327-8486**
Mon-Fri 9am-5pm www.earthtones.com
Provides long distance and wireless phone service, internet access. Donates 100% of profits to grassroots environmental organizations.

Red Jellyfish
Mountain View • **888-222-5008**
www.redjellyfish.com
Offers internet access and e-mail accounts, mobile phone recycling. Donates funds to conservation groups protecting rainforest and jaguar habitats.

Sonopia
1370 Willow Rd. Menlo Park 94025 • **877-595-0557**
www.sonopia.com
Wireless phone service donating 5% of monthly bill to conservation organization of customer's choice.

 GREEN TIP

Unplug chargers (for cell phones, iPods and other devices) when not in use. Only 5% of the power drawn by a cell phone charger is used to charge the phone. The other 95% is wasted when it is left plugged into the wall.

 Utilities

Some utility companies and their customers are starting to recognize that their energy choices have a direct and lasting impact on the environment. There are clean, alternative energy choices out there, but be careful, some are more benign than others. For instance, many utilities consider nuclear energy a clean alternative energy choice. The same goes for large hydroelectric projects, regardless of their impact on wild rivers. Dig into those pages that come with your bill. You'll be surprised. When you do, we think you'll find energy efficiency and conservation are the best choices you can make.

Check to see if your utility is doing its best to minimize the greenhouse gas emissions that result from its operations. Does it protect its watershed lands? What about its support for solar power and other renewables? Are rebates for energy-efficient appliances offered? Does the company make donations to environmental organizations and help with habitat restoration on company-owned lands? (Utilities are very large landowners.)

We have identified some utility companies that are moving in the right direction. It's up to you to check the fine print.

SORTING THROUGH SERVICES

Burbank Water and Power
164 W. Magnolia Blvd. Burbank 91502 • **818-238-3700**
Mon-Fri 8am-5pm www.burbankwaterandpower.com
Green Energy Champion program allows residents and businesses in Burbank to choose a percentage of green power they want to receive at a premium of 2¢/kWh.

Glendale Water and Power

141 N. Glendale Ave. Level 2 Glendale 91206 • **818-548-3300**
Mon-Thu 8:30am-5:30pm Fri 8:30am-4:30pm www.glendalewaterandpower.com
Offers customers option to support clean energy at a premium flat rate of 2.5¢/kWh.

Los Angeles Dept. of Water & Power (LADWP)—Green LA

111 N. Hope St. LA 90012 • **800-342-5397 (800-DIAL-DWP)**
Mon-Fri 10am-7:30pm www.ladwp.com
Green LA program allows customers to choose green power for up to 100% of their electric bill at a premium of 3¢/kWh.

Pasadena Water and Power

150 S. Los Robles Pasadena 91101 • **626-744-6970**
Mon-Fri 7:30am-5:30pm www.pwpweb.com
Offers Green Power Program allowing customers to purchase clean energy in blocks of 1,000 kWh or at a premium of 2.5¢/kWh.

Burial Services

There are more burial and cremation options than most people are aware of, many of them less polluting and more meaningful than traditional practices. With cremation, ashes can be buried, spread over a chosen area (in some cases a protected natural area that furthers conservation work), preserved in an urn, or used to create lasting ocean reefs.

Similarly, there are a variety of more sustainable options for whole body burial. For example, one form of green burial entails preserving the body with dry ice or refrigeration and wrapping it in either a cotton or hemp shroud before placing it in the grave, in a biodegradable pine, cardboard, or wicker box, without using a concrete burial vault. (Conversely, an embalmed body goes into the ground with toxic formaldehyde and mercuric chloride in it.)

Some burial services have conservation areas where remains are buried within land that is cared for in an ecologically sound and sustainable manner. Embalmed remains are not allowed in these areas. Native vegetation, such as a memorial tree, may be planted over or near the grave in place of conventional monuments.

Many funeral services and even traditional cemeteries are also willing to accommodate a variety of end-of-life rituals, both old and new. Ask about natural alternative preservation and presentation options and other new burial service choices.

> The centers listed here offer some or all of the options outlined above, and work to encourage and employ environmentally sustainable practices in the services they provide. There are, however, no consistent criteria across these types of businesses upon which to base leaf awards.

Eternal Reefs, Inc.

P.O. Box 2473 Decatur GA 30031 • **888-423-7333**
Mon-Fri 8am-6pm www.eternalreefs.com
Burial service for people and pets creates living memorials to preserve, protect, and enhance the marine environment using cremated remains.

Green Burial Council
Santa Fe NM • **888-966-3330**
www.greenburialcouncil.org
Nonprofit organization promoting sustainable deathcare practices.
Resource for information on local eco-friendly burial service providers;
assists with green burial arrangements.

Nature's Passage
Amityville NY • **800-407-8917**
By appt. www.naturespassage.com
Burial service offering environmentally-friendly burials at sea; seaborne and
airborne ash scattering; biodegradable internment vessels and natural fiber
shrouds.

Neptune Society
562 S. Palos Verdes St. San Pedro 90731 • **310-831-0664**
4312 Woodman Ave. 3rd Flr. Sherman Oaks 91423 • **818-845-2415**
By appt. www.neptunesociety.com
Cremation service whose primary focus is scattering cremated remains at
sea or returning ashes to the family. Offers the Neptune Memorium Reef:
loved ones' keepsakes or cremated remains may be placed into concrete
structures that form reef.

Sea Services
888-551-1277
By appt. www.seaservices.com
Provides sea burial services of cremated remains; biodegradable ocean
urns available.

 DID YOU KNOW?

Last year conventional deathcare practices caused us to bury:

- 800,000 gallons of formaldehyde-based embalming fluid,
  regarded as a "known carcinogen" by the World Health
  Organization;

- more metal to create caskets than was used to build the
  Golden Gate Bridge; and

- vaults using enough reinforced concrete to build a two-lane
  highway from San Francisco to Phoenix.

Our thanks to Joe Sehee, founder of The Green Burial Council
(www.greenburialcouncil.org), for the above information.

Home, Green Home

BY MARY CORDARO AND STEVE GLENN

It's time to remodel the house that Jack built. And redecorate. Our homes have some serious issues, and it's about time we address them.

Here's the bottom line—homes built in conventional ways are wasteful, resource intensive, and not sustainable in their design, use of materials, or in their function. Not only that, they include materials and systems that can pollute the indoor environment. We can do better; and we are doing better at H3Environmental and LivingHomes.

At LivingHomes, we are committed to building homes that are as healthy as possible and that minimize the resources they use for their construction, operation, and eventual decommission. (Construction detritus makes up 40% of all landfill mass.) We use sustainable, healthier building materials, as well as energy-efficient environmental systems and products.

Our goal is to achieve "zero" impact in six areas: water, energy, waste, emissions, carbon, and ignorance. (Of course, dealing with that last one has to come first.) At LivingHomes, we use LEED® (Leadership in Energy and Environmental Design), the most recognized national green building rating system, to evaluate our choices of products and systems. LEED also gives you as a consumer an objective, third-party way to understand and differentiate between homes that claim to be "green." We built the nation's first LEED Platinum homes (their highest level of certification), and we won't build homes that aren't at least LEED Silver-certified.

At H3 Environmental, where we provide healthy home products, consulting, and education, we think entering our homes shouldn't be a health risk. Unfortunately, many of today's building materials and products, in combination with our indoor lifestyles, make them so. We now know how important it is to "cure" unhealthy indoor environments. We must avoid materials that off-gas, pollute the air or trap moisture that can create mold, cleaning products that are toxic and chemical-laden, and fire retardants that lace our furniture.

In addition, we can select building materials, energy systems, bedding, cookware, appliances, and furniture that reflect our commitment to personal health, the health of our homes, and the health of the Earth. By reducing our exposure to chemicals, mold, electromagnetic fields, and toxic heavy metals, we reduce the toxic burden on the earth from the manufacture, use, and disposal of them.

Combining sustainable building methods with healthy materials and efficient systems will result in cleaner air, cleaner water, and cleaner soil. Our homes will once again nourish our minds and souls which will, in turn, guide us toward the necessary changes we need to make to protect and restore our planet.

MARY CORDARO

Mary Cordaro is president of H3Environmental (www.h3environmental. com), a healthy bedroom products company, and has been consulting/ educating on the healthy home since 1989. Mary created a luxury line under her own name, called The Mary Cordaro Collection™ of Healthy, Organic Beds and Bedding. Mary is a certified Bau-Biologist.

STEVE GLENN

Steve Glenn is the founder and CEO of LivingHomes, LLC, a developer and builder of modern, prefabricated homes, designed by world-class architects. LivingHomes feature healthy, green materials and energy systems at a great price/value (www.livinghomes.net).

Bed and Bath

The cotton in conventional bedding, bath towels, and linens requires significant chemical inputs for its growth and processing. Choose furnishings that are made from organic or sustainable fabrics or recycled materials. Begin to think about how these items are produced. Is their manufacture sustainable? Are the dyes and coatings they contain nontoxic? Your interest will spark increased supply of sustainably produced bed and bath furnishings.

And remember, you spend about a third of your life in bed so the mattress you sleep on should be good for you. Look for mattresses, toppers, and box springs made with organic and chemical-free materials, particularly wool. Wool naturally wicks moisture away from the body, thereby creating a healthier, allergen- and mold-free environment. You may also want to consider box springs and bed frames that are manufactured with sustainable or FSC-certified wood.

Businesses that offer bed and bath furnishings are evaluated based on the percentage of products stocked that are characterized by one or more of the following:

- produced with nontoxic or low-toxic materials;

- made with renewable, natural, or recycled materials;

- sustainably manufactured; and/or

- sustainably manufactured and locally or domestically produced.

⬩ at least 25% of products meet the above criteria.

⬩⬩ at least 50% of products meet the above criteria.

⬩⬩⬩ at least 75% of products meet the above criteria.

⬩⬩⬩⬩ at least 90% of products meet the above criteria.

If the establishment sells mattresses, we evaluated the percentage of total mattress stock made with 100% organic and chemical-free materials.

⬩ at least 25% of mattresses meet the above criteria.

⬩⬩ at least 50% of mattresses meet the above criteria.

⬩⬩⬩ at least 75% of mattresses meet the above criteria.

⬩⬩⬩⬩ at least 90% of mattresses meet the above criteria.

At Home Naturally ⬩⬩⬩⬩
Sherman Oaks • **818-988-4441**
By appt. www.athomenaturally.com
Provides organic and fair trade beds, bedding, and linens. Rating applies to linens, mattresses, and bedding.

French General ✐✐✐
1621 Vista del Mar Ave. Hollywood 90028 · **323-462-0818**
By appt. www.frenchgeneral.com
Household textiles made from hemp: sheets, towels, and bath mats. Rating applies to linens.

Green Cradle ✐✐✐✐
13344 Ventura Blvd. Sherman Oaks 91423 · **818-728-4305**
Mon-Sat 10am-6pm www.greencradle.com
Specializing in organic and all natural bedding and mattresses. Rating applies to linens, mattresses, and bedding.

Green for Baby ✐✐✐✐
2989 E. Thousand Oaks Blvd. Thousand Oaks 91362 · **805-230-2201**
Tue-Fri 10am-6pm Sat 11am-6pm www.greenforbaby.com
Organic cribs, baby clothing, linens, and accessories; adult organic mattresses. Rating applies to linens, mattresses, and bedding.

H3Environmental ✐✐✐✐
818-766-1787
By appt. www.h3environmental.com
The Mary Cordaro Collection® of naturally healthy, organic beds and bedding for adults, children, and infants. Bed and bath linens. Rating applies to linens, mattresses, and bedding.

Hästens ✐✐✐✐
8675 Washington Blvd. Culver City 90232 · **310-558-3155**
Mon-Fri 10am-7pm Sat 10am-6pm Sun 11am-5pm www.hbeds.com
All beds are tested and confirmed 100% natural. Certified by Oeko-Tex Standard 100. No chemicals used. Rating applies to mattresses and bedding.

Kelly LaPlante Organic Interior Design ✐✐✐✐
1501 Main St. Ste. 101 Venice 90291 · **310-581-6450**
Mon-Sat 10am-6pm Sun by appt. www.kellylaplante.com
Eco-friendly beds, bedding, and linens. Rating to linens, mattresses, and bedding.

Livingreen Store & Gallery ✐✐✐✐
10000 Culver Blvd. Culver City 90232 · **310-838-8442**
Mon-Sat 10am-5pm www.livingreen.com
Complete line of natural mattresses and bedding products. Rating applies to linens, mattresses, and bedding.

Organic Rush ✐✐✐✐
962 Mission St. South Pasadena 91030 · **626-799-8099**
Mon by appt. Tue-Sat 11am-6pm Sun 12pm-5pm www.organicrush.com
Organic beds, bedding, and linens for babies and adults. Rating applies to linens, mattresses, and bedding.

PJs Sleep Company ✐
415 N. Fairfax Ave. LA 90036 · **323-782-9767**
Mon-Fri 10am-7pm Sat-Sun 10am-6pm www.pjssleep.com
Carries organic fiber bedding, mattresses, and pajamas; recycles old mattresses. Rating applies to mattresses and bedding.

Soft Forest ✐✐✐✐
146 S. Lake Ave. Ste. 106 Pasadena 91101 · **626-796-1805**
Mon-Sat 9:30am-6pm Sun 12pm-5pm www.softforest.com
Carries linens, towels, robes, socks, shawls, hair wraps, and accessories; all bamboo, naturally antibacterial and allergen-free. Rating applies to linens.

What you choose to buy for your home has a direct effect on both your personal health and the health of the planet. Many conventional pieces of furniture use formaldehyde as a binder, are coated with toxic finishes, use synthetic fillers, and can off-gas harmful chemicals. But there are a growing number of alternatives available that are both more healthful and sustainably produced.

To avoid chemicals from new materials and save money, shop at unfinished wood furniture stores and finish the items with plant-based, natural finishes. Look for wood products that have the Forest Steward-ship Council (FSC) seal indicating they come from sustainably man-aged forests. Consider buying used furniture items but avoid all pieces containing vinyl (PVC) and pieces that may contain lead-based paint.

Wall-to-wall carpeting may look and feel pretty but the nylon variety is made from a chemical stew that takes a long time to fully off-gas. This can cause irritation to babies, children, and anyone who is chemically sensitive. When possible, look for all-wool carpeting with natural fiber backing made of jute or latex. Better still, choose carpeting made from 100% post-consumer recycled food and drink containers or other materials. Not only does its manufacture keep plastic out of the landfill, it is superior to lower grade virgin fibers on a number of counts—fewer emissions, better stain resistance, increased color fastness.

Check into other flooring alternatives too—recycled-content tile, cork, sustainably harvested wood, real linoleum, and area rugs made with natural materials. Many companies offer alternatives to standard fibers: jute, sisal, bamboo, and seagrass are among the most common.

The stores listed here are evaluated based on the percentage of furniture, flooring, carpeting, and/or décor sold that is sustainably manufactured; sustainably manufactured and locally produced; nontoxic or low-toxic; made with renewable, natural, or recycled materials—or some combina-tion of these.

> ✐ at least 25% of products sold meet the above criteria.
>
> ✐✐ at least 50% of products sold meet the above criteria.
>
> ✐✐✐ at least 75% of products sold meet the above criteria.
>
> ✐✐✐✐ at least 90% of products sold meet the above criteria.

Andrianna Shamaris ✐
3835 Cross Creek Rd. Ste. 9 Malibu 90265 • **310-456-2243**
Mon-Sat 10am-6pm Sun 11am-6pm www.andriannashamaris.com
Indonesian furniture handmade from recycled teak, bamboo, and some iron/metal.

At Home Naturally ✐✐✐
Sherman Oaks • **818-988-4441**
By appt. www.athomenaturally.com
Provides organic, healthy, natural, and fair trade carpets, rugs, flooring
products, and furniture for the entire home and family.

Bamboo 2000 ✐✐✐✐
420 S. First St. Burbank 91502 • **800-311-1116**
By appt. www.bamboo2000.com
Flooring made from bamboo, cork, and reclaimed wood. Services include
sales, installation, sanding, and finishing.

Cisco Brothers ✐✐
440 N. La Brea Ave. LA 90036 • **323-932-1155**
5955 S. Western Ave. LA 90047 • **866-247-2652**
474 S. Arroyo Pkwy. Pasadena 91105 • **626-584-1273**
Hours vary by location www.ciscohome.net
Chemical-free furniture handcrafted in Los Angeles from sustainably
harvested alder.

Cliff Spencer Furniture Maker ✐✐✐✐
13435 Beach Ave. Marina Del Rey 90292 • **310-699-6013**
By appt. www.cliffspencer.net
Custom-made furniture and cabinetry using FSC certified wood, reclaimed
lumber; nontoxic, water- and plant oil-based finishes.

Contempo Floor Coverings ✐
902 S. Barrington Ave. LA 90049 • **310-826-8063**
2460 Overland Ave. LA 90064 • **310-837-8110**
Hours vary by location www.contempofloorcoverings.com
Environmentally-friendly, nontoxic flooring and carpeting.

Culver Furniture ✐
4366 Sepulveda Blvd. Culver City 90230 • **310-397-6734**
Mon-Sat 9:30am-6pm Sun 12pm-5pm www.culverfurniture.com
Unfinished, formaldehyde-free, and FSC certified wood furniture;
environmentally-friendly paints, stains, and finishes.

DAO (Design Around Objects) ✐
8767 Beverly Blvd. LA 90048 • **310-289-8717**
Mon-Fri 10am-6pm Sat 11am-6pm Sun by appt. www.daohome.com
Home furnishings and accessories made from reclaimed, recycled, and
naturally felled wood; local artisan influence on design; objets d'art.

Discover Flooring ✐✐
1149 N. La Brea Ave. LA 90038 • **323-436-6298**
Mon-Fri 8am-5pm Sat 8am-4pm www.discoverflooring.com
Eco-friendly flooring: FSC certified hardwood; bamboo, cork, linoleum,
marmoleum, recycled glass, natural carpets.

Dom LA Showroom ✐
9030 Wilshire Blvd. Beverly Hills 90211 • **310-246-9790**
Mon-Fri 9am-6pm Sat 11am-5:30pm www.domshowrooms.com
Carries Italian furnishings and Valcucine energy- and water-efficient green
kitchen design accessories and hardware.

Ekla Home (Denizen Design Gallery) 🌿🌿🌿🌿
8600 Venice Blvd. LA 90034 • **310-838-1959**
Tue-Sat 11am-6pm Sun 12pm-5pm www.denizendesigngallery.com
Wood furniture reclaimed from industrial buildings in Los Angeles; nontoxic organic sofas, chairs, and beds.

French General 🌿🌿🌿
1621 Vista del Mar Ave. Hollywood 90028 • **323-462-0818**
By appt. www.frenchgeneral.com
Household window treatments, bedding, and décor items made from hemp; hemp-based oil paints. Offers craft classes using recycled materials.

Green Wood Installations 🌿🌿🌿🌿
570 E. Las Flores Dr. Altadena 91001 • **818-521-5762**
By appt. www.greenwoodinstallations.com
Woodwork and cabinetry using sustainable materials and functional, ecological design.

Ikea 🌿
600 N. San Fernando Blvd. Burbank 91502 • **818-842-4532**
20700 S. Avalon Blvd. Carson 90746 • **310-527-4532**
Daily 10am-9pm www.ikea.com
Wide selection of home furnishings made from renewable, recovered, and reused materials.

InterfaceFlor 🌿🌿🌿
1343 Fourth St. Santa Monica 90401 • **310-451-4191**
Mon-Fri 9am-5pm Sat by appt. www.interfaceflor.com
Innovative modular carpet tiles for the home and office; proactive environmental responsibility and commitment to eco-design.

Kelly LaPlante Organic Interior Design 🌿🌿🌿🌿
1501 Main St. Ste. 101 Venice 90291 • **310-581-6450**
Mon-Sat 10am-6pm Sun by appt. www.kellylaplante.com
Eco-friendly furniture and interior design.

Kellygreen Design & Home 🌿🌿🌿🌿
4008 Santa Monica Blvd. LA 90029 • **323-660-1099**
Tue-Sun 11am-7pm www.kellygreendesign.net
Eco-friendly products for a green home and lifestyle.

Linoleum City 🌿
4849 Santa Monica Blvd. Hollywood 90029 • **323-469-0063**
Mon-Thu 8:30am-5:30pm Fri 8:30am-7pm Sat 9am-5pm www.linoleumcity.com
Selection of cork, bamboo, linoleum, carpet, and recycled rubber flooring.

Livingreen Store & Gallery 🌿🌿🌿🌿
10000 Culver Blvd. Culver City 90232 • **310-838-8442**
Mon-Sat 10am-5pm www.livingreen.com
Environmentally-friendly flooring; green furniture and décor products.

Media Noche 🌿
1200 N. Alvarado St. LA 90026 • **213-353-4995**
Tue-Sat 11am-7pm Sun 12pm-5pm www.myspace.com/shopmedianoche
Solid wood furniture made with reclaimed materials; vintage furniture. Found object art.

Modern Child 🌿🌿🌿
610 Hampton Dr. Venice 90291 • **310-452-6961**
Tue-Sat 12pm-6pm www.modernchild.net

Modern Child (cont.)

Sustainably designed furniture, décor, and clothing items for children, babies, and home.

Mortise & Tenon 🌿

729 Pacific Coast Hwy. Hermosa Beach 90254 • **310-374-8108**
446 S. La Brea Ave. LA 90036 • **323-937-7654**
Hours vary by location www.mortisetenon.com
Handcrafted reclaimed wood furniture: chairs, tables, armoires, bureaus, and home office systems.

Natural Carpet Company, The 🌿🌿🌿

2014 S. Lincoln Blvd. Venice 90291 • **310-664-1420**
Mon-Fri 9am-5pm Sat 9:30am-4pm www.naturalcarpetcompany.com
Specializes in handmade natural fiber carpets, rugs, wallcoverings, and furnishings; natural wool, hemp, bamboo, silk, seagrass, cotton.

Nikzad Import, Inc. 🌿🌿

538 N. La Cienaga Blvd. LA 90048 • **310-657-6662**
Mon-Fri 8am-5pm www.nikzadflooring.com
Sells rapidly renewable natural hardwood flooring.

Organic Rush 🌿🌿🌿

962 Mission St. South Pasadena 91030 • **626-799-8099**
Tue-Sat 11am-6pm Sun 12pm-5pm www.organicrush.com
Sustainably manufactured children's beds, cribs, changing tables, high chairs, and shelves.

RC Green by Robert Craymer 🌿🌿🌿

300 S. La Brea Ave. LA 90036 • **323-933-6499**
Mon-Fri 10am-6pm Sat 10am-5pm Sun by appt. 11am-4pm
www.robertcraymer.com
All natural, green furniture designer and manufacturer; interior design services.

Smith & Hawken 🌿🌿

370 N. Canon Dr. Beverly Hills 90210 • **310-247-0737**
780 S. Sepulveda Blvd. El Segundo 90245 • **310-726-7341**
519 S. Lake Ave. Pasadena 91101 • **626-584-0644**
Hours vary by location www.smithandhawken.com
Sustainably harvested timber furniture; natural and organic gardening supplies.

Stranger Furniture 🌿🌿🌿

3202 E. Foothill Blvd. Ste. 6H Pasadena 91107 • **626-405-0927**
By appt. www.strangerfurniture.com
Furniture made with sustainable materials: salvaged wood, recycled lumber, timber from well-managed forests, nontoxic finishes.

Tara Home 🌿

6810 Melrose Ave. LA 90038 • **323-933-4477**
245 Main St. Venice 90291 • **310-452-8272**
Mon 11am-5pm Tue-Sat 11am-7pm Sun 11am-5pm www.tara-home.com
Combines antique materials, reclaimed teak and rosewood, and architectural elements to create contemporary furnishings.

Todd Birch Floor Coverings 🌿🌿

2535 W. 237th St. Ste. 109 Torrance 90505 • **310-326-7629**
Mon-Fri 8am-6pm Sat by appt.
Natural linoleum, bamboo, sustainably harvested wood flooring, and carpets made from corn fiber, sisal, and seagrass.

Twenty Gauge 🍃🍃🍃

3225 Helms Ave. LA 90034 • **310-945-5438**
Mon-Sat 10am-7pm Sun 10am-6pm www.twentygauge.com
Eco-friendly steel furniture restoration using powder coating; desks,
credenzas, file cabinets, lockers, tables, bookcases, and other items.

Universal Hardwood Flooring and Moulding, Inc. 🍃

10889 Venice Blvd. LA 90034 • **310-839-9663**
Mon-Fri 8am-5:30pm Sat 9am-3pm www.universalwood.com
Environmentally-friendly wood flooring and products. Offers cork, reclaimed
and recovered wood, zero-VOC finishes, and formaldehyde-free adhesives.

Vernare 🍃🍃🍃🍃

607 N. Huntley Dr. West Hollywood 90069 • **310-659-6400**
Mon-Fri 10am-5pm Sat-Sun by appt. www.vernare.net
High-end multiline interior/exterior showroom specializing in green and
sustainable furniture, textiles, lighting, carpets, garden features, and
accessories.

Viesso 🍃🍃🍃

2834 Colorado Ave. Ste. 53 Santa Monica 90404 • **310-453-3604**
Mon-Fri 12pm-7pm Sat 12pm-5pm www.viesso.com
Custom-made furniture using FSC certified wood, bamboo, recycled or
natural fibers, and water-based glues and stains.

Forest Stewardship Council (FSC)

An international network promoting responsible management
of the world's forests. Through consultative processes, it sets
international standards for responsible forest management. The
FSC label provides assurance to the consumer that the wood has
been sustainably harvested.

Polyvinyl Chloride (PVC)

PVC is commonly used for plastic pipes and outdoor furniture. It is
seldom, if ever, recyclable. PVC plastics often contain phthalates,
chemicals that make the plastic soft and flexible. Phthalates are
known hormone disruptors and possible carcinogens.

Volatile Organic Compounds (VOCs)

VOCs are emitted as gases from certain solids or liquids. VOCs
include a variety of chemicals, some of which may have short-
and long-term adverse health effects. VOCs are especially
hazardous indoors where concentrations may be up to ten times
higher than outdoors. That "new carpet smell" and the smell of
fresh paint indicate the presence of VOCs.

Building Materials and Supplies

Almost every part of home building and furnishing can be made more environmentally sound. It may take more effort to find green building materials, but they are available and using them is worth the effort.

Green building materials save water, energy, and other natural resources. They offer better indoor air quality due to the presence of less-toxic paints and finishes. Green products include those made from recycled materials such as glass or metal, as well as sustainably harvested wood, or easily replenished materials like bamboo.

Specific examples of green building materials that are more and more easily obtainable include Agboard, a wood substitute made from agricultural waste or agricultural byproducts: recycled cotton (post-industrial denim) insulation; recycled rubber or plastic shingles; natural lime and clay plaster; tile made from recycled windshields or recycled bottles; recycled rubber flooring; linoleum (made from linseed oil, pine resin, and wood flour) flooring; recycled-content carpeting; and natural (non-vinyl) wall coverings.

To determine which building material and supply centers to include in the guide, we looked at the percentage of products and materials sold by these companies that are sustainably manufactured, nontoxic or low-toxic, and/or made with renewable, natural, or recycled materials.

   🌿   at least 25% of products/materials meet the above criteria.

   🌿🌿   at least 50% of products/materials meet the above criteria.

   🌿🌿🌿   at least 75% of products/materials meet the above criteria.

   🌿🌿🌿🌿   at least 90% of products/materials meet the above criteria.

All Shades of Green 🌿🌿🌿🌿
3038 Rowena Ave. LA 90039 • **323-665-7454**
Mon-Sat 11am-7pm Sun 11am-6pm www.allshadesofgreen.net
Offers reclaimed wood building materials, recycled content countertops and cabinetry, cork and bamboo flooring, dual flush toilets.

Anawalt Lumber 🌿
1001 N. Highland Ave. Hollywood 90038 • **323-464-1600**
11060 W. Pico Blvd. LA 90064 • **310-478-0324**
641 N. Robertson Blvd. West Hollywood 90069 • **310-652-6202**
Hours vary by location www.anawaltlumber.com
Carries some green building products: FSC certified pine, SFI certified decking.

Architectural Coatings + Design Center (ac + dc) 🌿🌿🌿🌿
18424 Ventura Blvd. Tarzana 91356 • **818-757-3900**
Mon-Fri 7:30am-4pm Sat 9am-2pm www.acplusdc.com
Provides diverse selection of environmentally responsible interior paints and plasters.

Big Brand Water Filter, Inc. ✑✑✑✑
21947 Plummer St. Chatsworth 91311 • **818-340-7258**
Mon-Fri 8am-5pm www.bigbrandwater.com
Offers water purification and disinfection. Uses recycled packing materials.

Busy Bee Hardware ✑
1521 Santa Monica Blvd. Santa Monica 90404 • **310-395-1158**
Mon-Fri 8am-6pm Sat 9am-4:45pm
Family-owned hardware store carrying some eco-friendly products.

Crown City Hardware ✑
1047 N. Allen Ave. Pasadena 91104 • **626-794-0234**
Mon-Fri 7am-7pm Sat 8:30am-5:30pm Sun 10am-3pm
www.crowncityhardware.com
Carries Plan-It Hardware line of environmentally-friendly home
improvement products.

Epoxy Green ✑✑✑✑
602 Venice Blvd. Venice 90291 • **310-578-2123**
Mon-Sat 10am-6pm
Sustainable building and green home improvement materials for residential
and commercial projects. Green home design solutions; consulting
services.

Franklin's Hardware ✑
21936 Ventura Blvd. Woodland Hills 91364 • **818-347-6800**
Mon-Sat 8am-6pm Sun 9am-5pm www.franklinshardware.net
Plan-It Hardware line available; offers variety of sustainable home
improvement products.

H3Environmental ✑✑✑✑
818-766-1787
By appt. www.h3environmental.com
Air and water filtration products: under-counter triple water purifiers, whole
house chloramine removing filters, HEPA/carbon air filters with exclusive
EMF shielding.

Jill's Paint ✑✑✑✑
3534 Larga Ave. LA 90039 • **323-664-9067**
Mon-Fri 7am-5pm Sat 9am-5pm www.jillspaint.net
Carries no-VOC and low-VOC paint, prep, and paint stripper products;
nontoxic cleaning supplies.

Koontz Hardware ✑
8914 Santa Monica Blvd. West Hollywood 90069 • **310-652-0123**
Mon-Fri 8am-7pm Sat 8am-5:30pm Sun 10am-5pm www.koontz.com
Plan-It Hardware product line available.

Livingreen Store & Gallery ✑✑✑✑
10000 Culver Blvd. Culver City 90232 • **310-838-8442**
Mon-Sat 10am-5pm www.livingreen.com
Wide selection of counter tiles, coatings and wallcoverings, flooring, paint,
shower accessories, energy efficient lightbulbs; green building literature.

North Hollywood Hardware ✑
11847 Ventura Blvd. Studio City 91604 • **818-980-2453**
Mon-Fri 8:30am-6pm Sat 9am-5:30pm Sun 10am-4pm
www.northhollywoodhardware.com
Offers Plan-It Hardware product line: energy and water conservation
products, greener options for home cleaning and improvement projects.

Resource Conservation Group 🍃🍃🍃🍃
8981 Sunset Blvd. Ste. 312 West Hollywood 90069 • **213-278-2815**
By appt www.resourceconservationgroup.com
Offer reclaimed building materials: bricks, lumber, wood flooring.

SunAire 🍃🍃🍃🍃
12904 Riverside Dr. Sherman Oaks 91423 • **800-208-1137**
Mon-Thu 10am-3pm Fri 10am-2pm Sat-Sun by appt www.sunaire.com
Specializes in sale and installation of solar tube lighting and solar powered attic ventilation systems.

Virgil's Hardware Home Center 🍃
520 N. Glendale Ave. Glendale 91206 • **818-242-1104**
Mon-Fri 8am-7pm Sat 8am-6pm Sun 9am-5pm
Carries Plan-It Hardware products: energy and water conservation items, eco-friendly cleaning supplies, home improvement merchandise.

Salvaged Architectural Elements

The purchase and reuse of recycled and salvaged goods and materials has grown more popular as the world's resources are getting depleted and landfills overflow. Unwanted items and what may have once been demolition waste products are finding new life at salvage yards and "resource malls."

You may find the perfect door, window, or claw foot bathtub at one of the businesses we have listed below. By doing so, you will have taken another step on the path to a zero-waste society, a key goal of the organizations and businesses we've found.

Although salvaged materials represent the truest form of recycling, their content may or may not be "green." They may have lead paint or other toxic finishes, or they could contain formaldehyde or other toxins. For this reason, we cannot offer leaf awards in this category. Nevertheless, these businesses deserve our strong support in that they don't require the use of new materials, they keep used materials out of the landfill, and the salvaged items can be refurbished with natural, nontoxic materials or finishes. To further evaluate each business, we also looked at what percentage of the overall salvaged products they carry were locally sourced.

B & B Lumber
8040 Lankershim Blvd. North Hollywood 91605 • **818-983-1645**
Mon-Sat 8am-5pm
Carries used lumber and sustainable building materials.

Barnwood Group Demolition and Construction
Santa Ana • **714-769-2246**
By appt.
Provides deconstruction and restoration services; sells used barnwood, lumber, and other home construction materials. Serves greater Los Angeles area.

Big Daddy's Antiques
13100 S. Broadway LA 90061 • **310-769-6600**
Mon-Sat 9am-5pm www.bdantiques.com
Architectural salvage services; repairs made for custom furnishings.

European Reclamation & Earth Ceramics
4520 Brazil St. LA 90039 • **818-241-2152**
Mon-Fri 8am-4pm, Sat-Sun by appt www.historictile.com
Carries reclaimed architectural pieces from Spain, France, and England.

Freeway Building Materials
1124 S. Boyle Ave. LA 90023 • **323-261-8904**
Mon-Sat 8am-4pm
Salvaged building materials; antiques from the 1940s and earlier.

Habitat for Humanity Home Improvement Store
17700 S. Figueroa St. Gardena 90248 • **310-323-5665**
Tue-Sat 9am-6pm www.shophabitat.org
Offers salvaged materials: doors, appliances, tile, furniture. Accepts donations of used building materials. Please call before dropping off.

Liz's Antique Hardware
453 S. La Brea Ave. LA 90036 • **323-939-4403**
Mon-Sat 10am-6pm www.lahardware.com
Carries vintage and contemporary door, window, and furniture hardware; lighting and accessories.

Los Angeles Online County Materials Exchange
900 S. Fremont Ave. Third Flr. Annex Alhambra 91803 • **888-253-2652**
www.ladpw.org/epd/lacomax
Free online service for conservation of landfill space. Find and post listings for reusable architectural elements.

Nuñez & Sons
4042 Cesar Chavez Ave. LA 90063 • **323-266-0518**
Mon-Sat 7am-5pm Sun 9am-1pm
Salvaged building material: used, construction grade lumber and plywood.

Olde Good Things
1800 S. Grand Ave. LA 90015 • **213-746-8600**
Mon-Sat 9am-6pm Sun 12pm-5pm www.oldegoodthings.com
Large warehouse and showroom offers recycled architectural and antique artifacts.

Pasadena Architectural Salvage
30 S. San Gabriel Blvd. Pasadena 91107 • **626-535-9655**
Tue-Sun 10am-6pm www.pasadenaarchitecturalsalvage.com
Offers architectural antiques circa 1880-1930s: glass doors, claw-footed bathtubs, stained glass windows; plumbing, lighting, doors, windows, gates, and more.

Reclaimed Wood Products
11655 Wicks St. Sun Valley 91352 • **818-508-0100**
By appt www.reclaimedwoodproducts.com
Large inventory of reclaimed wood products: stud materials, dimensional lumber, and custom millings.

Resource Conservation Group
8981 Sunset Blvd. Unit 312 West Hollywood 90069 • **213-278-2815**
By appt www.resourceconservationgroup.com

Resource Conservation Group (cont.)
High-quality, environmentally-friendly reclaimed building materials: flooring, lumber, and fencing.

ReUse People of America, The
LA • **310-946-3179**
Tue-Sat 9am-6pm www.thereusepeople.org
Nonprofit organization promoting building deconstruction practices: donation, salvage, and distribution services; project management and consultation.

Santa Fe Wrecking Co.
1600 S. Santa Fe Ave. LA 90021 • **213-623-3119**
Mon-Fri 8am-5pm Sat-Sun 9:30am-3pm www.santafewrecking.com
Buys and sells architectural salvage materials: doors, tubs, sinks, mantels, hardware, lighting, and more.

Scavenger's Paradise
5453 Satsuma Ave. North Hollywood 91601 • **323-877-7945**
Mon-Sat 10am-4:30pm www.scavengersparadise.com
Carries vintage and antique columns, iron, garden pieces, doors, windows, lighting, hardware, furniture, and stained glass.

SGV Habitat for Humanity Builder's Surplus Store
770 N. Fair Oaks Ave. Pasadena 91103 • **626-792-3838**
Tue-Sat 9am-5pm www.sgvhabitat.org
Home restoration, construction, and maintenance services. Sells new and used products: antique doors, windows, tile, and lighting materials.

Silver Lake Architectural Salvage
1065 Manzanita St. LA 90026 • **323-667-2875**
Tue-Sat 11am-5pm
Salvaged goods: cabinets, doors, windows, lighting, pedestal sinks, tubs, flooring, antique stoves, and hardware. Walk-through remodeling and consulting service.

Nurseries and Garden Supplies

GREENING YOUR SPACE

When doing your gardening and yardwork, check out the nurseries that offer organic options. Choosing organic plants, seeds and starts, soil, potting mixes, fertilizers, and pest control products will promote better stewardship of the land and create a healthier home environment for you.

The plants garden centers sell may come from small, local growers or from large ones scattered across the United States. The market has more or less split: small local retailers tend to buy and sell plants from small local growers, whereas the large growers tend to sell to big-box retailers.

Growers who meet specific standards may qualify for organic certification. In addition, two programs address sustainability within the nursery industry—VeriFlora and Circle of Life. Growers that demonstrate sustainable practices that can then be documented are eligible for certification. Such practices include integrated pest management, water conservation measures, habitat preservation, reduced use of plastics, and fair labor practices.

To determine which nurseries and garden centers to include in the guide, we checked into the percentage of plants sold that were grown organically and that were native to the region. In addition, we asked about the plant starts and the planting mixes sold. We also checked into the availability of nontoxic pest management solutions.

    ∅   At least 25% of relevant products meet the above criteria.

    ∅∅   At least 50% of relevant products meet the above criteria.

    ∅∅∅   At least 75% of relevant products meet the above criteria.

    ∅∅∅∅   At least 90% of relevant products meet the above criteria.

Anawalt Lumber *∅*
1001 N. Highland Ave. Hollywood 90038 • **323-464-1600**
11060 W. Pico Blvd. LA 90064 • **310-478-0324**
641 N. Robertson Blvd. West Hollywood 90069 • **310-652-6202**
Hours vary by location www.anawaltlumber.com
Nursery carries some organic soils, fertilizers, insecticides, and native plants.

Barrister's Garden Center *∅∅*
915 El Centro St. South Pasadena 91030 • **626-441-1323**
Tue-Sun 9am-5:30pm
Organic soils and fertilizers, nontoxic pest treatments, native plants.

California Nursery Specialties Cactus Ranch *∅∅∅*
Reseda • **818-894-5694**
Sat-Sun 11am-5pm
Water-wise grower. Sells large selection of cacti and succulents, all grown in organic soil.

Grow Your Own *∅∅∅∅*
3715 Cahuenga Blvd. Studio City 91604 • **818-985-4769**
Daily 11am-7pm www.hydrodiscountcenter.com
Organic soils, nutrients, growing mediums, base additives, pesticides, disease control and hydroponic equipment.

Million Trees LA *∅∅∅∅*
LA • **800-473-3652**
www.milliontreesla.org
Offers program through L.A. Department of Water & Power that provides up to seven free shade trees to every Los Angeles city resident who qualifies.

Sego Nursery, Inc. *∅*
12126 Burbank Blvd. Valley Village 91607 • **818-763-5711**
Mon-Sat 8am-5pm Sun 9am-4pm
Full-service, family-owned and -operated gardening center with organic starts and soils; some nontoxic pest management solutions.

Smith & Hawken *∅∅∅*
370 N. Canon Dr. Beverly Hills 90210 • **310-247-0737**
780 S. Sepulveda Blvd. El Segundo 90245 • **310-726-7341**
519 S. Lake Ave. Pasadena 91101 • **626-584-0644**
Hours vary by location www.smithandhawken.com

GREENING YOUR SPACE

Smith & Hawken (cont.)

Natural and organic garden supplies; sustainable home and garden décor; outdoor solar lighting.

Theodore Payne Foundation ✏✏✏✏

10459 Tuxford St. Sun Valley 91352 • **818-768-1802**
Seasonal hours www.theodorepayne.org
Nonprofit California native plant nursery. Sells plants, seeds, and books.

Virgil's Hardware Home Center ✏

520 N. Glendale Ave. Glendale 91206 • **818-242-1104**
Mon-Fri 8am-7pm Sat 8am-6pm Sun 9am-5pm
Carries organic fertilizers and soils.

✏ GREEN TIP

Look for compostable pots when you purchase plants at garden centers. Although relatively new, they are available. Materials used to make the containers include rice hulls and other biodegradable plant-based materials. When you have to purchase plastic pots, check with garden centers and farmers' market growers to see if they can reuse containers that would otherwise be thrown away.

✏ DID YOU KNOW?

Every year, the horticultural industry disposes of:

- 130,000,000 pounds of greenhouse film
- 140,000,000 pounds of plastic pots
- 170,000,000 pounds of plastic ground cover

(Source: Texas A&M University)

GREENING YOUR SPACE

Garden and Landscape Design and Services

Well-planned landscaping can conserve water, attract and protect wildlife, keep your house cooler in summer, save you money, and even feed you!

Land that is cared for naturally feels better and can actually take less maintenance in the long run. In contrast, a yard that is maintained with pesticides and other chemicals can pose a threat to your family and pets, while artificially keeping plants alive with soil-depleting chemical fertilizers.

Our list consists of garden and landscape designers, landscape architects, arborists, and garden maintenance companies and workers whose main or sole purpose is offering environmentally sound gardening and landscaping services to homeowners and other non-commercial customers.

Businesses listed may offer one or more of the following: organic gardening services, planting, and maintenance of native and drought-tolerant species, use of Integrated Pest Management (IPM) techniques, designing water conservation or reclamation systems into garden plans, and/or creating wildlife habitat gardens.

> To be listed, at least 25% of time and/or projects in a given year must be devoted to environmentally sound landscaping and gardening practices. We also looked at how long the principal or firm had been providing sustainable landscape and gardening services. Note that some of these businesses and/or their employees may also be LEED® (Leadership in Energy and Environmental Design) accredited.

ALD Landscape
1821 Lincoln Blvd. Venice 90291 • **310-578-8488**
By appt. www.aldco.com
Design/build firm specializing in drought-tolerant, sustainable gardens, hardscapes, outdoor rooms, patios; uses sustainable wood and recycled concrete.

Artecho Architecture and Landscape Architecture
1639 Electric Ave. Ste. A Venice 90291 • **310-399-4794**
By appt. www.artecho.com
Residential, commerical, and landscape architecture using recycled materials and incorporating contemporary green design.

C & K Landscape Design Inc.
P.O. Box 441 Topanga 90043 • **818-353-7030**
By appt. www.candklandscapedesign.com
Designs, builds, and maintains custom residential landscaping; specializes in low-water, low-maintenance, and sustainable outdoor living spaces.

Campbell & Campbell
1425 Fifth St. Santa Monica 90401 • **310-458-1011**
By appt. www.campbellcampbell.com
Specializes in sustainable urban design, architecture, landscape architecture, and planning projects.

Campion Walker Garden Design, Inc.
1044 Palms Blvd. Venice 90291 • **310-392-3535**
By appt. www.campionwalker.com
Full-service landscape design and installation; garden maintenance; specializes in drought-tolerant plants.

Comfort Zones Garden Design
3782 Redwood Ave. LA 90066 • **310-398-0406**
By appt.
Garden design using organics, native plants; sustainability consulting, xeriscaping, integrated pest management, wildlife habitat.

Deming Design, LLC
LA • **310-694-0711**
By appt. www.demingdesign.com
Sustainable interior and landscape design for commercial and residential applications.

Dennis Design Group
915 1/2 South Holt Ave. LA 90035 • **310-493-3972**
By appt. www.dennisdesigngroup.com
Sustainable interior design, architecture, and landscaping; feng shui.
LEED AP.

Dezine, Inc.
607 N. Huntley Dr. West Hollywood 90069 • **310-360-3961**
By appt. www.dezinela.com
Interior and landscape design firm specializing in custom green
environments.

Dry Design
5727 Venice Blvd. LA 90019 • **323-954-9084**
By appt. www.drydesign.com
Landscape architecture and building design firm integrating surrounding
environmental elements into projects.

Environmental Concepts, Inc.
5519 S. Centinela Ave. LA 90066 • **310-302-9292**
By appt. www.envconcepts.com
Landscape and installation contractors using organic and natural
pesticides.

Flower to the People, Inc.
11409 Charnock Rd. Mar Vista 90066 • **310-312-5076**
Mon-Fri 9am-5pm www.flowertothepeople.com
Exterior designers utilizing sustainable, natural plants and materials with
water- and energy-efficient practices.

Gabriela Yariv Landscape Design
606 Venice Blvd. Ste. G Venice 90291 • **310-301-7234**
By appt. www.gabrielayariv.com
Full-service residential garden design firm offering site observation and
environmentally sensitive landscapes.

Garden Retro
North Hollywood • **818-765-1704**
By appt. www.gardenretro.com
Landscape design and garden maintenance using all natural, organic
products and sustainable practices.

Gardens by Mary Kay
Santa Monica • **310-395-1081**
By appt.
Consultation, design, and installation with a specialty in Mediterranean and
Californian natives, xeriscaping, Weathermatic systems, and sustainable
gardens.

Gary's Greenery, Inc.
2364 Kerwood Ave. LA 90064 • **310-991-2331**
By appt. www.garysgreenery.com
Designs and installs sustainable outdoor spaces. Uses green mulches,
organic soil conditioners, and edible gardens.

Gaudet Design Group
1756 22nd St. Santa Monica 90404 • **310-828-4908**
By appt. www.gaudetdesigngroup.com
Landscape architecture professionals using xeriscape principles.

Harmony Garden

Valley Village • **818-505-9783**
By appt. www.harmonygardens.net
Landscape architect providing garden design consultation; specializes in drought-tolerant landscapes.

Heart Beet Gardening

LA • **310-460-9365**
By appt. www.heartbeetgardening.com
Designs, builds, and maintains organic vegetable and edible gardens for residences and schools.

Homegrown

LA • **323-336-1284**
By appt. www.homegrownlosangeles.com
Designs and maintains organic gardens for private residences throughout Los Angeles.

Invisible Gardener, The

11902 Whitewater Ln. Malibu 90265 • **310-457-4438**
By appt. www.invisiblegardener.com
Consultant for organic lawn, tree, and rose care; natural pest control.

Jettscapes Landscape

Santa Monica • **310-392-4375**
By appt.
Designs and installs sustainable, regionally appropriate, water-efficient gardens.

JN Landscaping and Maintenance

12335 Santa Monica Blvd. Ste. 301 LA 90025 • **310-577-9378**
Mon-Fri by appt.
Offers organic fertilizer and mulching, planting of native and drought-resistant plants, drip irrigation, and soil amending.

Joan Booke Landscape Contractor

Pacific Palisades • **310-459-6976**
By appt.
Installs organic and chemical-free gardens using reused materials; services include irrigation, hardscape, lighting, and installation-removal.

Kathy's Landscaping

Venice • **310-399-7390**
By appt.
Design, consultation and installation; specializes in drought-resistant landscapes.

Kitchen Garden

3922 Glencoe Ave. Venice 90291 • **310-908-2345**
By appt.
Designs and installs edible organic gardens.

Knowlton Oaks

LA • **818-957-8432**
By appt.
Oak tree specialist; residential work, no removals, only organic methods.

L.A. Design Associates, Inc.

1601 Abbot Kinney Blvd. Venice 90291 • **310-455-6026**
By appt. www.ladainc.com

L.A. Design Associates, Inc. (cont.)
Sustainably oriented design firm practicing landscape architecture and site planning.

Le Quattro Stagioni
11693 San Vicente Blvd. Ste. 502 LA 90049 • **310-452-5064**
By appt.
Garden restoration and maintenance using nontoxic products, beneficial insects, water efficiency, and natural composts, mulches, and fertilizers.

Linda Estrin Garden Design
Oak Park • **818-707-0031**
By appt. www.legardendesign.googlepages.com
Sustainable landscape design, planting, and hardscape. Mediterranean and native plants, sustainable materials for responsible water and energy use.

Mark Tessier Landscape Architecture
1424 Fourth St. Ste. 234 Santa Monica 90401 • **310-395-3595**
By appt. www.marktessier.com
Full-service landscape architect for residential, institutional, and public sectors; organics, water conservation and reclamation; wildlife habitat gardens.

Mayita Dinos
Culver City • **310-838-5959**
By appt. www.mayitadinos.com
Landscape design and consultation; low-impact hardscape, softscape, and water conservation. Recommends and manages landscape contractors.

Mook's Arbor Systems, Inc.
Woodland Hills • **818-888-8742**
By appt.
Certified arborist. Specializes in diagnosis and treatment of turf, shrub, plant, and tree conditions.

New Growth Landscaping Co.
P.O. Box 3224 Covina 91722 • **626-967-4753**
By appt.
Natural landscaping and maintenance services; organic soils, fertilizers, and pest management products.

Organic Edible Gardens
LA • **310-471-7592**
By appt. www.organicediblegardens.com
Designs and maintains organic, sustainable herb and vegetable gardens year-round.

Quiet Garden Landscaping
11150 Ventura Blvd. Studio City 91604 • **818-515-4874**
www.quietgardenlandscaping.com
Full-service landscaping service using only battery, electrical, or conventional hand tool gardening equipment; xeriscaping and water conservation.

RK Landscape, Inc.
2318 Pier Ave. Santa Monica 90405 • **310-452-0007**
By appt.
Landscape contracting provides sustainable gardening, organic plants, and detail maintenance.

Robert Cornell and Associates
1211 Sinaloa Ave. Pasadena 91104 • **626-398-5581**
By appt. www.robertcornell.com
Environmentally sensitive landscape design and installation. Over 25 years experience.

SB Garden Design
2801 Clearwater St. LA 90039 • **323-660-1034**
Mon-Fri 9am-5pm www.sbgardendesign.com
Residential landscape design using sustainable design principles, native and water-efficient plants.

Sowing Machine, The
LA • **310-339-4220**
By appt.
Designs and installs wood and masonary structures, ponds, and softscapes; specializes in drought-tolerant gardens.

Stephanie Wilson Blanc Garden Design
Pacific Palisades • **310-459-3131**
By appt.
Designs habitat gardens emphasizing the use of native plants and sustainable practices.

StudioX
1503 Cahuenga Blvd. LA 90028 • **323-464-5316**
By appt. www.xavierstudiox.com
Interior and landscape design fusing elements of art and ecology to create minimal impact on the natural world.

Swamp Pink Landscape Design
125 N. Orange Dr. LA 90036 • **323-394-9693**
By appt. www.swamppink.com
Sustainable landscape design solutions and community-based conservation projects.

Terra Bella Landscape Design
LA • **310-398-3878**
By appt. www.terrabellalandscape.com
Modern residential landscape design specializing in xeriscape and low-maintenance gardens.

Tikotsky and Associates Landscape Architects
11969 Iowa Ave. LA 90025 • **310-820-3787**
By appt. www.tikotsky-associates.com
Sustainable landscape design using renewable energy, graywater, edible gardens, green roof systems, and water collection.

Tree Preservation, Inc.
South Pasadena • **626-441-4555**
By appt.
Eco-friendly irrigation, garden work, and landscaping. Serves all of Southern California.

Trilling Landscape and Design
11664 National Blvd. Ste. 353 LA 90064 • **310-390-4648**
By appt. www.trillinglandscape.com
Landscape design focused on native, drought-resistant plants; high-efficiency irrigation, composting, and vegetable gardens.

True Gardener

1925 Century Park E Ste. 2000 LA 90067 • **818-427-0442**
By appt.
Organic garden consultation, design, installation, irrigation, and maintenance.

Water's Edge Gardening

1637 Westerly Terrace LA 90026 • **213-713-7157**
By appt.
Certified arborist and horticulturalist offering consultation, maintenance, and design services; uses native plants.

Wild Gardens

LA • **310-390-3778**
By appt.
Landscape designer with specialty in water-efficient gardens.

William Hefner Architecture

5820 Wilshire Blvd. Ste. 500 LA 90036 • **323-931-1365**
By appt. www.williamhefner.com
Custom sustainable architecture; interior and landscape design using active and passive solar, xeriscaping, and natural materials and products. LEED AP.

Xeric Designs

Santa Monica • **424-645-9293**
By appt. www.xericdesigns.com
Landscape designer and installer specializing in native species and low-water landscaping.

Yard Design

1203 N. Sweetzer Ave. Ste. 314 LA 90069 • **323-822-7525**
By appt. www.yarddesign.net
Landscape design, installation, and maintenance using eco-friendly irrigation and native plants.

✐ GREEN TIP

Tired of mowing that lawn? Does your water bill make you see red instead of green? Maybe it's time for xeriscaping, an environmentally conscious form of landscaping that uses indigenous and drought-tolerant plants, drip irrigation systems, and mulch to conserve as much water as possible.

✐ GREEN TIP

Still hungry for change? Why not apply the principles of permaculture to your yard? Permaculture adopts methods and practices from ecology, appropriate technology, and sustainable agriculture providing the techniques to establish productive environments to supply food, energy, shelter, and other material and nonmaterial needs.

Alternative Energy Contractors

You may be in a position to directly affect your carbon footprint and consumption of conventional energy by using alternative energy. The companies listed below specialize in alternative energy systems: design, installation, service, and/or repair. They may offer free consultation to help you decide which is the best energy alternative for you. (Also, you might check with your utility company for a similar consultation and alternative energy plan. Likewise, utility companies as well as city, state, and federal agencies sometimes offer help in the form of rebates and tax incentives to homeowners who qualify.)

Because the work these groups do is so varied (from design to repair), they have not been leaf-awarded. However, to be included in the guide, at least 25% of their total annual number of projects must deal primarily with the installation, repair, servicing, or design of alternative energy systems. We also looked at how many years experience they have in providing alternative energy products and services.*

*Greenopia is not responsible for the outcome or performance of the work/service/products/materials of any listed company or individual. When hiring a professional or tradesperson, it is up to you to verify the experience and skills of the listed practitioners. For California, you can check on the status of a contractor's license by going to www.cslb. ca.gov. These businesses were selected and reviewed for residential projects only. We did not investigate, nor is the guide intended to cover, commercial contractors.

Photovoltaic (PV)

A solar power technology that uses solar cells to convert light from the sun into electricity.

Absolutely Solar
LA • **323-665-3192**
By appt. www.absolutelysolar.com
Design and installation of solar photovoltaic systems.

ACME Environmental Group
3200 Airport Ave. Ste. 18 Santa Monica 90405 • **310-397-2199**
By appt. www.acmegreen.com
Specializes in radiant heating, solar thermal energy, high-efficiency boilers, and high-velocity air conditioning.

Advanced Solar
818-894-8580
By appt. www.advancedsolarpower.com
Solar water heating, pool heating specialists.

Akeena Solar
22661 Lambert St. Ste. 204 Lake Forest 92630 • **888-253-3628**
By appt. www.akeena.net

Akeena Solar (cont.)
Design and integration of solar power systems for residential and commercial applications. Serves all of Southern California.

All Valley Solar, Inc.
12128 Sherman Way North Hollywood 91605 • **800-400-7780**
By appt. www.allvalleysolar.com
Design, installation, and service for solar PV, hot water, and pool systems.

Ameco Solar
1480 E. 28th St. Signal Hill 90755 • **562-595-9570**
By appt. www.amecosolar.com
Design and installation of solar electric, hot water, and pool heating systems since 1974.

Auto & Marine Machine Shop
13110 Washington Blvd. Culver City 90066 • **310-823-4334**
Mon-Fri 8am-5:30pm
Installs solar powered lighting systems; designs, builds electric cars and motorcycles.

Bella Electric
10025 Burin Ave. Inglewood 90304 • **310-293-8569**
By appt. www.bellasolar.com
Full-service electrical company specializing in solar and wind power, electric car charging stations.

Buel Solar
415 S. Topanga Canyon Blvd. Unit 184 Topanga 90290 • **310-455-1288**
By appt. www.buelsolar.com
Residential and commercial photovoltaic solar system installation; solar energy power parts, kits.

California Green Designs
4900 Hesperia Ave. Encino 91316 • **888-422-4733**
Mon-Fri 8am-5pm www.ca-green.com
Designs and installs residential and commercial solar energy systems.

California Solar
65 W. Easy St. Ste. 103 Simi Valley 93065 • **805-522-2747**
Mon-Fri 7am-5pm www.californiasolar.com
Installation and design of solar pool heating, radiant heating, and solar electric systems.

Citizenrē Renu
Reserve online www.citizenre.net
Solar energy company that pays for, installs, owns, and operates residential solar systems, available for rent at a flat monthly fee.

Energy Efficiency Solar
308 West Monterey Ave. Pomona 91768 • **909-865-8561**
By appt. www.eesolar.com
Designs and installs energy-efficient systems using photovoltaic and solar electric technologies.

Enviro Plumbing
2633 Lincoln Blvd. Ste. 606 Santa Monica 90405 • **310-450-7208**
By appt. www.enviroplumbing.com
Specializes in installation of solar water heating, radiant floor heating, tankless water heaters, dual flush toilets, and water reclamation systems.

Environmental Solar Design, Inc.
11237 Magnolia Blvd. North Hollywood 91601 • **818-762-6624**
Mon-Fri 9am-5pm Sat 9am-1pm www.esolardesign.com
Design, installation, and service of solar panels, hot water, and solar electric systems.

Foxx Power
12120 Washington Blvd. Culver City 90066 • **877-369-9228**
Mon-Fri 9am-5:30pm www.foxxpower.com
Offers 100% green lithium battery solutions lasting 5-7 years.

Gaiam Real Goods Solar
Santa Monica • **888-212-5638**
By appt. www.realgoodssolar.com
Full-service residential solar design and installation.

Go Solar Company
145 S. Glen Oaks Blvd. Unit 435 Burbank 91502 • **818-566-6870**
By appt. www.solarexpert.com
Installs and repairs residential PV, solar pool heating, and solar hot water systems.

Golden Energy
2630 S. La Cienega Blvd. LA 90034 • **310-204-3900**
By appt. www.goldenenergy.com
Designs, installs, and sells renewable energy systems; solar, radiant heating, and whole-building energy modeling.

Jo-Mi Plumbing and Solar
2011 Sawtelle Blvd. LA 90025 • **310-473-8111**
By appt.
High-efficiency solar water heating, solar pool heating; plumbing services.

Lee Rhoads Solar Design, Consulting, and Sales
20044 Valley View Dr. Topanga 90290 • **310-455-2958**
By appt. www.solarconsulting.org
Designs and sells photovoltaic and thermal solar systems for domestic and commercial applications. Free consultation in Topanga area.

PacWind, Inc.
23930 Madison St. Torrance 90505 • **310-375-9952**
By appt. www.pacwind.net
Provides small vertical axis wind turbines (VAWT) converting wind energy to electrical power for residential and commercial application.

PermaCity Solar
11977 San Vicente Blvd. LA 90049 • **866-976-5279**
By appt. www.permacity.com
Designs and installs residential and commercial solar electric and solar thermal systems.

Solar Electrical Systems
742 Hampshire Rd. Ste. A Westlake Village 91361 • **866-747-6527**
Mon-Fri 8am-5pm www.solarelectricalsystems.com
Solar electrical system design and installation; residential and commercial services.

SolarCity
10451 Jefferson Blvd. Culver City 90232 • **310-362-7505**
Mon-Fri 9am-5pm www.solarcity.com
Designs, engineers, and installs solar electric systems; energy efficiency consultation. Provides financing.

🏠 Building and Design Professionals and Tradespeople

More professionals are "going green" thanks to increased consumer demand and their own awareness of the impact they can have on the planet. However, not all green building and design professionals are experienced in all areas, so check into their primary focus and field of expertise. Review references and take a look at their portfolios. Visit their project sites, if possible.

The green home building industry is changing quickly. More products are available; more sustainable design options are being introduced. Look for professionals who are up-to-date and who specialize in your need, be it interior or exterior design, "green" construction, or environmental consulting. Within each of these areas there are further distinctions. You may be seeking better water use and reclamation, a chemical-free environment, solar energy installation, use of green materials, or another eco-oriented construction project. Be very clear about what you would like before you hire someone for your job.

The professionals listed here were chosen because of their experience in sustainable or green building design and/or construction. At least 25% of their annual projects must have a green, environmentally-oriented approach. We also looked at the number of years they have been practicing green design or building out of their overall number of years in business or years of experience. Because these businesses couldn't be measured against a single objective standard, we did not grant leaf awards in this category.*

Greenopia is not responsible for the outcome or performance of the work/service/products/materials of any listed company or individual. When hiring a professional or trade listed below, it is up to you to verify the experience and skills of the listed practitioners. For California, you can check on the status of a contractor's license by going to www. cslb.ca.gov. The businesses listed below are selected and reviewed for residential design and construction only. We did not investigate, nor is the guide intended to cover, contractors whose primary focus is commercial projects.

GREENING YOUR SPACE

U.S. Green Building Council (USGBC)

A nonprofit membership organization made up of leaders from all sectors of the building industry working to promote buildings that are environmentally responsible and healthy places to live and work.

Leadership in Energy and Environmental Design (LEED®)

LEED's Green Building Rating System™ is the national benchmark for the design, construction, and operation of high performance green buildings. LEED also offers a professional accreditation exam for building professionals, who have demonstrated a thorough understanding of green building practices and principles and the LEED Rating System (LEED accredited professional, or LEED AP).

Build It Green

A nonprofit membership organization that promotes healthy, energy- and resource-efficient buildings in California. Offers Certified Green Building Professional Training in residential design and construction for building, real estate, and other professionals. Build It Green also offers green home tours. Check their website for locations and times.

ARCHITECTS

Alexander Elias Architecture, Inc.
10746 Molony Rd. Culver City 90230 • **310-839-5892**
By appt. www.eliasarchitecture.com
Architects employing the USGBC's LEED rating system as a guideline for achieving the highest level of sustainability.

Architerra Studio
1132 Greenacre Ave. West Hollywood 90046 • **310-497-9103**
By appt. www.architerrastudio.com
Full-service architectural firm committed to sustainable design solutions. USGBC member.

Artecho Architecture and Landscape Architecture
1639 Electric Ave. Ste. A Venice 90291 • **310-399-4794**
By appt. www.artecho.com
Architecture and landscape architecture using recycled materials and contemporary green design; interior design services.

Caldwell Architects
3107 Washington Blvd. Marina del Rey 90292 • **310-306-2449**
By appt. www.caldwellarchitects.com
Provides architecture, planning, and interior design services. LEED AP, USGBC member, AIA member.

Casasco Studios, Architecture & Town Planning
710 Ocean Park Blvd. Ste. 1 Santa Monica 90405 • **310-399-1206**
By appt. www.casasco.net
Architectural design utilizing sustainable planning, systems, and materials.

Cindy Grant Architecture, Inc.
Sherman Oaks • **818-379-9566**
By appt. www.cindygrant.com
Sustainable design integration in custom residential and commercial projects. USGBC member.

Coscia Day Architecture and Design
12732 Maxella Ave. LA 90066 • **310-399-1613**
By appt. www.cosciaday.com
Eco-friendly, custom, modern architectural and interior design for residential and commercial projects.

Dake Wilson Architects
2906 Rowena Ave. LA 90039 • **323-662-6500**
Mon-Fri 9am-5pm www.dakewilson.com
Residential and commercial architectural and interior design focusing on sustainability. LEED AP, USGBC member.

Davida Rochlin Architecture
11973 San Vincente Blvd. Ste. 213 LA 90049 • **310-476-1987**
By appt. www.davidarochlin.com
Specializes in green and sustainable architecture for custom residential homes; offers environmental consulting and interior design services.

Design*21
5757 Uplander Way Ste. 202 Culver City 90230 • **310-574-8805**
Mon-Fri 8am-6pm www.godesign21.com
European and contemporary architecture and interior design using sustainable materials.

Design Forward
30 N. Raymond Ave. Ste. 804 Pasadena 91103 • **626-796-2566**
By appt. www.designforward.net
Designs sustainable residential buildings using recycled products and renewable energy; provides environmental consulting services. CA Straw Building Association member, AIA member.

Design Studios/LRC AIA
7717 Hollywood Blvd. Ste. 2 LA 90046 • **323-876-0430**
Mon-Fri 9am-5pm
Architects and associated contractors emphasizing environmental stewardship and LEED principles.

Drexel Design
8253 Mannix Dr. LA 90046 • **323-654-0406**
Mon-Fri 9am-5pm
Architectural firm specializing in eco-friendly, functional, elegant design; offers interior design services. USGBC member.

Dry Design
5727 Venice Blvd. LA 90019 • **323-954-9084**
By appt. www.drydesign.com
Landscape architectural and building design firm integrating surrounding environmental elements into projects.

Duvivier Architects
308 Westminster Ave. Venice 90291 • **310-399-4944**
By appt. www.idarchitect.com

Duvivier Architects (cont.)

Architect committed to all aspects of sustainability, emphasizing the relationships between buildings and their surrounding natural environments; environmental consulting services. LEED AP, USGBC member.

Ecotech Design

8834 Hollywood Hills Rd. LA 90046 • **323-270-5502**
By appt. www.ecotechdesign.com
Emphasis in solar and environmental design in both residential and commercial projects, with modular and prefab expertise; environmental consulting services. USGBC member.

Environmental Systems Group

9192 Crescent Dr. LA 90046 • **323-656-6549**
By appt.
Environmentally sensitive firm providing architecture and planning for residential and commerical projects.

Eric Lloyd Wright Architecture & Planning

24680 Piuma Rd. Malibu 90265 • **818-591-8992**
By appt. www.elwright.net
Organic architecture and interior design applying ecological design principles and sustainable materials; environmental consulting. LEED AP, USGBC member, Build It Green certified.

Gray Matter Architecture

639 E. Channel Rd. Santa Monica 90402 • **310-454-7960**
By appt. www.graymatterarchitecture.com
Architectural firm focused on sustainable design. LEED AP.

Green Studio of Architecture + Design

Encino • **818-705-3121**
Mon-Thu 8am-5pm Fri 8am-2pm www.greenstudioarchitecture.com
Architectural and interior design firm specializing in self-sustaining, zero-energy living. LEED AP, USGBC member.

Greenform

6404 Hollywood Blvd. Ste. 314 LA 90028 • **323-550-1055**
By appt. www.greenform.net
Green building and sustainability consultation; LEED management. LEED AP, USGBC member.

Hinerfeld-Ward, Inc.

310-842-7929
By appt. www.hwiconstruction.com
Sustainable architectural design, construction, and environmental consulting. Specializes in residential and commercial tenant improvements requiring fast-tracking and design/build collaborations.

HOF Architecture, Inc.

7825 McConnell Ave. LA 90045 • **310-695-7664**
By appt. www.hofarchitecture.com
Full-service architectural firm specializing in site planning and renewable energy systems; interior design services. USGBC member, AIA member.

James Heimler, Architect, Inc.

19510 Ventura Blvd. Ste. 210 Tarzana 91356 • **818-343-5393**
By appt. www.jhai-architect.com
Architectural firm for residential, commercial, industrial, and institutional projects. Member of Los Angeles Eco-City Council. LEED AP, USGBC member.

Janaki Welch Design and Construction
1348 Abbot Kinney Blvd. Venice 90291 • **310-918-2420**
By appt.
Residential and commercial architectural and interior design, general
construction. Bau-Biologie certified.

John Friedman
701 E. Third St. Ste. 300 LA 90013 • **213-253-4740**
By appt. www.jfak.net
Architectural firm incorporating environmental design into building plans.
LEED AP, USGBC member.

John Trautmann Architects
2904B Colorado Ave. Santa Monica 90405 • **310-453-1620**
By appt. www.jtarchitects.com
Green architectural and interior design firm. LEED AP, USGBC member.

KAA Design Group
4201 Redwood Ave. LA 90066 • **310-821-1400**
By appt. www.kaadesigngroup.com
Residential and commercial architecture, landscape, interior design, and
graphic design services. LEED AP, USGBC member.

Kanner Architects
1558 10th St. Santa Monica 90401 • **310-451-5400**
Mon-Fri 8:30am-5:30pm www.kannerarch.com
Sustainable design and materials for residential and commercial buildings
and interiors. LEED AP, USGBC member.

Koffka/Phakos Design
6404 Hollywood Blvd. Ste. 405 LA 90028 • **323-461-0050**
By appt. www.koffkaphakos.com
Architecture, interior design, and consulting services. LEED AP, USGBC
member, Build It Green certified.

Koning Eizenberg Architecture
1454 25th St. Santa Monica 90404 • **310-828-6131**
By appt. www.kearch.com
Contemporary aesthetic design; committed to providing sustainable,
community-oriented architecture. LEED AP, USGBC member.

Levitt + Moss Architects
3400 Airport Ave. Ste. 20 Santa Monica 90405 • **310-398-0850**
By appt. www.levittmoss.com
Architectural firm specializing in custom residential design; commericial
projects. LEED AP, USGBC member.

Marmol Radziner Prefab
12210 Nebraska Ave. LA 90025 • **310-689-0089**
Mon-Fri 8:30am-5:30pm www.marmolradzinerprefab.com
Sustainably designed and constructed prefabricated homes, delivered
complete with custom options; environmental consulting services. LEED AP,
USGBC member.

Moule & Polyzoides
180 E. California Blvd. Pasadena 91105 • **626-844-2400**
By appt. www.mparchitects.com
Sustainable architecture and urban design practices. LEED AP, USGBC
member.

Nadel Architects, Inc.
1990 S. Bundy Dr. 4th Flr. LA 90025 • **310-826-2100**
Mon-Fri 8:30am-5:30pm www.nadelarc.com
Full-service architectural firm offering master planning and feasibility
studies. LEED AP, USGBC member.

Newman Building Designs
1501 Main St. Venice 90291 • **310-581-6452**
By appt. www.newmanbuildingdesigns.com
Green building design for residential, commercial, and restaurant
applications; interior design and environmental consulting services. LEED
AP, USGBC member.

Office of Mobile Design
1725 Abbot Kinney Rd. Venice 90291 • **310-439-1129**
By appt. www.designmobile.com
Sustainable architectural design utilizing green materials and technologies;
specializes in custom prefab housing.

Polly Osborne Architects
1525 S. Sepulveda Blvd. Ste. D LA 90025 • **310-477-2855**
By appt. www.osbornearchitects.com
Green architects leading residential and small commercial LEED projects.
USGBC member, Build It Green certified.

Profeta Royalty Architecture
127 Broadway Ste. 204 Santa Monica 90401 • **310-260-8808**
By appt. www.profetaroyalty.com
Architectural and interior design firm. LEED AP, USGBC member.

Pugh + Scarpa Architecture
2525 Michigan Ave Bldg. F1 Santa Monica 90404 • **310-828-0226**
By appt. www.pugh-scarpa.com
Innovative and sustainable architectural and interior design; environmental
consulting. LEED AP, USGBC member.

Ramer Architecture
3231 Ocean Park Blvd. Ste. 222 Santa Monica 90405 • **310-452-2994**
By appt. www.ramer.com
Sustainable architectural and design firm. Principal architects are LEED AP.

Richard Best Architect
8800 Venice Blvd. Ste. 302 LA 90034 • **310-280-0999**
Mon-Fri 9am-5pm www.richardbestarchitect.com
Architect and interior design specialist for custom hillside homes. Uses
LEED principles. USGBC member.

Roger East Architects
821 Traction Ave. Ste. 104 LA 90013 • **213-620-0633**
By appt. www.rogereastarchitects.com
Custom sustainable residential architecture and modern prefabricated
systems. USGBC member.

Sander Architects
2524 Lincoln Blvd. Venice 90291 • **310-822-0300**
By appt. www.sander-architects.com
Residential, commercial, and institutional architectural and interior design.
Uses components of prefab technology to create custom homes. LEED AP.

Sco Studio
13456 Washington Blvd. Venice 90292 • **310-821-5200**
By appt. www.scostudio.com
Green architectural firm specializing in alternative energy, efficient water systems, and permaculture; environmental consulting services. LEED AP, Build It Green certified.

Scott Hughes Architects
1322 Pacific Ave. Venice 90291 • **310-399-5757**
By appt. www.sharc.com
Architectural and interior design firm emphasizing site environment as planning element. LEED AP, USGBC member.

Shubin + Donaldson Architects Inc.
3834 Willat Ave. Culver City 90232 • **310-204-0688**
By appt. www.shubinanddonaldson.com
Project types include commercial, residential, hotel and hospitality, single-family, mixed-use, and multi-family; consulting services and interior design. LEED AP, USGBC member.

Sorensen Architects
22774 Pacific Coast Hwy. Malibu 90265 • **310-456-1860**
Mon-Fri 8:30am-5:30pm www.sorensenarchitects.com
Architectural and interior design firm incorporating environmentally conscious design solutions into residential building projects. LEED AP.

Steven Ehrlich Architects
10865 Washington Blvd. Culver City 90232 • **310-838-9700**
By appt. www.s-ehrlich.com
Green-focused architecture and interior design. LEED AP, USGBC member.

Studio Nova A Architects, Inc.
4337 W. 59th St. LA 90043 • **323-292-0909**
By appt. www.studionovaa.com
Architects work to produce sustainable building projects; interior design services. LEED AP, USGBC member.

Studio of Environmental Architecture (formerly Syndesis, Inc.)
1920 Olympic Blvd. Santa Monica 90404 • **310-829-9932**
By appt. www.studioea.com
Focuses on design and construction of environmentally responsible residential and commercial buildings; interior design and environmental consulting. LEED AP, USGBC member, Build It Green certified.

Studio RMA
135A S. Topanga Canyon Blvd. Topanga 90290 • **310-455-7504**
By appt. www.studiorma.com
Architectural firm specializing in prefab, concrete composite, LEED certified homes; uses SCIP building technology and engineering for sustainable, fire-proof homes. USGBC member.

Tierra Sol y Mar, Inc.
601 Rose Ave. Venice 90291 • **310-392-2775**
By appt. www.tierrasolymar.com
Green design architectural and consulting firm utilizing solar energy, graywater, and straw bale.

Tighe Architecture
1632 Ocean Park Blvd. Santa Monica 90405 • **310-450-8823**
By appt. www.tighearchitecture.com

Tighe Architecture (cont.)

Architectural firm providing building and interior design, construction, and environmental consulting services. LEED AP, USGBC member.

Totum

3231 Ocean Park Blvd. Ste. 218 Santa Monica 90405 • **310-396-9036**
By appt. www.totumconsulting.com
Full-service firm offering sustainable design and construction management. LEED AP.

Tracy A. Stone Architect

2041 Blake Ave. LA 90039 • **323-664-0202**
Mon-Fri 9am-6pm Sat-Sun by appt. www.tracystonearchitect.com
Modern green architecture for commercial and residential projects; interior design and environmental consulting services. LEED AP, USGBC member.

Translation of Space

P.O. Box 2035 Venice 90294 • **310-383-8840**
By appt. www.tos-arc.com
Ecologically sustainable, contemporary architecture. USGBC member.

W3 Architects, Inc.

1337 Palms Blvd. Venice 90291 • **310-396-5885**
By appt. www.w3architects.com
Integrates solar and sustainable technologies into high-level architecture; principal architect has over 25 years experience in passive solar design. Offers consulting services. USGBC member.

Wick Architecture and Design

1820 Ashmore Pl. LA 90026 • **323-644-9867**
By appt. www.wickarch.com
Architectural firm specializing in sustainable modern design. LEED AP.

William Hefner Architecture

5820 Wilshire Blvd. Ste. 500 LA 90036 • **323-931-1365**
By appt. www.williamhefner.com
Custom sustainable architecture; interior and landscape design using active and passive solar, xeriscaping, and natural materials and products. LEED AP.

BUILDERS AND GENERAL CONTRACTORS

Gaia Builders

2658 Griffith Park Blvd. Ste. 727 LA 90039 • **323-428-5005**
By appt. www.gaiabuilders.com
Specializes in eco-friendly home design and building; remodeling and new construction; distributes composting toilets.

Go Green Construction

9300 Texhoma Ave. Northridge 91325 • **818-718-7477**
By appt. www.gogreencalifornia.com
Green contractors offering services for remodeling, new construction, LEED planning and certification, and consultation. LEED AP, USGBC member.

Green Properties, Inc.

468 N. Camdon Dr. Ste. 200 Beverly Hills 90210 • **310-273-3001**
Mon-Fri 9am-5pm www.greenpropertiesinc.net
Home design and construction, environmental consulting; creates and supports eco-friendly, sustainable, healthy lifestyles. LEED AP, USGBC member.

Hinerfeld-Ward, Inc.
310-842-7929
By appt. www.hwiconstruction.com
Sustainable architectural design, construction, and environmental consulting. Specializes in residential and commercial tenant improvements requiring fast-tracking and design/build collaborations.

Icaza Construction
Manhattan Beach • **310-480-0385**
By appt. www.icazaconstruction.com
Custom builder specializing in green projects; serves the Beach Cities. LEED AP, Build It Green certified.

Janaki Welch Design and Construction
1348 Abbot Kinney Blvd. Venice 90291 • **310-918-2420**
By appt.
Residential and commercial architectural and interior design, general construction. Bau-Biologie certified.

LivingHomes
2910 Lincoln Blvd. Santa Monica 90405 • **310-581-8500**
By appt. www.livinghomes.net
Modern prefabricated green home builders. LEED AP.

Marmol Radziner Prefab
12210 Nebraska Ave. LA 90025 • **310-689-0089**
Mon-Fri 8:30am-5:30pm www.marmolradzinerprefab.com
Sustainably designed and constructed prefabricated homes, delivered complete with custom options; environmental consulting services. LEED AP, USGBC member.

Minardos Construction
2800 28th St. Ste. 170 Santa Monica 90405 • **310-450-6900**
Mon-Fri 9am-5pm www.minardos.com
Residential and commercial builders specializing in green construction.

Red Barn Prefab
1357 Vienna Way Venice 90291 • **310-463-0211**
By appt. www.redbarnprefab.com
Provides environmentally sensitive modular prefabricated homes.

TNT Building Corporation
13636 Ventura Blvd. Ste 401 Sherman Oaks 91423 • **818-995-4868**
Mon-Fri 8am-5pm www.tntbuilding.com
General contractor that supports environmentally responsible building practices in residential and commercial remodels, tenant improvements, and ground up construction.

WholEarth™ Development Corporation
Simi Valley • **818-266-3834**
By appt. www.wholearthbuilder.com
Whole system design and construction of 100% solar-powered, sustainable homes and buildings. USGBC member.

ENVIRONMENTAL CONSULTING

All Shades of Green
3038 Rowena Ave. LA 90039 • **323-665-7454**
Mon-Sat 11am-7pm Sun 11am-6pm www.allshadesofgreen.net
Environmental consultant provides green building technical advice; resource directory for green building professionals. Build It Green certified.

Eco Consulting LA
149 S. Barrington Ave. Ste. 142 LA 90049 • **310-795-3138**
Mon-Fri 8am-6pm www.ecoconsultingla.com
Provides eco-friendly options for healthier homes, events, and lives. USGBC member, Build It Green certified.

Environmental Inspection Services
1311 Marine St. Santa Monica 90405 • **310-396-6532**
By appt.
Environmental home inspections: asbestos, lead, radon, mold, moisture, and EMFs.

Environmental Inspections and Solutions
P.O. Box 5713 Sherman Oaks 91413 • **866-821-5713**
By appt. www.eisinc.ca
Inspects homes and offices for air quality, off-gassing, water intrusion, mold, EMFs, and chemicals.

Environmental Testing and Technology
5431 Avenida Encinas Ste. F Carlsbad 92008 • **760-804-9400**
By appt. www.etandt.com
Indoor air quality testing: EMFs, RRFs, mold, and other environmental and general health concern factors.

EPD Consultants
411 N. Harbor Blvd. Ste. 304 San Pedro 90731 • **310-241-6565**
By appt. www.epd-net.com
Provides consulting services for sustainable water reuse, treatment, and disposal. LEED AP.

Green Built Consultants
2444 Hill St. Santa Monica 90405 • **310-749-5766**
By appt. www.greenbuiltconsultants.com
Works with homeowners, architects, contractors, and builders on eco-friendly residential and commercial projects. USGBC member.

Green Life Guru
11040 Santa Monica Blvd. Ste. 470 LA 90025 • **888-326-8884**
By appt. www.greenlifeguru.com
Provides sustainable living solutions that save money, reduce waste, and minimize exposure to health hazards. LEED AP, Build It Green certified.

Green Living Lifestyle
8383 Wilshire Blvd. Ste. 99 Beverly Hills 90211 • **310-432-7245**
By appt. www.greenlivinglifestyle.com
Environmental consultants and project managers assist clients in greening homes, businesses, and events; provides green cleaning solutions.

Green Queen™, The
Woodland Hills • **310-383-6977**
By appt. www.thegreenqueencorner.com
Consulting services for a green home, lawn, and garden.

Greenform
6404 Hollywood Blvd. Ste. 314 LA 90028 • **323-550-1055**
By appt. www.greenform.net
Green building and sustainability consultation; LEED management. LEED AP, USGBC member.

Healing Spaces by Design
235 E. Colorado Blvd. Ste. 1712 Pasadena 91101 • **626-826-9580**
Mon-Fri 9:30am-3pm www.healingspacesbydesign.com
Green building and interior design consulting for a healthier, more
sustainable environment; Green Point Rating home performance testing.
USGBC member, Build It Green certified.

Homage Design
LA • **213-507-7373**
By appt. www.homagedesign.com
Provides consulting services integrating ecologically sustainable design
and materials and LEED certification. LEED AP, USGBC member.

Lead Tech Environmental
605 S. Pacific Ave. Ste. 202 San Pedro 90731 • **310-831-2479**
Mon-Fri 9am-5pm
Environmental consultants specializing in remediation for homes with lead-
based paint, asbestos, and mold problems.

Low Impact Living
6399 Wilshire Blvd. Ste. 500 LA 90048 • **323-965-9100**
By appt. www.lowimpactliving.com
Energy assessment and green design consultation. LEED AP, USGBC
member.

Mary Cordaro, H3Environmental
818-766-1787
By appt. www.h3environmental.com
Healthy home consultant since 1989 providing solutions to indoor air
problems and general home environment improvement. Integrates Building
Science and Bau-Biologie.

Moss Cadora Green Consulting and Development
Santa Monica • **310-907-5079**
By appt. www.mosscadora.com
Green consulting firm specializing in on-site home evaluation, project
coordination, and management of home renovation; architect, developer,
and contractor consulting services. LEED AP, USGBC member.

Paradigm Project, LLC, The
1834 N. Harvard Blvd. Ste. 5 LA 90024 • **323-363-5260**
By appt. www.blueplanetparadigm.com
Designs and builds green homes; offers environmental consulting, home
energy performance testing. LEED AP, USGBC member, Build It Green
certified.

Santa Monica Green Building Program
1212 5th St. 1st Flr. Santa Monica 90401 • **310-458-8549**
Mon-Fri 9am-5pm www.smgreen.org
Liaison for City of Santa Monica Green Building regulations, incentives, and
outreach; provides free green building consultation to residents. LEED AP.

Sustainable Design Source
712 Radcliffe Ave. Pacific Palisades 90272 • **310-573-1885**
By appt. www.sustainabledesignsource.com
Advises homeowners and architects on sustainable building materials,
methods, and practices.

INTERIOR DESIGNERS

Alison Pollack Earth Friendly Interior Design
22434 Marlin Pl. West Hills 91307 • **818-888-6250**
By appt. www.earthfriendlyinteriordesign.com
Specializes in nontoxic and sustainable interior design; offers green consulting. USGBC member.

Andersen-Miller Design
10000 Culver Blvd. Ste. 200 Culver City 90232 • **310-202-8900**
By appt. www.andersenmillerdesign.com
Offers sustainable residential interior and architectural design.

Astrid Design
1309 Berkeley St. Ste. B Santa Monica 90404 • **310-828-8855**
By appt.
Full-service interior design firm offering green consulting and education services.

Deming Design, LLC
LA • **310-694-0711**
By appt. www.demingdesign.com
Interior and landscape design services promoting sustainable practices for residential and commercial clients.

Dennis Design Group
915 1/2 South Holt Ave. LA 90035 • **310-493-3972**
By appt. www.dennisdesigngroup.com
Sustainable interior design, architecture, and landscaping; feng shui. LEED AP.

Dezine, Inc.
607 N. Huntley Dr. West Hollywood 90069 • **310-360-3961**
By appt. www.dezinela.com
Interior and landscape design firm specializing in custom green environments.

Ecology By Design
10721 Ashton Ave. LA 90024 • **310-470-8055**
By appt.
Specializes in bringing health and sustainability to home design; offers environmental consulting.

Epoxy Green
602 Venice Blvd. Venice 90291 • **310-578-2123**
Mon-Sat 10am-6pm
Consultants specializing in interior design using eco-friendly products and technologies.

Heidi Toll Design
Sherman Oaks • **818-906-2444**
Mon-Thu 9am-5pm www.heiditolldesign.com
Utilizes sustainability principles in new home construction and interior design.

Inviro Design
West Hills • **310-403-3435**
By appt. www.invirodesign.com
Interior design and consulting services using innovative materials and technologies to help save energy, reduce waste, and improve air quality.

Kelly LaPlante Organic Interior Design
1501 Main St. Ste. 101 Venice 90291 • **310-581-6450**
Mon-Sat 10am-6pm Sun by appt. www.kellylaplante.com
Interior designer specializing in sourcing sophisticated, sustainable
furnishings. LEED AP.

Kim Colwell Design
323-309-2945
By appt. www.kimcolwelldesign.com
Residential and commercial interior design and space revitalization using
sustainable and vintage materials.

Kronos Interior Design
13428 Maxella Ave. Ste. 274 Marina del Rey 90292 • **310-344-3443**
By appt.
Interior designer incorporating natural fibers, textiles, and sustainable
flooring in mid- to high-end residential projects.

Lucas Studio, Inc.
636 N. Almont Dr. West Hollywood 90069 • **310-858-6884**
Mon-Fri 9am-6pm www.lucasstudioinc.com
Boutique residential interior design firm utilizing local vendors and eco-
friendly materials.

Lucinda Bailey Interior Design
Pasadena • **626-351-7695**
By appt.
Residential interior design firm emphasizing use of salvaged materials;
green consulting services. Serves Pasadena area only.

Picket Design Associates
9020 Linblade St. Culver City 90232 • **310-558-5500**
By appt. www.pickettdesigns.com
Provides interior design and planning services. LEED AP, USGBC member.

RC Green by Robert Craymer
300 S. La Brea Ave. LA 90036 • **323-933-6499**
Daily 11am-6pm www.robertcraymer.com
Custom green interior design services; 100% all natural, sustainable
furniture designer and manufacturer.

Sanctuary Living Designs
Woodland Hills • **323-371-3603**
By appt.
Offers eco-conscious interior design services; provides catalogue of
vendors promoting sustainable choices.

Van Patter Design, Inc.
4929 Sycamore Terrace LA 90042 • **323-344-8266**
By appt. www.vanpatterdesign.com
Provides green interior design for the entertainment industry; residential
and commercial construction projects.

TRADESPEOPLE

Alert Insulation
15913 Old Valley Blvd. La Puente 91744 • **626-945-0158**
Mon-Fri 8am-5pm
Contractor specializing in building insulation using bounded cotton and
recycled denim; residential and commercial projects.

Conserve Energy Services

3940 Laurel Canyon Blvd. Ste. 252 Studio City 91604 • **800-771-8479**
By appt. www.conserveenergyservices.com
Provides nontoxic home cellulose insulation, solar screen installation, free home inspections; offers information on energy efficiency program incentives and rebates.

Enviro Plumbing

2633 Lincoln Blvd. Ste. 606 Santa Monica 90405 • **310-450-7208**
By appt. www.enviroplumbing.com
Specializes in installing solar water and radiant floor heating, tankless water heaters, dual flush toilets, and water reclamation systems. USGBC member.

Environmental Home Improvement

6440 Bellaire Ave. North Hollywood 91606 • **818-508-1415**
By appt. www.ehomeimprove.com
Remodeling contractor focusing on healthy, sustainable, energy-efficient living spaces.

Everguard Home Insulation

Woodland Hills • **818-348-1460**
By appt. www.everguardinsulation.com
Insulation contractors work to reduce customer home energy costs.

Greenspace Building, Inc.

5616 W. Washington Blvd. LA 90016 • **310-488-2929**
By appt. www.greenspacebuilding.com
Building professionals working specifically with sustainable, renewable, and nontoxic materials; specializes in concrete.

Izhak's Custom Interiors

6824 Bryanhurst Ave. LA 90043 • **323-752-8800**
By appt. www.izhaks.com
Architectural woodworking, cabinets, and furniture using sustainable materials.

Jo-Mi Plumbing and Solar

2011 Sawtelle Blvd. LA 90025 • **310-473-8111**
By appt.
Offers energy-efficient hot water, solar pool heating, and general plumbing services.

Michael Levey Plumbing

1625 S. Livonia Ave. LA 90035 • **310-201-0197**
Mon-Fri 7am-6pm www.michaelleveyplumbing.com
Licensed plumber focused on water conservation. Specializes in whole-house water filters, on-demand tankless water heaters, graywater systems, and low-flow appliances.

Militello Plaster

4445 Zocalo Cir. Thousand Oaks 91362 • **805-531-0067**
By appt.
Plastering specialist using 100% green, nonsynthetic products: natural plaster, gypsum, and lime.

Naturalwalls

1341 E. Colorado Blvd. Ste. 201 Pasadena 91106 • **626-398-9383**
By appt. www.naturalwalls.com
Full-service artisan plaster company utilizing natural materials to create interior and exterior finished surfaces. USGBC member.

Nicholas Paint and Design

LA • **310-925-1801**
By appt.
Painting specialists using natural, zero-VOC paint; custom color mixing and matching.

Pacific Environmental Engineering Corp.

315 Indiana St. Ste. D El Segundo 90245 • **310-414-9974**
By appt. www.4voc.com
Environmental ground and air cleaning; offers pollution-control equipment and services.

Poly-Tech Environmental Heating, Ventilation, and Air Conditioning

P.O. Box 856 Simi Valley 90362 • **805-306-0354**
By appt.
Indoor air quality specialist providing energy-efficient and nontoxic heating, air conditioning, ventilation, and air purification.

 Recycling Centers and Services

"Reduce, reuse, recycle" is still the most logical and powerful protocol for personal consumption and use of natural resources in whatever form they might take. Tossing goods into the recycling bin should be what we do after reducing our consumption and reusing existing materials.

But when it comes time to recycle something, there are many avenues from which to choose. You can bring your recyclables to city-operated or privately owned recycling centers. There are also recycling services that come to you, either by directly picking up your recyclables curbside or by providing boxes or envelopes for mailing in such things as toner cartridges, cell phones, and other small electronics. Follow their directions for sorting, sending, and/or setting out materials for pick up.

The recycling centers and services below are listed here as resources. Many offer curbside recycling of a variety of items. Others are drop-off locations. However, because there is no objective means of awarding leaves in this category, we have not done so.

GREENING YOUR SPACE

Active Recycling

2000 W. Slauson Ave. LA 90047 • **323-295-7774**
Daily 6:30am-4:45pm
Accepts cardboard, paper, scrap metal; pickup available by appt. Call before 2pm for next-day service.

Burbank Recycle Center

500 S. Flower St. Burbank 91502 • **818-238-3900**
Mon-Fri 8am-5pm Sat 8am-4pm www.burbankrecycle.org
State certified bottle and can recycler. Electronic waste drop-off available to Burbank residents only.

California Integrated Waste Management Board (CIWMB)
www.ciwmb.ca.gov
Online resource promoting Zero Waste California in partnership with local government, industry, and the public.

California Recycles
1932 Cotner Ave. LA 90025 • **310-478-3001**
Mon-Fri 8:30am-5pm Sat by appt. www.californiarecycles.com
Offers electronic waste recycling solutions; biodegradable kitchenware and recyclable office products.

Cartridge World
Emeryville • **510-594-9900 or 888-997-3345**
www.cartridgeworld.com
Online resource locating nearby facilites for inkjet cartridge recycling and refilling. Assists in setting up cartridge recycling program/bin at businesses and schools.

Craigslist.org
www.losangeles.craigslist.org
Online service for people to buy and sell used items.

Freecycle.org
www.freecycle.org
Online local network providing individuals and nonprofits an electronic forum; post and find offers for unwanted, free items.

L.A. Shares
3655 S. Grand Ave. Ste. 280 LA 90007 • **213-485-1097**
Mon-Fri 8am-4pm www.lashares.org
Material reuse program that redistributes donations from local businesses to nonprofit organizations and schools.

Los Angeles County Environmental Resources, Dept. of Public Works
900 S. Fremont Ave. 3rd Flr. Annex Alhambra 91803 • **888-253-2652**
http://ladpw.org/epd
Provides information about recycling used motor oil, old medicine, tires, yard waste, household hazardous waste, Christmas trees, and more.

Los Angeles Services Hotline, City of
Dial "311"
Hotline for questions about recycling and all other services provided by the City of Los Angeles.

Planet Green
20724 Lassen St. Chatsworth 91311 • **818-725-2596**
Mon-Fri 8am-4:30pm www.planetgreenrecycle.com
Recycling center accepting printer cartridges, cell phones, non-biodegradable plastics, metals, and other refuse.

Recycler.com
www.recycler.com
Provides free classified searches and free private party advertising of used items; connecting buyers, traders, and sellers since 1973.

S.A.F.E. Collection Center and Free Mulch
1400 N. Gaffey St. San Pedro 90731 • **800-988-6942**
Mon-Fri 8am-4pm www.lacity.org
Hazardous waste drop-off site accepting paint, solvents, automotive fluids, batteries, bulbs, and electronics.

Santa Monica Recycling Center, City of

2411 Delaware Ave. Santa Monica 90404 • **310-453-9677**
Mon-Fri 8am-5pm, Sat 8am-2pm www.smgov.net
Sorts and buys cans, glass, plastic, paper products, and cardboard.

Santa Monica Refuse Transfer Station

2401 Delaware Ave. Santa Monica 90404 • **310-829-7323**
Mon-Sat 6am-2pm www.smgov.net
Full-service waste disposal facility accepting scrap metal, tires, organic
waste, construction and demolition debris, electronics, cardboard, and
refuse.

So Cal Computer Recyclers

1320 240th St. Harbor City 90710 • **800-727-3292**
Mon-Fri 9am-5pm www.socalrecyclers.com
Recycles office and home electronics regardless of age or usability:
printers, computers, fax machines, monitors, keyboards, cell phones, TVs.

Southern California Disposal and Recycling

1908 Frank St. Santa Monica 90404 • **310-828-6444**
Mon-Fri 5am-2pm, Sat 6am-1:30pm www.scdisposal.com
Refuse and recycling center dedicated to diverting materials from landfills.
Accepts all recyclables, e-waste, yard trimmings, and refuse.

Stimson's Recycling

6040 Venice Ave. LA 90034 • **323-525-1687**
Mon-Sat 8:30am-5pm Sun 9am-3pm
Drop-off site for all plastics, glass, aluminum, and scrap metal.

WBi Recycling

8201 Woodley Ave. Van Nuys 91406 • **818-700-6899**
Mon-Fri 8am-5pm www.wbirecycling.com
Partners with recycling centers and remanufacturing facilities to recycle
inkjet and toner cartridges.

West Los Angeles Recycling Center

4422 W. Jefferson Blvd. LA 90016 • **323-737-8923**
Mon-Sat 8am-4pm
Drop-off site for containers, newspapers, scrap metal, and cardboard.

 Household Hazardous Waste Disposal

Households are no longer allowed to put certain wastes in the trash,
including:

- all household batteries
- toxic cleaning supplies
- fluorescent and other mercury-containing light bulbs and lamps
- aerosols
- mercury thermometers and thermostats
- hobby and pool chemicals
- toxic gardening products (fertilizer, herbicides, pesticides)
- fire extinguishers
- oil-based paints, thinners, and stains

GREENING YOUR SPACE

Public hazardous waste programs collect these wastes (and others) from households and small businesses. Appointments and proof of residency are sometimes required to participate. These programs provide safe disposal options, but the best way to keep the planet healthy is to reduce your use of toxic materials in the first place.

Electronics (E-waste) are generally not accepted at hazardous waste drop-off sites but there are a number of electronics recycling centers and E-waste drop-off locations in the area. If the item is under five years old, it can sometimes be donated to an electronics refurbishing/reuse program.

Generally speaking, it is illegal to throw out all electronics. They must either be donated for refurbishment or recycled at an appropriate location. A number of disposal options are listed below.

Electronic Waste (E-waste)

E-waste consists of any broken or unwanted electrical or electronic appliance. This includes computers, entertainment electronics, mobile phones, handheld devices, and other items. Many components of such equipment are toxic and exposure to the heavy metals they contain can be hazardous.

East San Fernando Valley S.A.F.E. Center
11025 Randall St. Sun Valley 91352 • **800-988-6942**
Mon, Sat-Sun 9am-3pm www.lacsd.org/info/hhw_e_waste
Household hazardous waste collection center open to all Los Angeles County residents. Accepts paint, solvents, automotive fluids, batteries, bulbs, pool chemicals, and electronics.

Gaffey Street S.A.F.E. Collection Center
1400 N. Gaffey St. San Pedro 90731 • **800-988-6942**
Fri-Sun 9am-3pm www.lacsd.org/info/hhw_e_waste
Household hazardous waste collection center open to all Los Angeles County residents. Accepts paint, solvents, automotive fluids, batteries, bulbs, pool chemicals, and electronics.

Hyperion S.A.F.E. Collection Center
7660 W. Imperial Hwy. Gate B Playa Del Rey 90293 • **800-988-6942**
Sat-Sun 9am-3pm www.lacsd.org/info/hhw_e_waste
Household hazardous waste drop-off site open to all Los Angeles County residents. Accepts paint, solvents, automotive fluids, batteries, bulbs, pool chemicals, and electronics.

Los Angeles-Glendale S.A.F.E. Collection Center
4600 Colorado Blvd. LA 90039 • **800-988-6942**
Sat-Sun 9am-3pm www.lacsd.org/info/hhw_e_waste
Household hazardous waste drop-off site open to all Los Angeles County residents. Accepts paint, solvents, automotive fluids, batteries, bulbs, and electronics.

Los Angeles Services Hotline, City of
Dial "311"
Hotline for household hazardous waste questions and information regarding all services provided by the City of Los Angeles.

One-Day HHW/E-Waste Collection Events
www.lacsd.org/info/hhw_e_waste
Online resource for temporary neighborhood drop-off locations for household hazardous waste.

Santa Monica Household Hazardous Waste Center, City of
2500 Michigan Ave. Santa Monica 90404 • **310-458-2213**
Wed-Fri 7am-1pm Sat 7am-3pm www.smgov.net/epd/residents/hhw
Household hazardous waste center accepting paint, batteries, solvents, pesticides, cleaners, pool chemicals. Available to City of Santa Monica residents.

U.C.L.A. S.A.F.E. Center
550 Charles E. Young Dr. LA 90095 • **800-988-6942**
Thu-Sat 8am-2pm www.lacsd.org/info/hhw_e_waste
Household hazardous waste collection center open to all Los Angeles County residents. Accepts paint, solvents, automotive fluids, batteries, bulbs. Electronics accepted Saturday only.

Washington Blvd. S.A.F.E. Center
2649 E. Washington Blvd. LA 90021 • **800-988-6942**
Fri-Sun 9am-3pm www.lacsd.org/info/hhw_e_waste
Household hazardous waste collection center open to all Los Angeles County residents. Accepts paint, solvents, automotive fluids, batteries, bulbs, pool chemicals, and electronics.

✐ WRITE A REVIEW

Many people begin their journey to green living by changing their home environment. You can provide a great benefit to others by sharing your insights and experiences at greenopia.com: What did you think about the options and choices you were given, or the quality of the products and services? How was your experience with these providers? Was the cost in line with what you were getting? Let us know!

REDUCE YOUR IMPACT—IT'S EASY

- Use cloth bags or boxes for lunches instead of paper bags.
- Use washable cloth towels and napkins instead of paper towels and paper napkins.
- Stash reusable bags in your car, bike, or purse to take along when shopping.
- Use an erasable note board instead of paper notes.
- Buy products that come without boxes or excess packaging.
- Buy refillable or bulk products to reduce packaging and waste.
- Send holiday greetings electronically over the internet.
- Take advantage of public and school libraries.

REUSE OR REPURPOSE ORDINARY "TRASH" ITEMS

- Reuse large and/or padded envelopes and boxes for mailings.
- Reuse paper that has been printed on one side as scratch paper.

RECYCLE WHAT YOU DO USE

- Much of your daily waste can be recycled at the curb.
- Make sure old phone books and directories get into the recycle bin.
- Some programs now accept plastic bags.

BUYING RECYCLED BENEFITS ALL OF US BY SAVING:

- Natural resources—conserves land, reduces the need to drill for oil, mine for minerals, and desecrate forests.
- Energy—for example, producing aluminum by recycling takes 95% less energy than producing new aluminum from bauxite ore.
- Clean air and water—reduces amount of pollutants emitted during resource extraction, processing, and manufacturing.
- Landfill space—materials go into new products, not the landfill.
- Money and creating jobs—creates more jobs than landfills or incinerators and is often the least expensive waste management method for cities and towns.

What can be recycled curbside varies by municipality so check your city's or county's website for specifics. You can also log on to www.earth911.org, type in your zip code, and get all the local recycling information you need. Be sure to rinse all bottles, cans, containers, and foil food trays before placing them in the bin.

PAPER

- White, colored, shredded (unsoiled; no tissue or paper towels)
- Newspaper
- Magazines
- Catalogs
- Paperback books
- Paperboard (cereal boxes, etc.)
- Egg cartons
- Cardboard (flattened)
- Junk mail
- Nonmetallic wrapping paper
  (Note: staples, paperclips, labels, and tape are allowed)

CANS AND FOIL

- Steel
- Aluminum cans
- Metal food trays

GLASS

- Bottles, jars

PLASTIC

- #1 and #2 containers (beverage, milk, soda, water, detergent, shampoo, yogurt, margarine, etc.)

✐ DID YOU KNOW?

- Every year, over 40 tons of trash washes up on Los Angeles County beaches. Approximately 80% of that trash could have been recycled. The County of Los Angeles spends an average of $1.3 million cleaning the beaches after rainstorms every year.

- A plastic soda bottle will, on average, take about 450 years to biodegrade. Imagine all those soft drink bottles, still polluting the landscape 22 generations from now.

(City of Los Angeles Stormwater Program, Watershed Protection Division, Department of Public Works)

The plastics industry has developed a series of markers, usually seen on the bottom of plastic containers. **Despite the confusing use of the chasing arrow symbol, these markers do NOT mean the plastic can be recycled, nor do they mean the container uses recycled plastic.** The following markers **only identify the plastic type:**

- **1** - Polyethylene Terephthalate (PET or PETE)
- **2** - High-Density Polyethylene (HDPE)
- **3** - Polyvinyl Chloride or Vinyl (PVC or V)
- **4** - Low-Density Polyethylene (LDPE)
- **5** - Polypropylene (PP)
- **6** - Polystyrene (PS)
- **7** - Other (Polycarbonate)

Although almost everything made of plastic is marked with a recycling code, not all types can actually be recycled. Just remember:

- **Types 1** and **2** are widely accepted in container form.
- **Type 4** is sometimes accepted in bag form.
- **Types 6** and **7** (polystyrene and mixed or layered plastic, such as packaging pellets, meat trays, to-go clam-shell containers, and Nalgene bottles) have **virtually no recycling potential,** *and* are particularly **harmful to your health and the environment.**

You should place in your bin only those types of plastic authorized by your local recycling agency.

Besides their often limited recycling capability, there are many other reasons to limit your use of plastic. Its production poses serious health threats to the environment and humans. It is nearly impossible to completely dispose of (a "sea" of plastic coats the northern Pacific Ocean) and very little actually gets reused. Certain types of plastic are particularly harmful: #3 (PVC or V), #5 (PP), #6 (PS), and #7 (Other). These types should be completely avoided. Instead look for alternatives and ways you can reduce, reuse, and recycle!

GREENING YOUR SPACE

Until Electrics . . . the Mileage Test

BY CHRIS PAINE

The first car I ever owned was a used, green Ford Pinto. My Dad bought it as his company car, and I remember one of our first trips was to meet a young Bill Gates. Mr. Gates was peddling a new program called BASIC but, alas, the convention of the day was to finish high school before joining risky start-ups.

The first new car I ever bought was a silver GM EV1 in 1997. Electric cars had long been possible, but the technology was effectively squashed by cheap oil and the industrial monopoly serving the internal combustion engine. Those of us who drove these California-mandated electric cars discovered they were fast, nearly service free, and completely gas free. Plugging them in at home using off-peak electric power cost 70 cents "a gallon" or less if you had solar panels on your house. Imagine that! Given these advantages, 50 to 100 mile ranges and 2 to 4 hour charging times proved a much easier adaptation then we ever expected.

Fast-forward to 2008. The only electric cars you can buy are a handful of affordable, speed-limited neighborhood electric vehicles (see listings) and a hot but pricey sports car from a Silicon Valley start-up. With a range of 200+ miles and record-breaking acceleration, the Tesla kicks off a new generation of electric production vehicles.

And finally, old school car companies are reacting. With rising oil prices and public pressure, major manufacturers and aftermarket firms have announced plug-in hybrids. These include GM's Chevy Volt, Saturn's Vue, and Ford's Escape hybrid. It is up to us to keep the pressure on to bring flex-fuel plug-in hybrids to everyone. Utility companies say 150 million hybrid EVs could be charged at night without building a single additional power plant.

Until then, the mileage test is still the best place to start with any car or SUV. Hybrid vehicles should be compared with any high-mileage car. For instance, my 16-year-old niece recently bought a sub-compact with nearly the same miles per gallon as my parents' Prius. (Just so you know—my favorite feature of most hybrids is that the gas engine turns off in stop-and-go traffic.)

If you are willing to try alternative fuels today, consider specialty cars powered by electricity, renewable biodiesel, cellulosic ethanol, or natural gas. Our research does not support corn-based ethanol or current hydrogen fuel, but whatever you choose, it is surprisingly fun being an early adopter of cleaner energy. My friend Katie rediscovered the bus and light rail.

The right choice depends on you. Happy biking, carpooling, and riding smarter.

CHRIS PAINE

Chris Paine is the writer/director of *Who Killed the Electric Car* and an environmental activist. His prior projects include *Faster* and *No Maps for These Territories,* both of which he produced. He has been driving an electric car for over ten years.

GETTING AROUND

One of the most effective ways to start slowing global climate change is by driving less, and, when you do drive, by using a fuel-efficient, low-polluting vehicle.

The average new car is responsible for about two metric tons of carbon emissions each year. That means, if you're like many households and have a second car, your average annual emissions is up to 3.7 metric tons—and that doesn't even take into account the production of car or maintenance items.

So when it's time to clean up your corner of the sky, why not buy a high mileage vehicle or one that runs on biodiesel? Even electric cars are no longer out of the question. In fact, one of the most exciting areas of alternative energy use is the new crop of eco-friendly vehicles. After a century of reliance on gas-powered cars and trucks, there is a growing number of dealers dedicated to providing you with low-emission, fuel-efficient alternatives to yesterday's gas-guzzler.

Check out the diverse group below. We've found everything from green car brokers who can hook you up with biofuel vehicles to conventional car manufacturers with some super fuel-efficient and alternative fuel car models. We have not listed individual dealerships because there are so many, but the manufacturers listed below sell one or more alternative fuel or hybrid models. Check their websites for a dealership near you.

Hybrids can be a hot ticket to great MPG but not always. Be sure to check out the most fuel-efficient vehicle in its class (SUV, sedan, etc.) on www.fueleconomy.gov before making a decision. For simplicity, we have chosen to list only new vehicles that achieve 30+ miles per gallon in city driving (as of Feb 2008). Look to www.greenopia.com for updates on new makes and models that meet our criteria as they actually become available (not just promised).

The listed businesses are included as a resource for you. We have not leaf-awarded this category but if we've listed it, we are impressed. If you are looking for a way to create a major change in your own energy consumption, this is a key place to start.

AC Propulsion
441 Borrego Ct. San Dimas 91773 • **909-592-5399**
Mon-Fri 8am-5pm www.acpropulsion.com
Manufactures and sells electric vehicles and electric motors. Specializes in converting Toyota Scions to EV.

Auto & Marine Machine Shop
Venice • **310-823-4334**
Mon-Fri 8am-5:30pm
Designs and builds electric cars and motorcycles; installs solar-powered lighting systems.

Big Ass Motors
8815 Shirley Ave. Northridge 91324 • **818-882-4226**
Tue-Sat 10am-6pm www.bigassmotors.com
Motor scooter and moped dealership specializing in fuel-efficient
transportation logistics. Sells and services Zap and Skeuter brands.

BioBling
By appt. www.biobling.com
Online broker connecting people with biodiesel cars.

Biomoto
Santa Monica • **310-570-0547**
By appt. www.biomoto.org
Sells and services biodiesel vehicles.

Chrysler
www.gemcar.com
Manufactures the GEM neighborhood electric vehicles.

Edrive/Clean-tech
Contact via website for appt. www.edrivesystems.com
Converts hybrids to plug-in hybrids.

EnVironmental Motors
134 S. Glendale Ave. Glendale 91205 • **818-549-0000**
Daily 10am-7pm www.environmentalmotors.com
Green car dealership selling electric vehicles, high-mileage and ethanol-
ready cars, electric motorcycles, trucks, and scooters. Sells Zap, Zenn, and
smart® cars.

Ford Motor Co.
www.ford.com
Manufactures the Escape hybrid SUV.

General Motors Corporation
www.livegreengoyellow.com
Manufactures E85 FlexFuel vehicles.

Honda Motors
www.socalhonda.com
Manufactures the Civic and Accord Hybrids, Civic CNG, and the fuel-
efficient Fit.

LA BioCars
1539 E. Walnut St. Pasadena 91106 • **626-792-5755**
Mon-Sat 10am-7pm www.labiocars.com
Sells and services biodiesel- and vegetable oil- ready cars; other alternative
fuel vehicles available.

Lovecraft Biofuels
4000 Sunset Blvd. LA 90029 • **323-644-9072**
Mon-Sat 9am-6pm www.lovecraftbiofuels.com
Converts diesel vehicles to run on vegetable oil.

Mazda
www.mazda.com
Manufactures the Tribute hybrid SUV.

Mercury
www.mercuryvehicles.com
Manufactures the Mariner hybrid SUV.

Become a member greenopia.com

Miles Electric Vehicles
3100 Airport Ave. Ste. A Santa Monica 90405 • **310-390-4890**
Mon-Fri 9am-5pm Sat-Sun by appt. www.milesev.com
Manufactures and distributes 100% electric, zero emission cars and trucks.

Mini Cooper
www.miniusa.com
Small fuel-efficient vehicles made in England.

Nissan
www.nissanusa.com
Manufactures the Altima hybrid and the fuel-efficient Versa vehicles.

Pirate Solar
269 S. Beverly Dr. Ste. 528 Beverly Hills 90212 • **310-403-4952**
Daily 9am-6pm www.piratesolar.com
Provides solar designs for RVs, sailboats, homes, and all vehicle types.

Segway Los Angeles
1660 Ocean Ave. Santa Monica 90401 • **310-395-1395**
Mon-Sat 10am-7pm Sun 11am-7pm www.segway.la
Authorized Segway sales, rental, and service center.

Skeuter
12120 Washington Blvd. Los Angeles 90066 • **310-572-1065**
Mon-Fri 8:30am-5pm www.skeuter.com
Carries electric scooters and mopeds.

Smart®
www.smartusa.com
Manufactures the compact and fuel-efficient smart fortwo® vehicle. Sold at
Daimler Chrysler dealerships.

Solar Electrical Vehicles
742 Hampshire Rd. Ste. A Westlake Village 91361 • **805-497-9808**
Mon-Fri 8am-5pm www.solarelectricalvehicles.com
Installs solar roofs on hybrid and electric cars.

SoyCar
North Hollywood • **818-926-3920**
By appt. www.soycar.com
Modifies diesel engines to run on vegetable oil or biodiesel.

Tango
www.commutercars.com
Manufactures electric vehicles.

Tesla Motors
11163 Santa Monica Blvd. LA 90025 • **650-413-4000**
www.teslamotors.com
Manufactures and distributes a high performance electric vehicle.

Toyota
www.toyota.com
Manufactures the Prius and Camry hybrids and the fuel-efficient Yaris and
Corolla.

True Biofuels
2029 Blake Ave. LA 90029 • **213-291-8480**
600 Venice Blvd. Venice 90291 • **213-291-8587**
Hours vary by location www.truebiofuels.com
Vegetable oil conversions, specializing in Mercedes and Ford vehicles.

Wild Rose Motors

148 Lloyd Ave. Unit F Fullerton 92833 • **800-341-1012**
Mon-Fri 9am-6pm Sat 9am-4pm   www.vwtdionly.com
Specializes in sales and service of Volkswagen TDI vehicles. Modifies TDIs
to be more compatible with biodiesel.

Zap

www.zapworld.com
Manufactures neighborhood electric vehicles.

Zenn

www.zenncars.com
Manufactures neighborhood electric vehicles.

 Fueling Stations

As demand for alternative fuels and alternative fuel vehicles increases,
so will the number of fueling stations and programs. To locate your nearest clean fuel station, visit Clean Car Maps (www.cleancarmaps.com).
Simply select the fuel type you are interested in, followed by the relevant
region or county. To get you started right away, we have listed several
stations in the L.A. area and other online resources here.

Although not a leaf-awarded category, if you have an alternative fuel
vehicle, these stations and resources offer the kind of fuel, supplies,
and services that that will help you reduce your carbon footprint in a
very significant way.

Alternative Fuels

Vehicle fuels that aren't made from petroleum. The U. S.
Department of Energy officially recognizes the following:

- Alcohols—ethanol and methanol;
- Biodiesel—like diesel fuel but made from plant oil or animal fat;
- Compressed natural gas (CNG)—natural gas under high
  pressure;
- Electricity—stored in batteries;
- Hydrogen—a special type of gas. A hydrogen cell uses
  hydrogen as fuel and oxygen as oxidant;
- Liquefied natural gas (LNG)—natural gas that is very cold;
- Liquefied petroleum gas (LPG) (also called propane)—
  hydrocarbon gases under low pressure; and
- Liquids made from coal—gasoline and diesel fuel that do not
  come from petroleum.

Clean Car Maps

48 S. Chester Ave. Pasadena 91106 • **626-744-5600**
www.cleancarmaps.com
Online mapping resource for electric, CNG, ethanol, hydrogen, biodiesel,
and methanol fueling station locations.

Conserv Fuel
11699 San Vicente Blvd. Brentwood 90049 • **310-571-0039**
Daily 24 hrs. www.conservfuel.com
Fueling station providing biodiesel (B99), ethanol (E85), and three grades of gasoline. Also sells organic cotton and bamboo clothing.

ITL Cudahy Fuel Stop
8330 Atlantic Ave. Cudahy 90201 • **323-562-3230**
Mon-Fri 5am-7pm Sat 6am-2pm www.ifuel.net
B20 available at the pump; B99 sold in five-gallon containers, 55-gallon drums, and bulk.

LA Biodiesel Co-op
211 N. Ave. 21 LA 90031
20500 Madrona Ave. Torrance 90503
Daily 24 hrs. Access to members only www.biodiesel-coop.com
Sells biodiesel to members; provides public education on biodiesel.

OC Biodiesel
Laguna Hills • **949-244-2121**
Daily 8am-5pm Bulk delivery by appt. www.ocbiodiesel.net
Biodiesel sold in five-gallon poly containers and 55-gallon drums; pour spouts and drum pumps available.

Palisades Gas N Wash
890 Alma Real Dr. Pacific Palisades 90272 • **310-459-9181**
Daily 8am-5:55pm
Full-service station providing B99 biodiesel.

Standard Biodiesel
22020 Clarendon St. Ste. 202 Woodland Hills 91367 • **818-719-9967**
Mon-Fri 8am-6pm Delivery by appt. www.standard-biodiesel.com
Supplies biodiesel and blends for on- and off-road vehicles. Free delivery throughout greater Los Angeles area.

✐ GREEN TIP

Clean Car Maps has teamed with Better World Club, Automobile Club of Southern California, AAA of Northern California, and AAA Nevada to provide support while you're on the road. If you find yourself low on fuel, call one of the numbers below for an operator to direct you to the nearest alternative fueling station. *(This is a FREE service and you do not have to be a member.)*

Better World Club
In California, Nevada, and Arizona, call 866-238-1137 Mon-Fri 9am-5pm.

Automobile Club of Southern California
In southern California, call 800-400-4222 daily 24 hrs.

AAA of Northern California
In northern California and Nevada, call 800-861-7759 daily 24 hrs.

🌿 GREEN TIP

Idling your car for more than 10 seconds produces emissions at almost twice the rate of normal driving. For most cars built in the last 25 years, turning the car off and on again doesn't use extra gas or cause additional wear and tear and is far better for the air, our lungs, and greenhouse gas reduction.

🌿 GREEN TIP

Make sure your car's tires are inflated to the highest pressure recommended in your car's manual. Under-inflated tires cause your car to run less efficiently. If all Americans' tires were properly inflated, we could save around 2 billion gallons of gas each year.

🌿 GREEN TIP

Gasoline and diesel fuel account for all but about .25% of California's transportation fuel. Most California gasoline does contain a small amount of ethyl alcohol (also called ethanol), which increases the oxygen content of the gasoline for cleaner burning. (U.S. Department of Energy)

🚗 Auto Clubs

The best-known auto club is also in the business of lobbying for more roads and highways and less public transit, and working against better fuel economy and pollution controls. If this agenda isn't yours, look no further. We have found an alternative.

There is one national auto club that is environmentally friendly. This club offers the standard 24/7 roadside service, trip planning, and maps, but will also help you offset your carbon emissions, rent hybrids, and find the best eco-resorts. They also offer bicycle roadside assistance. What's more, they promote public transportation alternatives and other environmental causes.

We have listed the only widely available alternative auto club that actively works to protect the environment with its policies and revenue. Since there are limited options in this area, we have not leaf-awarded this category, but we applaud the efforts of the eco-friendly alternative.

GETTING AROUND

Better World Club
20 NW Fifth Ave. Ste. 100 Portland OR 97209 • **866-238-1137**
Mon-Fri 8:30am-5:30pm www.betterworldclub.com
Auto club with eco-friendly travel and roadside assistance services; discount on membership for hybrid owners.

Taxicab and Limousine Services

When you have to, or just want to leave your car at home and let someone else provide the transportation, it's good to know that you have some nifty, earth-friendly options.

Next time you call for a cab, look for a "green" one then sit back and enjoy the ride. And about that limo, whether you are headed for the airport or the prom, not only should there be room for your crew, it should be rollin' on the latest in eco-friendly fuels.

We have not leaf-awarded this category, since this service sector is one where new companies are just emerging or existing businesses are beginning to retire their low mileage, high emissions models and integrate alternative fuel vehicles into their fleets. However, the companies listed have at least 25% of their fleet running on an alternative fuel or hybrid system.

EcoLimo
Santa Monica • **888-432-6546**
Daily 24 hrs. www.eco-limo.com
Environmentally-friendly chauffeured transportation using mostly hybrids and alternative fuel vehicles. Chauffeurs' uniforms made from recycled materials.

EcoNation
LA • **310-312-0820**
Daily 24 hrs. www.econation.com
Environmentally-friendly chauffeured transportation using a mix of hybrid and alternative fuel vehicles.

Euro Taxi of Santa Monica
Santa Monica • **310-828-4200**
Daily 24 hrs. www.eurotaxism.com
Santa Monica-based taxi company using biodiesel and CNG cars.

Evo Limo
LA • **310-642-8600**
Daily 7am-11:30pm www.evolimo.com
Eco-friendly luxury car service. Serving Los Angeles since 2002.

Solar Gondola
Venice • **310-633-4224**
Mon-Fri 9am-11pm Sat-Sun 10am-1am www.solargondola.com
Provides electric pedicab service for Santa Monica, Venice, Marina Del Rey, and beyond. Specializes in dates and parties.

Taxi! Taxi!
Santa Monica • **310-828-2233**
Daily 24 hrs. www.santamonicataxi.com
Taxi service using biodiesel and hybrid cars.

TZR.LA Transportation, Inc.
LA • **310-571-7777**
Daily 24 hrs. www.tzrla.com
Environmentally-friendly car service using Lexus hybrid SUVs and CNG vehicles.

GETTING AROUND

Car Rentals, Car Share Services, and Alternative Transportation

Do you have friends or family coming to town who need a set of wheels? Want to test drive a hybrid or biodiesel car? Ready to go car-free except once in awhile? Then check out these car rental and car share options. They are adding some gas-sipping and climate-conscious vehicles to their fleets.

We have not leaf-awarded this category because we have found that rental companies generally offer either alternative fuel vehicles exclusively (which we are all for) or, as with the large mainstream rental companies, are making an effort to supply some hybrids and alternative fuel vehicles (which we also want to recognize).

For those ready for a substitute for individual car ownership, we have listed a number of car share and carpool resources. For rental companies, those that offer alternative transportation options, or cars running on alternative fuels (biodiesel, electric plug-in, hybrid, CNG, and flex fuel) meet our criteria for inclusion.

Avis
800-352-7900
Daily 24 hrs. www.avis.com
Rents Prius hybrids at most Los Angeles area locations. Call or check website for a rental location near you.

Bio-Beetle
Venice • **877-873-6121**
Daily 24 hrs. www.bio-beetle.com
Offers B99-powered biodiesel rental vehicles.

eRideShare
618-530-4842
Daily 24 hrs. www.erideshare.com
Free service connecting commuters or travelers going the same direction.

EV Rental
5500 W. Century Blvd. LA 90045 • **877-EVRental**
Daily 24 hrs. www.evrental.com
Offers hybrid car rentals. Also sells pre-owned hybrid vehicles.

Hertz
800-654-3131
Daily 24 hrs. www.hertz.com
Prius hybrids available for rental at most Los Angeles area locations. Booking in advance is recommended. Call or check website for a rental location near you.

Midway Rideshare
4751 Wilshire Blvd. Ste. 120 LA 90010 • **877-VAN-RIDE**
Mon-Fri 7am-5pm www.midwayrideshare.com
Offers vanpools for people to commute from home to work.

Rideamigos.com

Daily 24 hrs. www.losangeles.rideamigos.com
Online resource for finding and matching parties interested in ride sharing
and commuting solutions in Los Angeles.

Segway Los Angeles

1660 Ocean Ave. Santa Monica 90401 • **310-395-1395**
Mon-Sat 10am-7pm Sun 11am-7pm www.segway.la
Authorized Segway sales, rental, and service center.

Zipcar

LA • **866-494-7227**
Daily 24 hrs. www.zipcar.com
Membership provides access to a nationwide fleet of vehicles for
individuals aged 18 to 75. Pay by the hour or day. Cars parked throughout
neighborhoods in Los Angeles area.

🚌 Public Transportation

That train ticket, transit pass, or bus transfer may not look like much,
but it is one of the most potent weapons you can use to combat global
warming and climate change. Research has demonstrated that when
compared to other household actions that limit carbon dioxide, taking
public transportation can be more than ten times greater in reducing this
greenhouse gas.

It takes one solo commuter of a household to switch from daily driving
to using public transportation, and he or she can reduce the household
carbon footprint by 10%. If one household's driver gives up that second
car and switches to public transit, a household can reduce its carbon
emissions up to 30%. And, not only is it the right thing to do, it reduces
that commute-related stress by letting someone else do the driving.

Check out the clean, safe, and reliable public transportation systems
available to you. You just might be surprised at how pleasant it can be.

We have listed contact numbers and web addresses for local public
transportation services. Get in touch with the organizations listed below,
and they will set you up with bus and train schedules and let you know
the closest pick-up spot to your home or office so you can be on your way.

BUS SERVICES

Beach Cities Transit

310-937-6660
www.redondo.org
North/South bus system covering Redondo Beach, Hermosa Beach,
Manhattan, and El Segundo with East/West connectivity to Torrance.

Big Blue Bus Santa Monica

310-451-5444
www.bigbluebus.com
Serves Santa Monica to Downtown Los Angeles.

Burbank Bus
818-246-4258
www.burbankbus.org
Serves Burbank area.

Culver Citybus
310-253-6510
www.culvercity.org
Municipal bus system serves Culver City.

Foothill Transit
626-967-3147
www.foothilltransit.com
Serves San Gabriel and Pomona Valley.

Gardena Municipal Bus Lines
310-324-1475
www.ci.gardena.ca.us/government/transportation
Municipal bus system service operating in the Gardena area.

Glendale Bus Line
818-548-3960
www.glendalebeeline.com
Serves Glendale area.

Greyhound Lines Inc.
800-231-2222
www.greyhound.com
Intercity bus transportation system across California and nationwide.

LAX FlyAway Bus Service
866-435-9529
www.lawa.org/flyaway
Bus service to and from LAX; locations at Westwood, Union Station, and Van Nuys.

Los Angeles Department of Transportation (LADOT)
(213, 310, 323, 818)-808-2273
www.ladottransit.com
Offers information on DASH, Commuter Express, City Hall Shuttle, Metrolink Shuttle, and City Ride services in Downtown Los Angeles.

Metro (L.A. County Metropolitan Transportation Authority)
800-COMMUTE
www.metro.net
Metro Bus and Metro Rail services throughout Los Angeles County. Information online for specific lines in your area, schedules, and maps; provides information on other travel services.

Palos Verdes Peninsula Authority
310-544-7108
www.palosverdes.com/pvtransit
Bus lines serving the Palos Verdes area.

Pasadena Area Rapid Transit
626-398-8973
www.ci.pasadena.ca.us/trans/transit
Bus system serving the Pasadena area.

Thousand Oaks Transit
805-375-5473
www.totransit.org
Bus lines serving the Thousand Oaks area.

Torrance Transit System
310-618-6266
www.ci.torrance.ca.us
Bus service covering the Torrance area with connections to Los Angeles and Long Beach.

TRAINS AND RAIL

Amtrak
800-872-7245
www.amtrak.com
Nationwide train service.

Metro (L.A. County Metropolitan Transportation Authority)
800-COMMUTE
www.metro.net
Metro Bus and Metro Rail services throughout Los Angeles County. Website offers information on specific lines, schedules, maps, and other travel services.

Metrolink
800-371-5465
www.metrolinktrains.com
Commuter train services for Southern California; check online for schedules, maps, and trip planning options.

OTHER SERVICES

Commute Smart
800-COMMUTE
www.commutesmart.info
Guide to carpooling, vanpooling, rail, and biking to work.

ExperienceLA.com
www.experiencela.com/gettingaround
Online resource for assistance in planning public transportation commutes through Los Angeles.

SoCal Transport
800-COMMUTE
www.socaltransport.org
Trip planning service for Southern California using various bus and rail lines.

GETTING AROUND

GREEN TIP

Walking, biking, and taking public transportation are among the most eco-friendly ways to get around. Instead of a new car, consider a new pair of shoes (sustainably made, of course!), hopping on your bike, or flagging down your local bus.

Although it is sometimes comforting to blame "industry" for all of our environmental ills, the fact is, each one of us contributes to the greenhouse gases (GHG) that increase global warming. The cars we drive, the flights we take, the products we buy, and the energy we use in our homes and apartments directly affects what happens to our planet. This is where "carbon offsets" come into play.

The idea behind carbon offsets is to counter the effects of the carbon emissions we produce by purchasing carbon offset credits from a third party who, in turn, uses those funds to engage in projects that capture and/or reduce greenhouse gases elsewhere. The goal is not only to lessen greenhouse gas emissions, but for us to recognize and take responsibility for the things we do which may have larger, or even global consequences.

First and most important, reduce your carbon footprint by becoming more eco-efficient. Then, look to carbon offsets as a way to mitigate the effects of what's left. You can select from a variety of programs— renewable energy, reforestation/tree planting, wind farms, and energy efficiency are among the most popular.

Because this is a new and emerging field, we have not leaf-awarded these organizations but they all provide customers with the means to calculate, and the opportunity to buy, carbon offset credits.

Carbon Footprint

The effect your actions and lifestyle have on global warming and climate change as measured in units of carbon dioxide. Biggest contributors include air and car travel, and electricity used in the home. Other factors include your diet (the average grocery store item is transported 1,500 miles before it reaches your table) and the clothing you wear (cotton grown in Turkey, sewn in China, sold at Target, for instance). For more information on offsetting your carbon footprint, see page 215.

Better World Club
20 NW Fifth Ave. Ste. 100 Portland OR 97209 • **866-238-1137**
Mon-Fri 8:30am-5:30pm www.betterworldclub.com
Provides carbon offsets for air travel; offers ecotourism and general travel services.

Buy Carbon
1220 W. Sixth St. Ste. 600 Cleveland OH 44113 • **216-522-8700**
Mon-Fri 9am-5pm www.buycarbon.org
Calculates carbon emissions and sells offsets. Issues carbon credits on behalf of Clean Air Conservancy.

Carbon Fund
1320 Fenwick Ln. Ste. 206 Silver Spring MD 20910 • **240-293-2700**
Mon-Fri 9am-6pm www.carbonfund.org
Sells carbon offsets for fees used to invest in alternative energy
development and reforestation.

Clean Air Cool Planet
100 Market St. Ste. 204 Portsmouth NH 03801 • **603-422-6464**
Mon-Fri 9am-5pm www.cleanair-coolplanet.org
Provides carbon offsets for emissions caused by auto travel; leads methane
capture projects.

Clean and Green
P.O. Box 803 Boulder CO 80306 • **877-USA-GREEN (872-4733)**
Mon-Fri 8:30am-5:30pm www.cleanandgreen.us
Provides community-based wind energy credits.

Climate Trust, The
65 SW. Yamhill St. Ste. 400 Portland OR 97204 • **503-238-1915**
Mon-Fri 8am-5:30pm www.climatetrust.org
Promotes climate change solutions by providing greenhouse gas offset
projects and advancing offset policy.

DrivingGreen
1990 W. New Haven Ave. Ste. 205 Melbourne FL 32904 • **321-409-7821**
Mon-Fri 8am-5pm www.drivinggreen.com
Calculates and sells carbon offsets for auto and air travel, events. Funds
support GHG emission-reduction projects managed by AgCert International.

Live Neutral
2601 Mission St. Ste. 401 San Francisco 94110 • **415-695-2355**
Mon-Fri 9am-6pm www.liveneutral.org
Enterprise of Presidio School of Mgmt. and Chicago Climate Exchange
providing education on GHG emissions; calculates and sells offsets for
carbon emissions.

NativeEnergy
823 Ferry Rd. P.O. Box 539 Charlotte VT 5445 • **800-924-6826**
Mon-Fri 8:30am-5pm www.nativeenergy.com
Uses carbon offset fees to build wind turbines on Native American lands.

Prairie Tree Project
7703 Ralston Rd. Arvada CO 80002 • **800-715-8753**
www.prairietreeproject.com
Calculates carbon footprints and sells offsets to fund tree plantings on the
Colorado prairie; provides strategies to help individuals and businesses
become carbon neutral.

Renewable Choice Energy
2500 55th St. Ste. 210 Boulder CO 80301 • **877-810-8670**
Mon-Fri 9am-6pm www.renewablechoice.com
Promotes the development of clean energy alternatives through a carbon
offset program.

Save Green Earth
www.savegreenearth.com
Calculates carbon footprint from the energy usage of your home and
vehicle. Carbon offsets fund environmental education, reforestation, and
technology.

GETTING AROUND

Sky Energy
2131 Woodruff Rd. Ste. 2100, Box 203 Greenville SC 29607 • **866-759-3637**
Mon-Fri 9am-5pm www.sky-energy.com
Renewable energy credits offset emissions by funding wind power.

Sustainable Travel International
P.O. Box 1313 Boulder CO 80306 • **720-273-2975**
www.sustainabletravel.com
Sells offsets to travelers and invests in renewable energy and reforestation projects.

Terra Pass
568 Howard St. 5th Flr. San Francisco 94105 • **877-210-9581**
Mon-Fri 9am-5pm www.terrapass.com
Offsets support projects designed to neutralize environmental impacts caused by travel and other means of energy consumption.

3 Phases Renewables
2100 Sepulveda Blvd. Ste. 37 Manhattan Beach 90266 • **310-939-1283**
Mon-Fri 8:30am-6:30pm www.3phasesrenewables.com
Provides individuals and businesses with direct access to competitive, sustainable, and renewable energy choices. Sells renewable energy credits (REC's).

FOR MORE INFORMATION

My Footprint
www.myfootprint.org
Offers the Ecological Footprint Quiz, assessing an individual's consumption rate of natural resources as compared to the global average.

Solar Electric Light Fund (SELF)
1612 NW. K St. Ste. 402 Washington DC 20006 • **202-234-7265**
Mon-Fri 9am-6pm www.self.org
Serves rural, off-grid families and communities in developing countries by providing clean, renewable energy opportunities and modern communications.

Stop Global Warming
By mail: 15332 Antioch St. Ste. 168 Pacific Palisades 90272 • **310-454-5726**
www.stopglobalwarming.org
Offers personal carbon dioxide calculator and tips for reducing carbon emissions.

┌─ ✐ **WRITE A REVIEW** ────────────────

Every time we leave our homes, we make choices that make a significant impact on our carbon footprint and thus on global warming. What are your experiences with the eco-friendly options that we've listed here? What have we missed? Drive your comments home on greenopia.com.

Going Carbon Neutral

Lots of things are going "carbon neutral" these days, but what does that really mean? Making something carbon neutral (also known as climate neutral) doesn't mean sucking up greenhouse gases or sticking a banana in the tailpipe. Carbon neutrality, or carbon offsetting, is the process by which global warming gases emitted by a certain activity, event, or process are calculated and then effectively offset by removing or preventing an equal amount of pollution elsewhere. These offsets usually involve renewable energy projects like wind power, solar, or methane; reforestation projects (trees absorb CO_2); or energy efficiency programs. Carbon offset actions can take place next door or on the other side of the world, but the desired goal is that they reduce the net amount of greenhouse gases released into the atmosphere.

If something's emissions can be calculated, then they can be offset. The list of neutralized events, companies, and products is growing fast. Music tours, restaurants, films, colleges, books (yes, *Greenopia*), web hosts, entire companies, and huge events like the Winter Olympics and the World Cup have all gone carbon neutral. But it's also something we can each do with our own actions.

The most common examples of carbon offsets for individuals are emissions from air travel, emissions from driving, and home or office energy use. There are a growing number of services out there that will help you calculate and offset your emissions if you wish to go carbon neutral, whether it's on a case-by-case basis (like air travel), or over time (like offsetting commuting or home energy use for the year). If the thing you want to offset is more complex (like an event, the production of a film, or a product) there are independent companies able to calculate the associated environmental footprint.

It should be noted that there is a certain amount of contention around the idea of carbon offsets. It is important that companies offering offsets have a reliable way of verifying their actions, such as using Green-e Certified renewable energy credits. Green-e has strict consumer and environmental safeguards. Green-e's goal is to build consumer confidence in renewable energy alternatives and provide customers with clear information about renewable energy options. Consumers can use the Green-e logo to quickly identify renewable energy options that meet Green-e's high standards.

(See www.green-e.org for more information.)

The Movement is Underway

BY ANDY LIPKIS

It's not that you can make a difference. It's that you do. And it's not only *you* that is making that difference, there's a legion of aware and like-minded people doing their best to make the world better as well. As documented by Paul Hawken in his new book, *Blessed Unrest,* we have a huge movement underway that no one saw coming. We're being called on to heal our planet. It's an environmental imperative and one for which I believe we are biologically programmed. And many of us are beginning to listen and answer the call.

We've been given the gift of all kinds of energy to support our healing work, including nutrients, species intelligence, passion, compassion, and creativity. But our lives are often filled with distractions that prevent us from committing to something meaningful. We're used to the idea that you can bury, toss, or push problems away, but we know there's no "away" anymore and we're surrounded by ecosystem damage as well as human pain and suffering.

So what do we do? You can begin by taking one step, and then the next; it's a slow walk that becomes a healthy habit. The positive results support you going even deeper, so your activism is sustained throughout a lifetime and inspires others around you.

The good news is that there is room for everyone's participation, for their own health and sanity—and the planet's. I am inspired when I see the excitement, concern, and dedication on the faces of TreePeople volunteers of all ages. We are now in the process of making Los Angeles into a functioning community forest.

For more than three decades, we've been working with local schools and community groups to plant and care for trees. More than two million schoolchildren county-wide have participated in our programs—learning, planting, nurturing, and protecting our city's life-support system.

I know the journey we face is a long one, and that there are no quick fixes. But I also know that the movement is underway and is unstoppable. Find a group or work alone. What matters is that you begin.

ANDY LIPKIS

Andy Lipkis began planting trees when he was 15 years old. He founded TreePeople and has served as its President since 1973. TreePeople has been a guiding light for the Citizen Forestry movement and also helped pioneer integrated urban ecosystem management (www.treepeople.org).

It's easy to be overwhelmed by the sheer number of environmental problems that plague our planet, but the organizations listed below are making a real difference. They inform and motivate, promote environmental awareness in different areas, and provide opportunities to get involved. Engaging with any one of these groups is a great way to learn about the problems your own community faces and to help find and implement the solutions to solve those problems.

All organizations in this section promote environmental preservation, conservation, education, or habitat management. They offer direct, local, community involvement through classes and/or environmental work programs. None operate on a for-profit basis.

Algalita Marine Research Foundation
148 N. Marina Dr. Long Beach 90803 • **562-598-4889**
Mon-Fri 10am-4pm www.algalita.org
Dedicated to protecting the marine environment through research, education, and restoration. Check website or call for volunteer opportunities.

Audubon Society
Los Angeles Chapter
7377 Santa Monica Blvd. West Hollywood 90046 • **323-876-0202**
www.laaudubon.org
Pasadena Chapter
1750 N. Altadena Dr. Pasadena 91107 • **626-355-9412**
www.pasadenaaudubon.org
San Fernando Valley Chapter
P.O. Box 7769 Van Nuys 91407 • **818-998-3122**
www.sfvaudubon.org
Santa Monica Bay Chapter
P.O. Box 35 Pacific Palisades 90272 • Contact via e-mail
www.smbas.org
Call or check websites for hours and meeting information
Promotes the enjoyment and protection of birds and other wildlife through recreation, education, conservation, and restoration. Field trips and volunteer opportunities available.

Ballona Creek Renaissance
P.O. Box 1068 Culver City 90232 • **310-839-6896**
www.ballonacreek.org
Promotes environmental, artistic, and educational projects that foster a communal commitment to the collaborative renewal of Ballona Creek and its watershed. Volunteer opportunities available.

Ballona Wetlands Land Trust
P.O. Box 5623 Playa Del Rey 90296 • **310-264-9468**
www.ballona.org
Nonprofit community organization dedicated to the acquisition, restoration, and preservation of the entire Ballona Wetlands ecosystem.

ADDING TO YOUR INVOLVEMENT

Beverly Vermont Community Land Trust
117 Bimini Pl. Ste. 201 LA 90004 • 213-383-8684
By appt.
www.urbansoil.net/wiki.cgi/The_Beverly_Vermont_Community_Land_Trust
Community development organization committed to creating permanent affordable, sustainable housing and commercial spaces in a context of land stewardship and integrating urban living with nature.

BringYourOwn.org
LA • 310-998-8616
www.bringyourown.org
Campaign encouraging people to reduce plastic waste by bringing reusable cups, bags, and utensils when shopping or eating out.

California Native Plant Society
Los Angeles/Santa Monica Mountains Chapter
15811 Leadwell St. Van Nuys 91406 • 818-881-3706
www.lasmmcnps.org
San Gabriel Mountains Chapter
1750 N. Altadena Drive Pasadena 91107 • Contact via e-mail
www.cnps-sgm.org
Member-based local chapters working to increase understanding and preservation of California's native flora. Monthly field trips; annual native wildflower show and plant sale; programs and events free to the public.

CALPIRG
3435 Wilshire Blvd. Ste. 385 LA 90010 • 213-251-3680
Mon-Fri 9am-5pm www.calpirg.org
Advocacy group working to protect and uphold public health and safety for Californians. Student membership, internships.

Center for Food & Justice
2106 Colorado Blvd. LA 90041 • 323-341-5099
Mon-Fri 9am-5pm www.foodandjustice.org
Works for better access to healthy foods. Promotes local and sustainably grown food.

Coalition for Clean Air
811 W. Seventh St. Ste. 1100 LA 90017 • 213-630-1192
Mon-Fri 9am-5pm www.coalitionforcleanair.org
Promotes clean air in California by advocating responsible public policy, providing technical and educational expertise, and encouraging community involvement.

Coalition on the Environment and Jewish Life of Southern California, The (CoejlSC)
3424 Motor Ave. Ste. 100 LA 90034 • 310-841-2970
Mon-Fri 9am-5pm www.coejlsc.org
Promotes environmental stewardship within faith communities through advocacy, education, and community partnerships.

Communities for a Better Environment
5610 Pacific Blvd. Ste. 203 Huntington Park 90255 • 323-826-9771
Mon-Fri 9am-5pm www.cbecal.org
Environmental health and justice nonprofit promoting clean air, clean water, and the development of toxin-free communities.

Community Coalition for Change
P.O. Box 59027 LA 90059 • 310-729-8726
Environmental justice organization advocating for urban communities affected by major pollution sources. Classes and service learning opportunities for youth.

Become a member greenopia.com

Concerned Citizens of South Central Los Angeles
4707 S. Central Ave. LA 90011 • 323-846-2500
Mon-Fri 10am-6pm www.ccscla.org
Fosters social justice and economic and environmental change within the
South Central Los Angeles community.

Del Amo Action Committee
1536 W. 25th St. Ste. 440 San Pedro 90732 • 310-769-4813
Environmental justice group serving as watchdog for toxic sites; advocates
for better enironmental policies.

Earth Day LA
1247 Lincoln Blvd. Ste. 253 Santa Monica 90401 • 888-295-8372
Mon-Fri 9am-6pm www.earthdayla.org
Sponsors Earth Day festivals in the Los Angeles region. Volunteer
opportunities available.

Earthways Foundation
20178 Rockport Way Malibu 90265 • 310-456-8300
www.earthways.org
Initiates environmental, social justice, and educational projects to increase
cultural consciousness and restore the planet's health.

East Yard Communities for Environmental Justice
2317 Atlantic Blvd. City of Commerce 90040 • 323-263-2113
Mon-Fri 9am-6pm www.eycej.org
Provides information on the health issues surrounding train and truck traffic
pollution. Advocates community involvement for policy reforms.

EndOil
P.O. Box 360465 LA 90036 • 323-930-9117
Mon-Fri 9am-5:30pm www.endoil.org
Educates and fosters direct action to promote energy alternatives and end
oil dependency.

Environment California
3435 Wilshire Blvd. LA 90010 • 213-251-3688
Mon-Fri 9am-5pm www.environmentcalifornia.org
State-based, nonpartisan environmental advocacy for the public interest.

Environment Now
2515 Wilshire Blvd. Santa Monica 90403 • 310-829-5568
Mon-Fri 9am-5pm www.environmentnow.org
Dedicated to preserving and restoring coastal freshwater and forest
ecosystems while improving air quality and advancing sustainability.

Environmental Change Makers
6700 W. 83rd St. Westchester 90045 • 310-670-4777
Meets 4th Thu of each month 7pm-9pm www.envirochangemakers.org
Monthly meetings with speakers, discussions, and movies on sustainability,
community-building, and environmental victories.

Environmental Media Association
5979 W. Third St. LA 90036 • 310-446-6244
Mon-Fri 9:30am-5:30pm www.ema-online.org
Mobilizes the entertainment industry in a global effort to educate people
about environmental issues and inspire them into action.

Farmlab
1745 N. Spring St. Ste. 4 LA 90012 • 323-226-1158

Farmlab (cont.)

Mon-Fri 10am-4pm www.farmlab.org

Multi-disciplinary investigation of land use issues related to sustainability, livability, and health; art production studio; public salons every Friday at noon.

Friends of Ballona Wetlands

7740 W. Manchester Ave. Ste. 210 Playa Del Rey 90293 • **310-306-5994**

Mon-Fri 10am-6pm Freshwater marsh open dawn to dusk

www.ballonafriends.org

Interpretive nature tours held the 2nd/4th Saturday and 2nd Sunday of each month. Restoration party held on the 4th Saturday of each month. Freshwater marsh located at Jefferson Blvd. and Lincoln Blvd.

Friends of the Los Angeles River

570 W. Ave. 26 Ste. 250 LA 90065 • **323-223-0585**

Mon-Fri 9am-5pm www.folar.org

Programs include river area cleanups, water quality monitoring, outdoor education, and walking tours.

Global Green USA

2218 Main St. 2nd Flr. Santa Monica 90405 • **310-581-2700**

Mon-Fri 9am-6pm www.globalgreen.org

Santa Monica-based national organization addressing climate change, weapons of mass destruction, and drinking water. Volunteer and internship opportunities.

Global Inheritance

LA • **213-683-8442**

By appt. www.globalinheritance.org

Organization designing large scale interactive programs and campaigns to empower people and inspire activism.

Green Building Council, Los Angeles Chapter

315 W. Ninth St. Ste. 312 LA 90015 • **213-689-9707**

www.usgbc-la.org

Dedicated to improving the economic, social, and environmental performance of Southern California regional development through the integration of green building practices.

Green Building Resource Center

2218 Main St. Santa Monica 90405 • **310-452-7677**

Tue-Wed 10am-3pm Thu 3pm-8pm Fri-Sun 10am-3pm

www.globalgreen.org/grbc/index.htm

Provides free design advice and information on environmentally-friendly building products and strategies.

Greenpeace

1727 N. Vermont Ave. Ste. 210 LA 90027 • **323-953-1366**

www.greenpeaceusa.org

Independent campaigning organization using peaceful direct action to expose global environmental problems and enforce solutions.

Habitat Works

La Crescenta • **818-353-4653**

www.habitatwork.org

Local stewardship benefiting the habitats of endangered and threatened species. Check website for single-day outings, weekend campouts, and backpacking trips.

Heal the Bay
1444 Ninth St. Santa Monica 90401 • **310-451-1500**
Mon-Fri 9am-5pm Closed 12:30pm-1:30pm www.healthebay.org
Helps protect the Santa Monica Bay and its watersheds through education, advocacy, beach cleanups, and a beach report card monitoring service. Volunteer opportunities available.

Healthy Homes Collaborative
514 S. Shatto Pl. Ste. 270 LA 90020 • **213-252-4411**
Mon-Fri 9am-5pm W. Hollywood clinic open Wed. 7pm Sat 10am
www.cesinaction.org/hfhfc.html
A collaboration of organizations working on issues of environmental neglect in housing, such as code violations and lead paint. Hosts bimonthly meetings and public education efforts for healthier homes.

Hollywood Beautification Team
P.O. Box 931090 Hollywood 90093 • **323-962-2163**
Mon-Fri 9am-4:30pm www.hbteam.org
Organizes community members to improve the Los Angeles environment by planting trees, abating graffiti, and removing trash. Education programs for children.

Koreatown Youth and Community Center
3727 W. Sixth St. Ste. 300 LA 90020 • **213-365-7400**
Mon-Fri 9am-6pm www.kyccla.org
Works to improve the Koreatown environment through tree planting, graffiti removal, and water conservation. Volunteer opportunities available.

Livable Places
634 S. Spring St. Ste. 727 LA 90014 • **213-622-5980**
By appt. www.livableplaces.org
Nonprofit organization advancing affordable, healthy Southern California communities through mixed-income housing developments and advocacy work.

Local Initiatives Support Corporation
1055 Wilshire Blvd. Ste. 1600 LA 90017 • **213-250-9550**
www.lisc.org
Intermediary for financial and technical assistance providing support to other nonprofits for affordable housing and revitalization projects.

Long Beach Alliance for Children with Asthma
2651 Elm Ave. Ste. 100 Long Beach 90806 • **562-427-4249**
Mon-Fri 8am-5pm www.lbaca.org
Partnerships improving the lives of children with asthma in the Long Beach community through healthcare delivery, outreach, education, and support systems.

Los Angeles Community Garden Council
2658 Griffith Park Blvd. Ste. 728 LA 90039 • **323-666-2137**
www.lagardencouncil.org
Committed to connecting people with garden space in their communities.

Los Angeles County Bicycle Coalition
LA • **213-629-2142**
Mon-Fri 10am-6pm www.labike.org
Member-supported coalition advocating safer streets for cycling and promoting the bicycle as a means of transportation. Safe cycling and road-sharing classes available to the public.

Los Angeles County Department of Public Health-Environmental Health

5050 Commerce Dr. Baldwin Park 91706 • **626-430-5200**
Mon-Fri 8am-4:30pm www.lapublichealth.org/eh
Promotes health and quality of life by identifying, preventing, and controlling harmful environmental factors in Los Angeles County. Information available on website.

Los Angeles Neighborhood Land Trust

315 W. Ninth St. Ste. 1002 LA 90015 • **213-572-0188**
Mon-Fri 9am-5pm www.lanlt.org
Advocates for the creation of community green and open space; brings awareness to the inequity of open space in Los Angeles' underserved neighborhoods.

Marine Mammal Care Center

3601 S. Gaffey St. San Pedro 90731 • **310-548-5677**
Daily 10am-4pm www.marinemammalcare.org
A hospital for ill, injured, and orphaned marine mammals. Tours, education, internships, and many volunteer opportunities available.

Natural Resources Defense Council

1314 Second St. Santa Monica 90401 • **310-434-2300**
Mon-Thu 9am-5:30pm Fri 9am-5pm www.nrdc.org
Marine mammals program, SoCal air quality and coastal waters programs, and public tours of Platinum LEED green building.

Nature Conservancy

523 W. Sixth St. Ste. 1216 LA 90014 • **213-327-0104**
Mon-Fri 9am-5pm www.nature.org
Natural conservation group sponsoring "adopt an acre" and "rescue the reef" programs. Call 800-84-Adopt.

North East Trees

570 W. Ave. 26 Ste. 200 LA 90065 • **323-441-8634**
Mon-Fri 9am-5pm www.northeasttrees.org
Designs, constructs, and preserves green spaces in the greater Los Angeles area. Check website for volunteer opportunities.

Pacoima Beautiful

11243 Glenoaks Blvd. Ste. 1 Pacoima 91331 • **818-899-2454**
Mon-Fri 9am-5:30pm www.pacoimabeautiful.org
Environmental health and justice nonprofit working for the creation of healthy, safe communities. Programs oriented toward youth, community-building, and healthy homes.

People for Parks

1216 S. Westlake Ave. LA 90006 • **213-487-9340**
Mon-Fri 9am-6pm www.peopleforparks.org
Aims to preserve and expand Los Angeles County park systems, natural areas, and open spaces and to increase youth recreational opportunities. Volunteer opportunities available.

Physicians for Social Responsibility

617 S. Olive St. Ste. 810 LA 90014 • **213-689-9170**
Mon-Fri 9am-6pm www.psrla.org
Brings together medical professionals and communities to promote environmentally sound public health policy. Volunteer opportunities available.

Planet Rehab

2745 W. Balepark Dr. San Dimas 91772 • **323-350-0873**
Mon-Fri 9am-5pm www.planetrehab.org
Dedicated to the preservation of rainforests and their native species.
Volunteer opportunities in fundraising, research, and membership
development.

River Project, The

3912 Laurel Cyn Blvd. Ste. 208 Studio City 91604 • **818-980-9660**
Mon-Fri 10am-5pm www.theriverproject.org
Encourages the responsible management and revitalization of watershed
lands and rivers through outreach, advocacy, scientific research, and
hands-on educational programs.

Santa Monica Bay Keeper

P.O. Box 10096 Marina Del Rey 90295 • **310-305-9645**
Mon-Fri 9am-5pm www.smbaykeeper.org
Volunteer programs include public outreach and education, Beachkeeper
program, advocacy, and kelp restoration.

Sierra Club, Los Angeles Chapter

3435 Wilshire Blvd. Ste. 320 LA 90010 • **213-387-4287**
Mon-Fri 10am-6pm www.angeles.sierraclub.org
Environmental outings; political and conservation activism. Promotes and
offers ecotourism.

South Bay Energy Savings Center

3868 Carson St. Ste. 110 Torrance 90503 • **310-543-3022**
Mon-Fri 9am-5pm www.sbesc.com
Energy and water conservation resource center and lending library.
Workshops on saving water, energy, and money open to the public free of
charge.

Southern California Wetlands Recovery Project–Los Angeles Task Force

700 N. Alameda St. 4th Flr. Annex LA 90012 • **818-590-9342**
www.scwrp.org
Works cooperatively with organizations and agencies to acquire and
restore rivers, streams, and wetlands in Southern California.

Stop Global Warming

By mail: 15332 Antioch St. Ste. 168 Pacific Palisades 90272 • **310-454-5726**
www.stopglobalwarming.org
Brings Americans together in a nonpartisan effort to acknowledge and help
stop global warming; provides climate change facts.

Strategic Actions for a Just Economy

152 W. 32nd St. LA 90007 • **213-745-9961**
By appt. www.saje.net
Center for economic justice, community development, and education
building economic power for the working class since 1996.

Surfrider Foundation, Malibu/West Los Angeles Chapter

P.O. Box 953 Malibu 90265 • **310-451-1010**
www.surfrider.org/malibu
Conservation and education nonprofit advocating for clean coastal water
and beach preservation, protection, and access. Volunteer opportunities
available.

Sustainable Business Council

www.sustainablebc.org

Sustainable Business Council (cont.)

Serves as a networking forum and industry advocate for Los Angeles regional businesses and individuals working with sustainable products and services. Volunteer opportunities available.

Sustainable Economic Enterprises of Los Angeles

6605 Hollywood Blvd. Ste. 220 LA 90028 • **323-463-3171**
Mon-Fri 9am-5pm www.see-la.org
Private, nonprofit community development corporation promoting sustainable food systems, social and cultural programs, and economic revitalization programs.

Sustainable Transport Club

9 Village Pkwy. Santa Monica 90405 • **310-450-7419**
Mon-Fri 9am-5pm www.sustainableclub.org
Community-based organizing and networking to advance sustainable transportation options from bicycles to biofuels and electric vehicles.

Sweatshop Watch

1250 S. Los Angeles St. Ste. 212 LA 90015 • **213-252-5945**
By appt. www.sweatshopwatch.org
Focuses on eliminating sweatshop exploitation in California's garment industry through public education, advocacy, and corporate accountability. Volunteer opportunities available.

Theodore Payne Foundation

10459 Tuxford St. Sun Valley 91352 • **818-768-1802**
Seasonal hours www.theodorepayne.org
Classes on horticulture, garden design, and native bird habitats; books and educational resources. Youth field trips available.

Transit Coalition, The

P.O. Box 567 San Fernando 91341 • **818-362-7997**
Mon-Fri 10am-4pm www.thetransitcoalition.us/index.htm
All-volunteer organization working with the community and transit users to demonstrate and mobilize a solid base of support to expand bike, bus, and rail systems.

Tree Musketeers

136 Main St. Ste. A El Segundo 90245 • **310-322-0263**
Mon-Fri 10am-6pm www.treemusketeers.org/tm06/index.asp
Youth-centered urban forestry: kids teach other kids to become active citizens and community leaders.

TreePeople

12601 Mulholland Dr. Beverly Hills 90210 • **818-753-4600**
Mon-Fri 9am-5pm; Coldwater Canyon Park is open year-round sunrise to sunset www.treepeople.org
Works with school children and their families, connecting communities to the natural world. Provides education and advocacy on tree care and sustainable water use; tree plantings and eco-tours. Volunteer opportunities available.

Trust for Public Land

570 W. Ave. 26 Ste. 300 LA 90065 • **323-223-0441**
Mon-Fri 9am-5pm www.tpl.org
National nonprofit land conservation organization preserving parks, community gardens, historic sites, and rural areas.

WestStart-CalStart

48 S. Chester Ave. Pasadena 91106 • **626-744-5600**

Become a member greenopia.com

WestStart-CalStart (cont.)
Mon-Fri 8am-5pm www.calstart.org
Sponsors programs supporting the growth of alternative transportation.

Windows-on-Our-Waters
2515 Wilshire Blvd. Santa Monica 90403 • **310-829-1229**
By appt. www.windowsonourwaters.org
Teaches school-children and the public about the negative effects of
marine pollution on environments and people.

 Environmental Education

If you want to study something in the environmental arena in depth, there
are a growing number of opportunities for further education. You'll find
opportunities in traditional and nontraditional settings: We think you'll be
amazed at the choices that are now available—for adults and children alike.
There are schools that offer environmental studies programs and ones
that incorporate sustainable living and real-world environmental issues
into their curriculum. And if you don't find what you are looking for here,
many of the environmental organizations we've listed in the previous
section also offer educational workshops or other learning options.

All of the organizations listed below provide ongoing environmental
education and many also provide community outreach. Some offer advanced degrees in environmental fields. Others are geared specifically
to educate and inspire adults and/or children to become good stewards
of the earth. Be sure to check the organizations' websites regularly
to see when classes are offered. Programs are listed based on their
primary educational focus and who they serve.

ACCREDITED UNDERGRADUATE, GRADUATE, AND POST-GRADUATE DEGREE PROGRAMS

Antioch University, Los Angeles
400 Corporate Pt. Culver City 90230 • **310-578-1080**
Mon-Thu 9am-6pm Fri 9am-1pm www.antiochla.edu
Offers undergraduate degrees in Liberal Studies and Urban Community
and Environment. Campus environmental policies encourage student
commitment to sustainability.

California State Polytechnic University, Pomona— John T. Lyle Center for Regenerative Studies
4105 W. University Dr. Pomona 91768 • **909-869-5155**
Mon-Fri 8am-5pm www.csupomona.edu/crs
Offers Master of Science degree in Regenerative Studies. Advances sustainability
principles through education, research, demonstration, and outreach.

California State University, Channel Islands— Environmental Science and Resource Program
1 University Dr. Camarillo 93012 • **805-437-8494**
Mon-Thu 11am-12pm http://esrm.csuci.edu

CSU Environmental Science and Resource Program (cont.)
Interdisciplinary program designed to give students a solid understanding of the environment from multiple, sometimes conflicting, perspectives.

California State University, Northridge—
Urban Studies and Planning Program
18111 Nordhoff St. Northridge 91330 • **818-677-2904**
Mon-Fri 8am-5pm www.csun.edu
Prepares students for careers in Urban Planning, Community Development, Environmental Analysis, Public Administration, and Resource Management.

Center for Environmental and Urban Studies
at Santa Monica College
1744 Pearl St. Santa Monica 90405 • **310-434-3909**
Mon-Fri 10am-5pm www.smc.edu/ceus
Information and resource center for students, faculty, and the surrounding community. Nucleus for campus environmentalism and university environmental programs.

Claremont McKenna College—Roberts Environmental Center
925 N. Mills Ave. W. M. Keck Science Center Claremont 91711 • **909-621-8190**
Seasonal hours www.roberts.cmc.edu
Offers undergraduate degree in Environment, Economics, and Politics (EEP).

Southern California Institute of Architecture
960 E. Third St. LA 90013 • **213-613-2200**
Mon-Fri 9am-6pm www.sciarc.edu
Core program focused on green building and sustainability.

University of California, Los Angeles—
Department of Urban Planning
337 Charles E. Young Dr. Ste. 3250 LA 90095 • **310-825-4025**
Mon-Fri 8am-5pm www.spa.ucla.edu/up
Offers an advanced degree in Urban Planning with an environmental focus.

ACCREDITED K-12 PROGRAMS

Crossroads School for Arts and Sciences
1714 21st St. Santa Monica 90404 • **310-829-7391**
Mon-Fri 8am-3pm www.xrds.org
Independent K-12 college preparatory school offering a multi-disciplinary education built on a progressive, developmental learning model.

EcoScholarship.com
By appt. www.ecoscholarship.com
Scholarships for high school seniors and college students aspiring to environment-oriented careers. Partially funded by proceeds from sale of the Green Coupon Book (myGreenSpark.com/eco).

Environmental Charter High School
16315 Grevillea Ave. Lawndale 90260 • **310-676-3107**
Mon-Fri 7:30-4:30 www.echsonline.org
Independent, college prep, public charter school open to students throughout LA County. Field trips and project-based learning apply academics to real-world environmental issues.

TeachingGreen
P.O. Box 754 Hermosa Beach 90254 • **310-372-7484**
www.teachinggreen.org
Nonprofit organization offering environmental education services and

TeachingGreen (cont.)

materials for school-children and adults, including workshops for adults and in-class presentations for children in grades K-12. Provides comprehensive, empowering environmental education to help people live sustainably.

Tom Bradley Environmental Science & Humanities Magnet
3875 Dublin Ave. LA 90008 • **323-292-8195**
Mon-Fri 8am-4:30pm www.lausd.k12.ca.us/Tom_Bradley_EL/
K-5 college prep school focusing on environmental science and the humanities.

Waldorf School, Highland Hall
17100 Superior St. Northridge 91325 • **818-349-1394**
Mon-Fri 8am-4pm www.highlandhall.org
Nursery, elementary, grade, and high school curricula emphasizing whole-child development and sustainable living.

Waldorf School, Pasadena
209 E. Mariposa St. Altadena 91001 • **626-794-9564**
Mon-Fri 8am-4pm www.pasadenawaldorf.org
Pre-school through eighth grade curricula focus on whole-child development and creating a sustainable world.

Waldorf School, Westside
17310 Sunset Blvd. Pacific Palisades 90272 • **310-454-7064**
Mon-Fri 8am-3pm www.wswaldorf.org
Eco-minded pre-K and elementary school with an emphasis on whole-child development and sustainable living.

GENERAL INTEREST - ADULTS

Aquarium of the Pacific
100 Aquarium Way Long Beach 90802 • **562-951-1630**
Daily 9am-5pm www.aquariumofpacific.org
Variety of adult and children's educational programs, cultural festivals, classes, guest lectures, and field trips contibute to conservation efforts, watershed and ocean literacy.

Arboretum, The
301 N. Baldwin Ave. Arcadia 91007 • **626-821-3222**
Daily 9am-4:30pm www.arboretum.org
A 127-acre botanical garden and historical site; free admission every 3rd Tuesday of the month.

Audubon Center at Debs Park
4700 N. Griffin Ave. LA 90031 • **323-221-2255**
Wed-Sat 9am-5pm www.audubondebspark.org
Urban nature center and park providing family-oriented education programs aimed at bringing together community members and local natural spaces. Center housed in LEED Platinum Building.

Bicycle Kitchen
706 Heliotrope Dr. LA 90029 • **323-NO-CARRO**
Mon 12pm-6:30pm, 6:30pm-9:30pm (Women only) Tue-Thu 6:30pm-9:30pm
Sat-Sun 12pm-6pm www.bicyclekitchen.com
Volunteer-run nonprofit helping residents learn to build, maintain, and ride bikes; Earn-A-Bike program for youths aged 12-18. Runs occasional workshops.

Bike Oven
3706 N. Figueroa St. LA 90065
Mon-Thu 7pm-10pm Sat-Sun 1pm-4pm www.bikeoven.com
Volunteer-run, donation-based bicycle repair collective.

Bikerowave
1816A Berkeley St. Santa Monica 90404
Mon, Wed-Thu 6:30pm-10pm Sat 1pm-7pm www.bikerowave.org
Westside do-it-yourself, donation-based bike wrenching space: volunteer
mechanics teach people to become self-sufficient in basic bike repair.

Cabrillo Marine Aquarium
3720 Stephen M. White Dr. San Pedro 90731 • **310-548-7562**
Tue-Fri 12pm-5pm Sat-Sun 10am-5pm www.cabrilloaq.org
Engages visitors in education, recreation, and research to promote knowledge,
appreciation, and conservation of Southern California's marine life.

California Conservation Corp—Los Angeles Service District
4366 S. Main St. LA 90037 • **213-744-2254**
Mon-Thu 6am-4:30pm, Fri 6:30am-3pm www.ccc.ca.gov
Work force development program training people ages 18-25 in life skills,
environmental conservation, fire protection, and emergency response.

California League of Conservation Voters
10780 Santa Monica Blvd. Ste. 210 LA 90025 • **310-441-4162**
Mon-Fri 9am-5pm www.ecovote.org
Nonprofit organization providing voter education, political campaign
partnerships, and legislative advocacy for California's environmental
causes.

Coalition for a Safe Environment
P.O. Box 1918 Wilmington 90748 • **310-834-1128**
By appt. www.coalitionfase.org
Public policy and environmental justice advocacy for public health and
safety regarding port, petroleum, and energy issues.

Cooperative Resources & Services Project (CRSP)—
Institute for Urban Eco-Villages at Los Angeles Eco-Village
117 Bimini Pl. LA 90004 • **213-738-1254**
By appt. www.laecovillage.org
Education, training, and resource center for small ecological cooperative
communities. Regularly-scheduled tours of Los Angeles Eco-Village,
workshops, and special events.

Creative Green Sustainability Coaching
By appt. • **323-935-1214**
Workshops covering waste reduction and recycling, composting, water
and energy efficiency, the nontoxic home, organic food, organic gardening,
permaculture, and other environmental isues.

Cyclists Inciting Change thru Live Exchange (C.I.C.L.E.)
4734 Eagle Rock Blvd. Ste. 1001 LA 90041 • **323-478-0060**
www.cicle.org
Los Angeles-based organization working to promote the bicycle as a viable,
healthy, and sustainable transportation choice.

De-Sal Response Group
2515 Wilshire Blvd. Santa Monica 90403 • **310-829-1229**
www.desalresponsegroup.org
Educates community groups about ocean water desalination programs.
Intern program for local college students.

Descanso Gardens
1418 Descanso Dr. La Cañada Flintridge 91011 • **818-949-4200**
Daily 9am-5pm www.descansogardens.org
Public gardens showcasing hearty native plants; horticulture and harvest

Descanso Gardens (cont.)

classes; environmental lecture series. Electric-powered tram. Day fees apply.

Earthworks Enterprises

LA • **626-523-6469**
Wed, Sat 7am-2:30pm
A program of the LA Conservation Corps enhancing the health and economic security of at-risk high school youth and low-income families and communities through organic, sustainable agriculture.

Eco-Home™ Network

4344 Russell Ave. LA 90027 • **323-662-5207**
By appt. www.ecohome.org
Sustainable urban living demonstration home with solar paneling, xeriscaped front yard, backyard composting, and organic gardening; $10 suggested donation.

Green Depot

P.O. Box 3096 Santa Monica 90408 • **310-351-7606**
Mon-Sat 8am-6pm www.greendepot.org
Promotes sustainable energy choices and practices through education, outreach, and environmental justice programs.

Healthy Child Healthy World

12300 Wilshire Blvd. Ste. 320 LA 90025 • **310-820-2030**
Mon-Fri 8:30am-5pm www.healthychild.org
Educates the public about environmental toxins affecting children's health.

Long Beach Marine Institute

6475 E. Pacific Coast Hwy. Ste. 281 Long Beach 90803 • **562-431-7156**
www.longbeachmarine.org
Educates the public about the California coast's resources, promoting the preservation of the Southern California coastal environment.

Los Angeles Eco-Village

117 Bimini Pl. LA 90004 • **213-738-1254**
By appt. www.laecovillage.org
Public demonstration of sustainable community development; shares processes, strategies, and techniques through tours, talks, workshops, and conferences.

Mary Cordaro, H3Environmental

818-766-1787
By appt. www.h3environmental.com
Lectures and classes on the healthy home; offers solutions for mold, chemicals, and electromagnetic fields. Integration of Bau-Biologie and Building Science.

Mountains Recreation and Conservation Authority

15061 Sunset Blvd. Pacific Palisades 90272 • **310-454-1395 x151**
www.mrca.ca.gov
Wide variety of free public programs, private naturalist-guided outings, and field trips for school groups.

Natural Resource Defense Council

1314 Second St. Santa Monica 90401 • **310-434-2300**
Mon-Thu 9am-5:30pm Fri 9am-5pm
Tours: Tue 11am, Thu 3:45pm or by appt.
Bookstore: Mon-Fri 12pm-4pm www.nrdc.org
Provides top-to-bottom tour of its LEED Platinum-certified building. Free and open to the public.

Nature of Wildworks

P.O. Box 109 Topanga 90290 • **310-455-0550**
By appt. www.natureofwildworks.org
Interactive wildlife educational programs enhance public understanding of native wildlife and the California environment.

New Earth

23200 Red Rock Rd. Topanga 90290 • **310-455-2847**
Open to public for events and by appt. www.newearthlife.org
Offers programs and services in environmental sustainability education, expression, and wellness.

Opportunity Green

1933 Manning Ave. Ste. 204 LA 90025 • **310-441-0830**
Mon-Fri 9am-5pm www.opportunitygreen.com
Offers conferences, monthly eco-salons, and eco-retreats for businesses and individuals that explore ways to implement initiatives for social, environmental, and economic sustainability.

Outward Bound, Los Angeles

2020 Lincoln Ave. Pasadena 91103 • **626-564-0844**
Mon-Fri 9am-5pm www.outwardbound.org
Provides five core challenge and adventure programs teaching long-term environmental education and stewardship training to youth and adults.

Path To Freedom

631 Cypress Ave. Pasadena 91103 • **626-795-8400**
Mon-Fri by appt. www.pathtofreedom.com
Educates individuals and families to integrate sustainable living practices into their daily lives. Sustainable Living Resource Center and Urban Homestead tours available by appt.

Resource Conservation District of the Santa Monica Mountains

P.O. Box 638 Agoura Hills 91376 • **818-597-8627**
Mon-Fri 9am-4pm www.rcdsmm.org
Working to enhance society's stewardship of local natural resources through scientific research, education, and leadership efforts.

Santa Monica Community Sustainability Liaison

200 Santa Monica Pier Santa Monica 90401 • **310-266-4616**
By appt. www.sustainablesantamonica.org
Sustainability liaison for the City of Santa Monica. Offers complimentary assistance to residents, businesses, and organizations needing information or resources relating to sustainability and the Sustainable City Plan.

School of Self Reliance

P.O. Box 41834 LA 90041 • **323-255-9502**
www.self-reliance.net
Teaches classes in outdoor survival and home skills in recycling, conservation, and gardening.

Star Eco Station

10101 W. Jefferson Blvd. Culver City 90232 • **310-842-8060**
Sep-Jun Fri 1pm-5pm Sat-Sun 10am-4pm Jul-Aug Mon-Fri 1pm-5pm
www.ecostation.org
Environmental science museum and exotic wildlife rescue facility. Events held year-round.

Sustainable Works

1744 Pearl St. Santa Monica 90405 • **310-458-8716**

Sustainable Works (cont.)

Mon-Fri 9am-5pm www.sustainableworks.org
Offers programs teaching sustainable practices in business, residential, and college communities.

TeachingGreen

P.O. Box 754 Hermosa Beach 90254 • **310-372-7484**
www.teachinggreen.org
Nonprofit organization offering environmental education services and materials for school-children and adults. Provides comprehensive, empowering environmental education to help people live sustainably.

Think Earth Foundation

5318 E. 2nd St. Ste. 512 Long Beach 90803 • **562-434-6225**
Mon-Fri 9am-5pm www.thinkearth.org
Coordinates environmental projects and partnerships; provides educational materials to schools.

TreePeople

12601 Mulholland Dr. Beverly Hills 90210 • **818-753-4600**
By appt. www.treepeople.org
Works with school-children and their families, connecting communities to the natural world. Provides education and advocacy on tree care and sustainable water use; tree plantings and eco-tours.

University of California Cooperative Extension— Common Ground Garden Program

4800 E. Cesar E. Chavez Ave. LA 90022 • **323-260-3348**
Mon-Fri 9am-5pm
http://celosangeles.ucdavis.edu/Common_Ground_Garden_Program/
Trains community volunteers and Master Gardeners to teach low-income Los Angeles County residents at community and school gardens to become successful gardeners, learn about nutrition, and gain increased access to fresh, low-cost produce.

Wildlife Waystation

14831 Little Tujunga Cyn. Rd. Sylmar 91342 • **818-899-5201**
Mon-Fri 7pm-5pm www.wildlifewaystation.org
Wild and exotic animal rehabilitation sanctuary educating the public about the global plight of wildlife; focus on ecosyststems affected by cities.

GENERAL INTEREST— YOUTH AND YOUNG ADULTS

Aquarium of the Pacific

100 Aquarium Way Long Beach 90802 • **562-951-1630**
Daily 9am-5pm www.aquariumofpacific.org
Variety of adult and children's educational programs, cultural festivals, classes, guest lectures, and field trips contibute to conservation efforts, watershed, and ocean literacy.

Audubon Center at Debs Park

4700 N. Griffin Ave. LA 90031 • **323-221-2255**
Wed-Sat 9am-5pm www.audubondebspark.org
Urban nature center and park providing family-oriented education programs aimed at bringing together community members and local natural spaces. Center housed in LEED Platinum Building.

Bicycle Kitchen

706 Heliotrope Dr. LA 90029 • **323-NO-CARRO**
Mon 12pm-6:30pm, 6:30pm-9:30pm (Women only) Tue-Thu 6:30pm-9:30pm

Bicycle Kitchen (cont.)

Sat-Sun 12pm-6pm www.bicyclekitchen.com
Volunteer-run nonprofit helping residents learn to build, maintain, and ride bikes; Earn-A-Bike program for youths aged 12-18. Runs occasional workshops.

California Safe Schools

P.O. Box 2756 Toluca Lake 91610 • 818-785-5515
Mon-Fri 9am-6pm www.calisafe.org
Children's environmental health nonprofit coalition committed to the health and safety of children, staff, and community members living and working near and on school sites.

Children's Nature Institute

2600 Franklin Canyon Dr. Beverly Hills 90210 • 310-860-9484
Mon-Fri 9am-5pm www.childrensnatureinstitute.org
Environmental education programs connecting children with nature in the greater Los Angeles area.

Earthworks Enterprises

LA • 626-523-6469
Sat, Wed 7am-2:30pm
A program of the LA Conservation Corps enhancing the health and economic security of at-risk high school youth and low-income families and communities through organic, sustainable agriculture.

Environmental Defenders Program, Los Angeles County Department of Public Works

LA • 310-551-5375
By appt. www.ladpw.org/epd/defenders
Educates and empowers elementary school kids in Los Angeles to protect the local environment. Offers free school assemblies for grades K-6.

Generation Earth

12601 Mulholland Dr. Beverly Hills 90210 • 818-623-4855
Mon-Fri 9am-5pm www.generationearth.com
Educates and empowers secondary school students to be active participants in waste reduction, recycling programs, and stormwater pollution prevention. Uses service learning approach integrated with academic study. Offers workshops for teens, teachers, and school administrators. Features annual "Battle of the Schools" competition.

Green Ambassadors

16315 Grevillea Ave. Lawndale 90260 • 310-940-1626
Daily 24 hrs. www.greenambassadors.org
Empowers youth to become agents of change in their communities through service-based learning, community partnerships, and cross-cultural global exchange.

Heal the Bay Santa Monica Pier Aquarium

1600 Ocean Front Walk Santa Monica 90401 • 310-393-6149
Tue-Fri 2pm-5pm Sat-Sun 12:30pm-5pm Shark Feedings Sun 3:30pm
www.healthebay.org/smpa
Educational programs for children and adults. Hands-on interactive aquarium with plant and animal life from Santa Monica Bay; field trip program.

Kidspace Children's Museum

480 N. Arroyo Blvd. Pasadena 91103 • 626-449-9144
Daily 9:30am-5pm www.kidspacemuseum.org
Promotes environmental stewardship through educational programs in science, nature, arts, and humanities utilizing creative learning and interactive play .

Los Angeles Conservation Corps
P.O. Box 15868 LA 90015 • **213-362-9000**
Mon-Fri 8am-5:30pm www.lacorps.org
Provides at-risk young adults and school-age youth with opportunities for success through job skills training, education, and work experience; emphasis on conservation and service projects.

Malibu Foundation for Environmental Education
1471 S. Bedford St. Unit 3 LA 90035 • **310-652-4324**
Mon-Fri 9am-5pm www.malibufoundation.org
Education programs dedicated to connecting kids to beaches and oceans through school assemblies and beach cleanups.

Mountains Recreation and Conservation Authority
15061 Sunset Blvd. Pacific Palisades 90272 • **310-454-1395 x151**
By appt. www.mrca.ca.gov
Wide variety of free public programs, private naturalist-guided outings, and field trips for school groups.

Outward Bound, Los Angeles Center
2020 N. Lincoln Ave. Pasadena 91103 • **626-564-0844**
Mon-Fri 9am-5pm www.outwardbound.org
Provides five core challenge and adventure programs teaching long-term environmental education and stewardship training to youth and adults. Offers a scholarship program to individuals and groups based on need or merit.

Roots & Shoots California Region
Berkeley • **510-420-0746**
Mon-Fri 9am-5pm www.rootsandshoots.org
Assists young people in the Los Angeles area to form service-learning groups to help people, animals, and the environment, locally and globally.

Santa Monica Mountain National Recreation Area
401 W. Hillcrest Dr. Thousand Oaks 91360 • **805-370-2301**
Daily 9am-5pm www.nps.gov/samo
Provides a variety of outdoor activities and educational programs for K-12 students and teachers.

Star Eco Station
10101 W. Jefferson Blvd. Culver City 90232 • **310-842-8060**
Sep-Jun Fri 1pm-5pm Sat-Sun 10am-4pm Jul-Aug Mon-Fri 1pm-5pm
www.ecostation.org
Environmental science museum and exotic wildlife rescue facility specializing in educational programs and events for kids.

TreePeople
12601 Mulholland Dr. Beverly Hills 90210 • **818-753-4600**
By appt. www.treepeople.org
Works with school-children and their families, connecting communities to the natural world. Provides education and advocacy on tree care and sustainable water use; tree plantings and eco-tours.

Wildlife on Wheels
P.O. Box 512 Sunland 91041 • **818-951-3656**
By appt. www.wildlifeonwheels.org
Nonprofit organization providing conservation education; brings animals and children together. Volunteer opportunities.

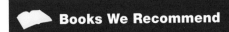
EATING OUT/EATING IN

The Art of Simple Food: Notes, Lessons, and Recipes from a Delicious Revolution
Alice Waters
Fresh and appealing low-stress dishes from the founder of Chez Panisse. Recipes are simple to prepare and reflect Alice's passion for flavor and locally produced, seasonal foods.

Everyday Greens: Home Cooking from Greens, the Celebrated Vegetarian Restaurant
Annie Somerville
Innovative vegetarian cooking. Title refers to Zen concept of everyday mindfulness. Recipes vary in complexity; all are inspired by readily available fresh and sometimes unusual ingredients.

Grub: Ideas for an Urban Organic Kitchen
Anna Lappé and Bryant Terry
Promotes benefits of sustainable eating. Provides how-to's for creating an affordable organic kitchen. Includes dozens of delectable recipes.

Hollywood Dish: More Than 150 Delicious, Healthy Recipes from Hollywood's Chef to the Stars
Akasha Richmond
Healthy and chic food with recipes and stories from an A-list Hollywood chef.

The Santa Monica Farmers' Market Cookbook: Seasonal Foods, Simple Recipes and Stories from the Market and Farm
Amelia Saltsman
The author shares her knowledge of and enthusiasm for the Santa Monica market. Recipes are delicious and accessible.

Your Organic Kitchen: The Essential Guide to Selecting and Cooking Organic Foods
Jesse Ziff Cool
Easy-to-prepare, delicious, healthy recipes listed by season. Clear format. Includes main dishes, side dishes, and desserts.

GETTING GOODS

Stuff: The Secret Lives of Everyday Things (New Report, No. 4)
John C. Ryan and Alan Thein Durning
Documents a day in the life of the average North American consumer and unravels the hidden costs of everything around us. Traces the environmental impact of consumer decisions.

GREENING YOUR SPACE

Cradle to Cradle: Remaking the Way We Make Things
William McDonough and Michael Braungart
Challenges the belief that human industry must damage the natural world. Guided by the principle that "waste equals food."

Food Not Lawns: How to Turn Your Yard into a Garden and Your Neighborhood into a Community
Heather C. Flores
Practical wisdom on ecological garden design and community-building; a permaculture lifestyle manual.

Green Building & Remodeling For Dummies
Eric Corey Freed
Step-by-step guide to Earth-friendly construction. Shows how to build responsibly, reduce waste, save money, and preserve the environment.

Naturally Clean: The Seventh Generation Guide to Safe and Healthy, Nontoxic Cleaning
Jeffrey Hollender, Geoff Davis, Meika Hollender, and Reed Doyle
Full of useful information on chemicals and cleaners to avoid. Very good resource section.

The Passive Solar House: The Complete Guide to Heating and Cooling Your Home
James Kachadorian
Proven techniques for building homes that heat and cool themselves using readily available materials and methods.

Prescriptions for a Healthy House, 3rd Edition: A Practical Guide for Architects, Builders, and Homeowners
Paula Baker-Laporte, Erica Elliot, and John Banta
Shows how to create interior spaces that promote physical health and well-being. Addresses every aspect of construction process.

SEEING THE WORLD

Lonely Planet Code Green: Experiences of a Lifetime
Kerry Lorimer
Travel publisher Lonely Planet's first ecotourism guide. Offers practical tips for socially and environmentally-responsible travelers, including how to immerse oneself in a culture and make a positive economic impact at the same time.

Fragile Earth: Views of a Changing World
Collins UK Staff (ed.)
Stunning photographs of the dramatic changes affecting today's world. Features satellite imaging and outstanding cartography.

ADDING TO YOUR INVOLVEMENT

The Consumer's Guide to Effective Environmental Choices: Practical Advice from the Union of Concerned Scientists
Michael Brower and Warren Leon
A guide to living responsibly. Outlines choices consumers can make to reduce their environmental impact. Includes priority actions in transportation, food, and household operations.

Green Living: The E Magazine Handbook for Living Lightly on the Earth
By the Editors of E/The Environmental Magazine
Practical tips for living a healthier, more eco-friendly life. Smart food choices, natural health care, socially responsible investing, healthy home care. Chapter-by-chapter resource list.

An Inconvenient Truth: The Planetary Emergency of Global Warming and What We Can Do About It
Al Gore
Eloquently outlines the necessity for immediate action to reduce global warming.

Stop Global Warming: The Solution is You! An Activist's Guide
Laurie David
Provides inspiration for global warming activists. Raises public awareness. Invites action. Lots of resource listings.

Worldchanging: A User's Guide for the 21st Century
Alex Steffen (ed.)
A compendium of the latest and most innovative solutions, ideas, and inventions for building a sustainable, livable, prosperous future.

REGION ONE
Westside including Malibu, Pacific Palisades, Santa Monica,
Venice, Culver City, Westwood, and Beverly Hills

REGION TWO
South Bay including Beach Cities from Playa del Rey to San Pedro,
and Inglewood, Hawthorne, Torrance, and surrounding areas of L.A.

REGION THREE
Hollywood to Downtown L.A. and surrounding areas,
and Glendale to Pasadena

REGION FOUR
San Fernando Valley, parts of Simi Valley,
North Hollywood, and Burbank

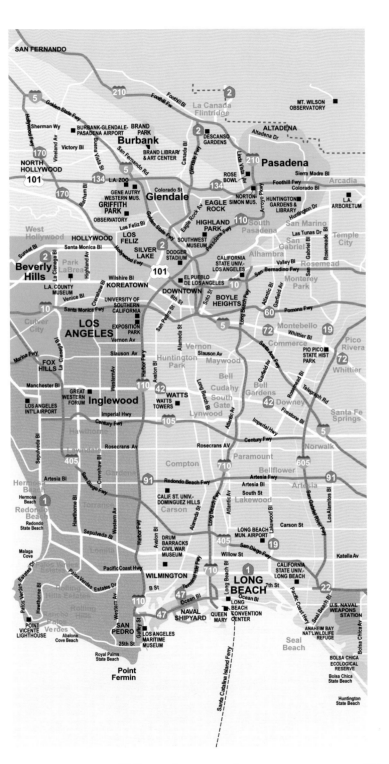

SAN FERNANDO

Burbank

NORTH
HOLLYWOOD

MT. WILSON
OBSERVATORY

La Canada
Flintridge

ALTADENA

Pasadena

Arcadia

L.A.
ARBORETUM

BRAND LIBRARY
& ART CENTER

DESCANSO
GARDENS

BRAND
PARK

BURBANK-GLENDALE-
PASADENA AIRPORT

Sherman Wy

Victory Bl

ROSE
BOWL

Sierra Madre Bl
Colorado Bl

Foothill Fwy

HUNTINGTON
GARDENS &
LIBRARY

San Marino

NORTON-
SIMON MUS.

L.A. ZOO

GENE AUTRY
WESTERN MUS.

Glendale

Colorado St

EAGLE
ROCK

GRIFFITH
PARK

OBSERVATORY

HIGHLAND
PARK

South
Pasadena

Alhambra

Temple
City

SOUTHWEST
MUSEUM

LOS
FELIZ

SILVER
LAKE

West
Hollywood

HOLLYWOOD

Rosemead

Monterey
Park

San Gabriel

CALIFORNIA
STATE UNIV.-
LOS ANGELES

DODGER
STADIUM

Beverly
Hills

Park
LaBrea

Santa Monica Bl

EL PUEBLO
DE LOS ANGELES

L.A. COUNTY
MUSEUM

KOREATOWN

Wilshire Bl

Venice Bl

BOYLE
HEIGHTS

DOWNTOWN

Montebello

Commerce

Pico
Rivera

UNIVERSITY OF
SOUTHERN
CALIFORNIA

Santa Monica Fwy

LOS
ANGELES

Culver
City

FOX
HILLS

EXPOSITION
PARK

Vernon Av

Whittier

PICO PICO
STATE HIST
PARK

Slauson Av

Huntington
Park

Maywood

Bell

Cudahy

Downey

Santa Fe
Springs

Bell
Gardens

WATTS
TOWERS

WATTS

South
Gate

Lynwood

GREAT
WESTERN
FORUM

Manchester Bl

Inglewood

Imperial Hwy

Hawthorne

LOS ANGELES
INT'L AIRPORT

Norwalk

Rosecrans AV

Rosecrans Av

Compton

Paramount

Bellflower

Artesia

Hermosa
Beach

Redondo
Beach

Redondo
State Beach

CALIF. ST. UNIV.-
DOMINGUEZ HILLS

Carson

Redondo Beach Fwy

South St
Lakewood

Artesia Bl

Torrance

LONG BEACH
MUN. AIRPORT

Carson St

Katella Av

Malaga
Cove

DRUM
BARRACKS
CIVIL WAR
MUSEUM

Willow St

CALIFORNIA
STATE UNIV.-
LONG BEACH

Pacific Coast Hwy

WILMINGTON

B St

LONG
BEACH

U.S. NAVAL
WEAPONS
STATION

Palos
Verdes
Estates

Rolling
Hills
Estates

Rolling
Hills

Rancho
Palos
Verdes

NAVAL
SHIPYARD

LONG
BEACH
CONVENTION
CENTER

QUEEN
MARY

Seal
Beach

ANAHEIM BAY
NAT'L WILDLIFE
REFUGE

BOLSA CHICA
ECOLOGICAL
RESERVE

POINT
VICENTE
LIGHTHOUSE

Abalone
Cove Beach

SAN
PEDRO

LOS ANGELES
MARITIME
MUSEUM

Bolsa Chica
State Beach

Royal Palms
State Beach

Point
Fermin

Huntington
State Beach

Santa Catalina Island Ferry

Write a review greenopia.com

Write a review greenopia.com